A STUDY OF
RUSALKI
SLAVIC MERMAIDS
of Eastern Europe

RONESA AVEELA

BENDIDEIA
PUBLISHING

Contents

Introduction

Mermaids. Beautiful and treacherous.

But there's so much more to them than that. This book in the "Spirits and Creatures" series is a breakout book. Instead of covering a variety of water spirits, I'll focus on Rusalki alone. These water maidens are popular throughout much of Eastern Europe: some good, others bad, but all are fascinating. You'll learn not only about these water spirits, but also about rituals and customs people practice that relate to the maidens, including special groups of people who heal diseases the Rusalki cause.

As I mentioned in the first book in this series, these looks at spirits and creatures are meant to be fun, more than academic, although they do contain many references from those who write in the academic world. Those authors present the facts, while I'd like to make those facts feel more alive through art, music, videos, and stories.

I hope you learn something, but most importantly, I hope you have an enjoyable journey into the world of Rusalki.

Rusalka Goddess. Illustration by Nelinda. © Bendideia Publishing.

Rusalka (Русалка)

Here the Rusalki, green-haired nymphs of wood
And water, gambolled in delight, or played
Upon the rivers, wringing their dark locks,
Plucked lilies from the fields of fragrant breath,
Or twined in chorus round the branching trees
That bent beside the limpid current's edge:
White hyacinths like snow-flakes fell around.[1]

Rusalka (singular); **Rusalki** or **Rusalky** (plural)

Name variations: russalka, rousalka, roussalka, roussilka, rousalia, roussalia, rusalia, rusanka, rusalja, rusávka, rusálaŭka, rosáŭka, rusál'nica, rusałka, rusawka

Related names: vodianikha, mavka, navka, vila (See more in the "Who's Who?" sidebar.)

Alternate names: demoness (*chertovka*), "demon" jokestress (*shutova*), tickler (*leskotukha* or *loskotukha*), abductor (*khitka* or *khitkha*),[2] bather (*kupálka*), spoiler (*kazýtka* or *smoljánka*), crooked one (*krivúcha*), iron one (*železnjáčka*)[3]

Slang: A term used to represent universal beauty.[4]
In a negative context, it's also a euphemism for women of non-traditional sexuality.[5]

Mankind's fascination with the sea has sparked imagination since the first person beheld its mighty waters. Curiosity led people to invent the means to travel across the great oceans and eventually explore beneath them, trying to discover their secrets. Throughout the centuries, millennia in fact, people have created myths and legends about creatures living within the sea's depths. One of the most alluring and formidable beings to inspire writers, artists, children, and adults is the mermaid, who has been forever immortalized in stories such as Hans Christian Andersen's *The Little Mermaid*. But there's more to this sea maiden than that story tells. In Slavic folklore, she's called a Rusalka and lives mostly in fresh-water bodies or swamps, rather than the sea.

Belief in the spirit was widespread across Eastern Europe: from Russia to the Czech Republic, from Poland to Bulgaria. Even today, she lives on in the minds and imaginations of many people.

Origins

These water spirits have existed far longer than the name Rusalka has been in existence (see "Etymology sidebar"), so what did people call them before "Rusalka" became popular?

Etymology

The name Rusalka may be derived from an old Slavonic word *rus* (river or stream), *ruslo* (river bed), or even *rosa* (dew) (Ralston, 139). Others have thought it comes from the word *rusyj/rusaja* (strawberry blond, golden [of hair]) (Dynda, 86). Many scholars, however, believe the name of the spirits comes from the spring *rusalia* festival. (You'll learn more about this in the "Rusalka Week" section.) Although the *rusalia* festivals have been mentioned between the twelfth and eighteenth centuries, the term "rusalka" is more recent, first appearing in the eighteenth century (Ivanits, 77).

Goddesses and Nature Spirits

As far back as the Neolithic era (7000 – 3500 BC), archaeologists have discovered artifacts that indicate societies worshiped female deities. Not wimpy, sidekick-to-men-only goddesses, but powerful ones, who ruled in their own right. They were linked to all life: "water, animals, plants, birth, life, death and regeneration."[6] During this era, women may have been the head of their households and leaders in the community. This, in part, was due to the fact they were able to prove their lineage from their mothers, while the paternity of a child wasn't always known.[7]

As time moved on and Christianity swept over the region, that state of mind changed. The Church suppressed the role of female deities as much as they repressed women.

> [T]he role of the sacred female deteriorated over time. Long ago people venerated her as the supreme creator. Over time she acquired a son or lover, then became the partner of a god with whom she ruled equally. Her status eroded later to sister, wife, or mother of the supreme god under whom she served. Finally, the male deity ruled as the supreme being, and the goddess was either demonized as a witch or monster; trivialized as an angel, nymph, or fairy; demoted to a subservient and docile saint or "good" wife; or dichotomized as a madonna/whore.[8]

Not only that, but sacred places and customs became profane or replaced with religious variations, and helpful spirits were deemed dangerous demons.

In ancient societies, people worshipped nature, especially water, and the spirits who lived there—but water spirits were also the most feared of those that roamed the community. Water spirits, who lived the farthest away from the homestead, were the most dangerous and cruelest among their brethren. They lured people into the water with the sole intent of causing them harm. The community never considered drownings to be accidents. Everyone who drowned was a victim of these spirits, who had dragged the unfortunate person beneath the surface.

Although some nature spirits with a connection to water caused death, others also brought life. Among these are the collective *beregini* fertility spirits and one-time Great Mother earth goddess called *Berehynia*, who "conveyed a message of female empowerment."[9] Some believe *beregini* are the ancestors of Rusalki, since these spirits brought moisture to the land. Their name possibly comes from *bereghy* ("riverbanks" or "shore"). Over time, the *beregini* also became associated with the home's hearth.

Rusalki, Minor Goddesses. Franciszek Siedleck, before 1934.
Franciszek Siedlecki (1867-1934) [Public domain], via Wikimedia Commons.

WHO'S WHO?

The names of spirits vary from one locality to the next. What is called a Rusalka in one place may be referred to as another name in a different geographical location. Rusalki also take on characteristics of other beings from folklore, while retaining their own name. The list below gives a brief description of a few of the most common spirits related to Rusalki.

Bereginia (pl. beregini): Ukrainian spirit of a drowned girl, with a fish tail. Also, the name for a goddess of Mother Earth.

Boginki: Female spirits whose name means "little goddesses." They stole human babies and replaced them with their own children, called "the changed ones."

Lesovikha: Female forest spirit who tickles people to death, steals cattle or makes them stray, and steals children. She's the consort of Leshy.

Mavka (pl. Mavky): A child who dies when her mother drowns her, or an unbaptized child who dies. She appears as a small baby or a beautiful, young girl with curly hair. The spirit's body may be transparent from behind, showing her internal organs. She cries like an infant at night, while rocking on branches, trying to attract people so she can tickle them to death. She may also laugh, giggle, or clap her hands. If baptized before seven years, she'll pass to the other side; if not, she becomes a water nymph.

Morske Deklice: Mention of the name Rusalki is rare in Slovenia. Instead, the water maidens are known as Morske Deklice, Povodna Vile, or White Women. They often help with field work and the harvest. Farmers repay them by leaving wicker baskets filled with food.

Navka (pl. Navky): Spirit of a child who dies at birth, or before birth if her mother dies a violent death. This spirit attacks women in childbirth. She's a spirit of the underworld, the land of the dead, called Nava, from which she gets her name (*nav'*, *navie* meaning a dead person). Instead of the river Styx, the soul crosses a sea called Nava to get to the other side. She may appear as a hideous, hairy creature, or like a huge, black bird, magpie, or bat. As with the Mavka, if she's baptized before seven years, her soul can travel to the other side.

Poludnica: Spirit dressed in white who appears at noon and wanders in the rye fields, making sure no one is working during her sacred time. Anyone who sees her becomes ill and dies.

Sky Women: Rusalki become Sky Women when they come out of the water. Thunder and lightning are believed to be the result of these spirits mating with the thunder gods.

Vila (pl. Vily), **Wila** (Poland), **Samovila** (Serbia and others), **Samodiva** (Bulgaria): Various forest nymphs. In northern and western Bulgaria, water nymphs are considered to be wood nymphs who appear during Midsummer's Week, while in southern Bulgaria, they are referred to as Samovili rather than Rusalki (or Roussalii).

Vodianikha: A female version of the Vodyanoy (or Vodnik), a water spirit who often sits on mill wheels. She's found more often in northern Russia, and is often considered the wife or concubine of the Vodyanoy.

Rusalki may also have been descendants of *Mokosh'*, goddess of fertility of both land and people, as well as spinning, weaving, and fishing. She protected women's fate and also provided moisture to the land, with rain being her milk. Over time, due to "dual faith," where Christian and pagan beliefs merged, she became connected to the Virgin Mary and the goddess Paraskevaand, who herself became known as Saint Paraskeva.[10]

As time progressed, some believe these fertility spirits became associated with the concept of the unclean dead, and so Rusalki came into existence.

Unclean Dead

Although different explanations exist about the origins of Rusalki, the most commonly accepted idea since the nineteenth century is that they're "unclean dead," sometimes called the "unquiet dead." These are people who have died a "bad" death: for example, they committed suicide or died from unnatural or premature causes, especially a violent death such as from strangulation. People feared these spirits, whom they believed were dangerous.

Mokosh and Dual Faith. Marek Hapon, 2011.
Mhapon [CC BY-SA 4.0 (https://creativecommons.org/licenses/by-sa/4.0)].

What's especially important to Rusalki, as you'll learn throughout this book, is that the unclean dead are also those who died during a *liminal* (that is, in between or transitional) phase of their life: before baptism, on the verge of marriage, or while giving birth. These bad deaths demonstrate "the absence of control, and uncanny presence of arbitrariness, contingency, and/or volition that goes against the social order, procreation, regeneration and moral code of the society."[11]

Those who died unclean did not receive proper Christian burial rites as the deceased were considered cursed. Because of their status as unclean dead, Rusalki are also classified as demons in some countries, because the spirits adhere to pagan customs or fall under the rule of the Devil, as the story below demonstrates. And, as you'll learn through various stories, they are unclean because they have no soul.

> One peasant woman accidentally suffocated all of her newborn children when she was sleeping with them and, in order not to hurt her last daughter, she didn't sleep with her even when she became an adult girl. Finally, the daughter, being already married, went to visit

her mother, who said to her: "My daughter, I have never slept with you; let's sleep together today."

The daughter agreed, and the same night her mother accidentally suffocated her. After the funeral, the mother was inconsolable. She went to the field one day and heard a voice: "Go to church on Annunciation day and, when they start singing the Cherubic Hymn, stand by the door; during that time all the devils will be coming out; you'll see your daughter among them. You let the devils pass by, and grab your daughter and hold onto her until the priest comes out and starts lecturing her!" The mother did so and brought her daughter home unharmed.[12]

It didn't matter whether the girl's death was her fault or not. She still became a Rusalka—and cursed.

What is missing here is any sense of equitable justice. Nature is presented here as being indifferent to notions of fairness; it makes but little difference whether the mermaid failed as a result of her own fault or her bad luck. What is crucial in both the folklore and its literary imitators is that she failed and therefore wasted her reproductive resources, the same potential celebrated in the fertility rites. This is what damns her.[13]

Water Nymph. Wilhelm Kotarbiński, before 1917.
Wilhelm Kotarbiński [Public domain], via Wikimedia Commons.

"RUSALKA. LAKE OF THE DEAD" (2018)

A house on the lake, even if it needs repair, seems like a wonderful gift. But then, it turns into a nightmare as a young woman (Lisa Grigorieva) haunts the place. The man she loved intends to marry someone else. She goes to the wedding and kills him, then drowns herself. Yup, all traditional Rusalki lore, except for the part where she kills him before she kills herself. She's buried next to the water, but as time passes, the water rises over her grave. Since she's already killed the man who spurned her, she has to get her revenge by killing other men who resemble him. In this way, she gets her revenge of the woman who stole her man. (Castro, "The Mermaid: Lake of the Dead.")

This film is in Russian, but you don't need to understand the words to feel the terror. You can watch the trailer here: https://www.youtube.com/watch?v=bTJ9RdH6BWk.

Drowned Women

Unlike other unclean dead, Rusalki are always female. The male version of the water spirit goes by a different name: Vodyanoy or Vodnik. In particular, Rusalki are spirits of young, unmarried (but often engaged) women or girls who have drowned—whether accidentally or intentionally—or died near water. They are restless, wandering spirits because they didn't complete motherhood, which was considered "the most important ritual transition in their life."[14]

They remain in this undead state, unable to move to the other side, until various conditions are met: 1) they live out what would have been their normal lifespan if they hadn't had a violent death or committed suicide, 2) they are avenged of their jilted lover, 3) they become human again through the miracle of the cross and baptism, or 4) until Christ returns to the world (what's commonly called "the second coming").

Rusalki wander around the place where they died, moaning about their untimely fate as you'll see in the story below.

> They tell that formerly the pond in the hollow was not large, but mighty deep. Well, a certain woman drowned in it. Even now she walks about the hollow crying in a thin voice, clad in a white shift with her tresses hanging loose. As soon as she sees anyone, she beckons him to her.
>
> It's clear that she's not at peace. You see, a funeral office wasn't sung for her and she died without confession. It was during Lent she drowned. And when the flood waters came, they swept the entire pond into the river, and they didn't find her. And it still happens that she climbs out onto the edge of the hollow, sits, and weeps. Many of us have seen her. Even dogs tuck their tails between their legs and begin to yelp and howl at her, only they don't go near her. On account of her the hollow is a bad place for us. You're seized with fright if you go by on nightly business.[15]

In some cases, Rusalki haunt deceitful lovers and seek revenge, unable to find peace until they are avenged. The story below tells of one jilted lover.

The story says that in one village a beautiful girl had drowned. Everyone felt sorry for her, the girl was kind and hard-working. And everyone judged and reviled the guy, because of whom she drowned: he was a partier and a drunkard. Since then, people began to see a beautiful rusalka by the lake. Once Mitka was fishing on the lake, and as always, had some vodka with him. The evening came quietly; the moon came out. And then he saw her. She swam along the moonlit path close to the boat and started calling him with beautiful translucent hands: "Come to me; I miss you," said the rusalka. He got scared and started telling her that it was her own fault, that he was joking when he was seeing another girl. The rusalka grabbed the boat and started rocking it. Mitka threw a bottle of unfinished vodka at her and started paddling very fast. He came to his senses only when he got home. Since that incident no one has seen drunk people at the lake.[16]

In this story, the jilted Rusalka doesn't get her revenge, because she was unable to murder her deceitful lover. But, then again, maybe she did get satisfaction. She took away something he loved dearly—alcohol. What kind of life would he endure from that point onward without being able to socialize with his drunken friends?

Many stories tell of unmarried women—quite often pregnant—who drown themselves (or even hang themselves) after being jilted by a lover.

My grandmother has told me this story. She knew a young girl; she worked for a landowner. The landowner had a young son; they liked each other. But he didn't care much about love. He had so many girls it was hard to count. And she was just a poor working girl. He slept with her and then dumped her. But she got pregnant and couldn't tell anyone but him. The young landowner didn't want to hear anything about the child, and she became a stranger to him. The poor grieving girl went to the lake and drowned herself while pregnant. The story says that she's pouring tears into the lake each night, and the lake, because of her bitter tears, replenishes during the night and dries up in the morning.[17]

Drowned Man in Rusalka's Embrace. Jacek Malczewski, 1888.
Jacek Malczewski [Public domain].

A few sources claim that any women who don't marry can become Rusalki when they die, because they're shirking their duty of being wives and mothers. Even married women who drown themselves because of unhappy marriages have the potential to become Rusalki.

At times, it's not even an act of violence or self-injury that causes girls to drown. Failure to wear a cross while in the water enables the Vodyanoy (male water spirit) to drag them under the surface and drown them. In such a way, he can then claim them for his own realm as brides or daughters.

Unbaptized Children

Similarly, infants who have died (by drowning, suffocation, abortion, or natural causes) before being baptized have the potential to become Rusalki. The same applies to unborn babies cursed by their mothers. Fireflies or lights that flicker above graves are believed to be the souls of these children.[18] In some areas of Eastern Europe, these little Rusalki are called Mavki or Navki.

These wandering souls run around clapping their hands and saying, "Ho, ho! my mother has brought me into the world and abandoned me without baptism."[19] They beg people to baptize them. If they're fortunate, someone will say, "I baptize you in the name of the Father, and of the Son, and of the Holy Ghost." This releases the child from earthly wanderings so she can proceed to her eternal home.

Often though, no one hears these laments, so faint are the cries. If people hear anything, they think it's "the wind whispering in the tree-tops or the breezes sighing through the water reeds."[20]

The child has a better chance of rescue if she waits near a church. Once a year, the priest holds a baptismal service there, and people pray for these lost souls. If the wandering spirit happens to be nearby and hears the rite, she'll be freed of living between worlds.

Some people once believed that cuckoos were the souls of these unfortunate children, and so they "baptized" every cuckoo they heard. Others would create an effigy of the bird and perform the rite, so that any unbaptized souls in the area would be freed by the ritual.[21]

If no one blesses them, or if the wandering souls miss the service for seven years, the spirits must plunge themselves into a river or other water body to become Rusalki. In the "Rusalki in Literature" section, you can read a tale about one such unbaptized girl on the verge of becoming a Rusalka.

Abducted Children

Often, a devil steals children, exchanging his own offspring for them. These human children—abducted and hidden in a dark, cold dungeon with little space to move—will curse their mothers for not protecting them. It's likely the mothers cursed their children in the first place by saying, "May the devil take you." Give him permission, and he'll snatch children the first moment he can. The devil gives these children to Rusalki to raise, and forces the innocent children to create and spread fires. Over time, the now-cursed female children become Rusalki.[22] Abducted boys become forest demons, rather than water spirits.

9

At other times, Rusalki themselves steal unbaptized human children for their own. Their desperate—and failed—attempts to nurse, however, result in the death of the infants. Since these babies haven't been baptized, they, too, become Rusalki or *rusalenji* (little Rusalki).

Ancestors

Unlike "bad" deaths from suicides and violence, natural causes of death are called "good" deaths. They're considered good because they follow the normal, expected order of life. An important aspect is that people have lived long enough to continue the cycle of life by having children.

These good deaths don't make spirits unclean; instead, the deceased become ancestral spirits, *rodiyelui*. They help their living relatives when called upon to do so. (These spirits were covered in more detail in *Household Spirits*, book 1 of this series.)

Although Rusalki are the souls of people the community once knew, these maidens are *not* classified the same as *rodiyelui*. The difference between ancestors and Rusalki is stated quite nicely below:

> Ancestors are the patrons of revival of crops in general—they are celebrated during the early spring, during sowing, as we have seen. But the period of crops ripening requires different patrons. Someone who would embody the fragile, transitional, vital and somewhat sexual nature of the process itself.
>
> Therefore, it makes sense that *rusalki*, the undead young maidens, are the patrons of the most delicate period of this process, the time of flowering of crops. The ambivalent and fragile ecological process needs to be guaranteed by equally ambivalent and fragile symbolic representations. *Rusalki* are simply *the personification of the eternal unripen-ness*.[23]

You'll learn later in this book what makes Rusalki "fragile," "transitional," "vital," and "sexual."

Appearance

As with most other mythological beings found across Eastern Europe, Rusalki vary in appearance from one geographic location to the next. They appear at times as white butterflies, the insect being a common depiction of souls in various cultures. They have also been described as "little doll-like people, birds, beasts, traditional mermaids, and young boys."[24] Other late-nineteenth century authors described them as sometimes being "tiny beings floating in the cup of the water-lily" and at others as "huge female forms which haunt the cornfields and steal the grain of the peasants."[25]

Aquatic Aspects

Most often in traditional folklore, Rusalki lack the fish tails other mermaids possess. However, Slavic literature in the nineteenth and twentieth centuries—influenced by stories such as Hans Christian Andersen's *The Little Mermaid* (1836)—introduced the half-woman, half-fish beings to "re-folklorize" the tales.[26]

Some stories also describe the spirits as having webbed fingers and toes, and having the ability to shape-shift into water creatures: white, migratory birds like swans and geese, snakes, silvery fish, toads, and frogs. It's interesting to note that all these creatures lay eggs, which from ancient times has been a symbol of renewal of life and fertility.[27]

The Swan Maidens. Walter Crane, 1894.
Walter Crane [Public domain].

Avian Features

Rusalki can appear as semi-human but with wings, and have been referred to as "swan maidens." When they put on white linen garments, the material behaves like "a second skin," transforming the spirits into birds or other creatures.[28]

> Their bird-like aspect was represented in folk costume as extra-long sleeves, like wings. In the tale of the Frog Princess, at the wedding feast, the Princess empties her drink into one long sleeve, and hides the bones of her swan-meat in the other. When the king commands her to dance: "she waved with the left sleeve and a lake appeared; she waved with the right and white swans were swimming on the water; the tsar and guests marveled." Legends of this kind formed the basis for Tchaikovsky's *Swan Lake* (1877), Dvořák's *Rusalka* (1990), and Chopin's *Les Sylphides* (1909).[29]

This visual representation of a goddess with extra-long sleeves appears in ancient imagery and on garments swan-girls wore during Rusalki dances performed in the 1930s.

Frog Tsarevna. Viktor Mikhailovich Vasnetsov, 1918.
Viktor Mikhailovich Vasnetsov [Public domain].

These maiden spirits may appear completely in the form of birds, as the teller of the tale below recounts.

> In the village of Dolgo on the Rusal'naia Day a peasant set out with his laborer for the forest to cut firewood. The peasant went about the forest, cut branches, and the hired man scooped what had been cut into one place. Suddenly a whole flock of *rusalki* in the form of birds attacked the peasant. They flew on him and pecked at him; and they would have pecked him to death, but the hired man ran up to his master at his cry. He rescued the peasant, hoisted him onto the cart, and drove him home. But all the same the peasant didn't get off free from his encounter with the *rusalki*. He began to get ill and soon died. They say that on this day one shouldn't work so as not to anger the *rusalki*.[30]

Their ability to shape-shift into birds has possible origins with the Greek Sirens.[31] This makes sense, because Rusalki, like the winged enchantresses, sing hypnotic songs to entice men to their death. However, in Slavic folklore, the Greek Sirens appear to have split into two entities: Rusalki and Sirins (or Sirens).

While Rusalki, in general, remain non-birdlike, they cause destruction by enchanting people with their songs. Slavic Sirens, however, are not evil; they are "songful birds of paradise perched on the Tree of Life— Sirin, Alkonost, and Gamaiun,"[32] who reward "the virtuous by flying down from heaven and singing to these fortunate few."[33] This fortune is short-lived, though, as those who hear the song forget everything and die.

Women

Most often, however, Rusalki appear as young women with large, voluptuous breasts and eyes that are pale or have no pupils.

Sirin, Alkonost, and Gamaiun.
[Public domain], via Wikimedia Commons.

On occasion, Rusalki have been described as having no breasts, because of their demonic nature, which was considered "inherently 'reversible' and inverted in comparison with the human world."[34] One account states:

> You've never seen rusalkas, but I have. They're very beautiful. I was working through the village, and one of them was in the vegetable patch sitting and giving me looks with her darting eyes. She's damned and she has no breasts. She's not a woman at all![35]

These ghostly figures have pale or translucent skin. Gogol, in *A May Night*, describes them as follows.

> Levko cast a glance at the lake-shore. In a silvery mist there moved, like shadows, girls in white dresses decked with May flowers; gold necklaces and coins gleamed on their necks [*typical wedding attire*]; but they were very pale, as though formed of transparent clouds. They danced nearer him, and he could hear their voices, somewhat like the sound of reeds stirred in the quiet evening by the breeze.[36]

Rusalki twist together wreaths of poppies and sedge, the grasses and weeds along the water's edge, to

Did you know?

Rusalki don't belt their garments, which was considered uncivilized among Russian peasants (Warner, 43).

adorn their long, loose-flowing tresses. Their hair color varies by location: green (Russia, Bulgaria), pale blond or strawberry blond, golden, light-brown (Ukraine), red, and black (Poland, forest Rusalki, while water Rusalki are fair-haired). In extreme cases, their hair can appear like Medusa's, a tangle of snakes.[37] Whatever the color, if you get close enough to them, their hair is likely to turn green and their faces become distorted.[38]

Rusalki's attire ranges from unbelted, transparent, white shifts or wedding robes to ragged clothing, and quite often nothing at all. Some even wear robes made of mist or green leaves.

Ralston describes them as follows:

> They are generally represented under the form of beauteous maidens with full and snow-white bosoms, and with long and slender limbs. Their feet are small, their eyes are wild, their faces are fair to see, but their complexion is pale, their expression anxious. Their hair is long and thick and wavy, and green as is the grass. Their dress is either a covering of green leaves, or a long white shift, worn without a girdle.[39]

The farther north you go (in Russian North, Volga, Ural, and Western Siberia regions),[40] the more vicious and monstrous Rusalki become. There, the spirits (sometimes called *lobasti*)[41] are far from how you'd envision mermaids. They're cadaverous old women, looking like drowned corpses.[42] Their long hair is unruly and green, and their eyes are green, glowing orbs. They have overly large, pendulous breasts, which they can toss over their shoulders. They've been described as "hideous, humpbacked, hairy creatures, with sharp claws, and an iron hook."[43] And that laughter you hear is not the giggling, playful sort; no, instead, they scream like savages, making a noise that verges on hysterical.

Getting to Know Rusalki

Rusalki are complex, unpredictable beings, whom humans both fear and respect, as well as show compassion toward the cursed spirits. Much about these dead maidens is dualistic: from their appearance (as you've already learned) to their actions and nature as well. They emerge from the water one week a year when crops are flowering, and the spirits bring both life and death, fertility and chaos. They are innocent maidens and seductive enchantresses. Vulnerable and dangerous. Demons and goddesses. They're stuck in a liminal state, not quite belonging in the world of either the living or the dead. Even the place where they live, water, is dualistic. In water, the supernatural or spiritual world overlaps the real world in "an ambivalent 'no man's land' … symbolic of the unconscious and the other world."[44]

It's here they live in underwater crystal palaces; the roads leading to them are covered with gold, silver gravel, and precious stones. At other times, they call nests of straw and feathers their home. They dwell at the bottom of fresh-water bodies—mainly lakes, rivers, streams, and brooks, as well as swamps—or hide among the reeds at secluded locations and even under waterfalls.

Did you know?

Rusalki can grow large enough to step across a stream if they see a man they want to enchant on the other side (Johnson, 155).

Bulgarian Rusalki reside at the end of the world in a land called Zmeykovo (Dragon Village), a mystical place that other spirits and supernatural creatures also call home. Some accounts say they live in the palace of the Sun, and like Rusalki from other countries, they come to the human world only once a year.

The spirits control the weather. At their command, clouds scatter so crops can ripen with the sun's heat, but Rusalki also command clouds to gather to prevent too much sun from withering the harvest. The spirits dance to bring rain to water the crops, but Rusalki can also cause strong winds to rip across the land if they're in a bad mood. People living along the seacoast tell tales of Rusalki who sometimes assist and other times thwart fishermen. They stir up the wind to bring men home safely, or they may cause fatal storms to sink boats and drown those brave enough to venture out onto the water.

Did you know?

You should pour out a bit of water you collect in a pail so you can set free any water spirit you may have captured (Bassett, 161).

When they leave the water during what is called Rusalka Week (which you'll learn more about later in this book), they frequent forests, fields, and meadows, and love to sit on tree branches, especially willow and birch.

Trees are sacred, especially the World Tree,[45] which has been called a tree of souls.

(As spirits of the dead, it was natural for them to live in the green trees, which ancient Slavic belief regarded as the homes of the departed.) When the sun has not yet entered "the abode of summer," the Rusalki can remain under water, but when the waters are warmed by the rays of life-giving light, they have to return to the trees, the houses of the dead.[46]

Their time spent beneath lakes and rivers attributes to their deathly pale skin, since they seldom see sunlight. Even when they do surface, they hide among the branches of trees gracing the shoreline. But remember, they're also spirits—sometimes ghostly images, other times solid forms that can interact with people—and so they are colored by death.

Rusalki are seldom alone, preferring to be among their sisters. They spend their time the way unmarried peasant girls do by singing, dancing, swimming, swinging, and laughing. As they swing from willow branches, they call out to one another: *"Kum! Kum!"* Like human girls, Rusalki are each other's *kum*, those who have sworn eternal friendship to one another. They giggle and admire themselves in mirrors while they sit on the riverbanks combing their hair to keep it moist. Failure to do so causes their hair to dry, and then Rusalki will die.

Rusalka. Сергей Панасенко-Михалкин, 1992.
Сергей Панасенко-Михалкин [CC BY-SA 3.0 (https://creativecommons.org/licenses/by-sa/3.0)], from Wikimedia Commons.

When they get bored, they may catch a flock of geese that have slept by the water. The spirits wrap themselves around the birds' wings, preventing them from flying away. If geese aren't around, they'll catch people to torment. Always carry wormwood with you if, for any reason, you must walk in the forest during Rusalka Week. The moment Rusalki discover you're there, they'll force you to answer their favorite rhyming riddle: "What do you have in your hands? *Poluin* (wormwood) or *petrushka* (parsley)."

Even if you've forgotten to carry wormwood, be sure to say, "*Poluin*."

Off the Rusalki will run, frustrated and crying, "Hide under the *tuin* (hedge)."

If you can, throw the wormwood into their eyes to make sure they leave you alone. You're doomed, however, if you forget the safe answer and instead say, "*Petrushka*."

The Rusalki will open their arms wide and rush at you, saying, "Ah! my *dushka* (sweetheart)."

If you fail to tell them you have parsley or incorrectly answer any of their riddles, they'll gang up and tickle you until you foam at the mouth as you'll discover in the poem below.[47]

> Whither, pretty maiden, speeding?
> Fast the Rusalque treads behind thee;
> Thus her ruby message pleading,
> In the trust that she may bind thee—
> > Riddles three
> > She's giving thee:—
> What without a root is growing?
> What without a bridle's flowing?
> What without a flower's blowing?
> Answer, maiden?—Still she flies.
> Without a root the stone upgrows,
> Without a stay the fountain flows,
> And fern without flower blows.
> > The maiden sad
> > No answer had.
> > She *tickled* dies.[48]

Although the following aren't specific to Rusalki, they're likely representative of other riddles the spirits may ask:

> "What is higher than the forest?" (*the moon*)
> "What is brighter than the light?" (*the ruddy sun*)
> "What is thicker than the forest?" (*the stars*)
> "What is there that's rootless?" (*a stone*)
> "What is never silent?" (*the sea*)
> "What is there past finding out?" (*God's will*)[49]

Another place Rusalki entertain themselves is by a mill. From a distance, you'll know they're dancing from the splashing of the water. They cry, "Kuku,"[50] as they cling to the wheel churning water. Don't let

Did you know?

The first time it thunders, Rusalki scurry back to the water or fly into the sky (Wikipedia, "Slavic water spirits").

Did you know?

A Rusalka may appear as a water snake that you can "milk" to bring rain (Anne & Myers, 64).

them catch you watching. As soon as they discover you peeping, they'll call you toward them. Run away if you can! You don't know whether they intend to harm you or merely have a little fun.

As a rule, they rarely attack women, girls, or children, although some people say Rusalki are even more violent toward females. They may lure children into the water with fruit baskets. When they do, it's likely due to the Rusalki's desire to nurture a child, which was an activity denied them during their life.

Men, however, are the primary targets of Rusalki. They desire the company of men, as lovers and husbands, who, like children, they were unable to obtain while they were alive. They love men and yearn to seduce them (often with ruinous results). When they bring men home to their crystal palace, the unfortunate men drown. A few stories say that these men don't die; quite the contrary, they remain forever young.[51]

What you know about mermaids in other cultures applies to Rusalki as well. They use their beauty and voices to lure men into the depths of the water. Overcome by desire, men can think of nothing but going toward the melody, and therefore the Rusalki. The result often is their death or, if they escape, a life of physical or mental illness filled with hallucinations.

Rusalki can change their looks depending on the man they're about to seduce. Does the gentleman prefer blondes? Voilà, blondes by the dozen—and buxom by nature, even if they weren't so in life.

If the spirits don't know a man's preferences (besides his often-jested "one-track mind"), Rusalki call out any man's name that crosses their mind as they're swinging in the tree branches. "Hey, Ivan!" or "Vanya sweetie!" is certain to grab the attention of some Russian walking near the riverbank. Even if it's not Ivan, if the man replies, the spirits have successfully trapped him with their power. The man will hurry their way, hypnotized by their siren-like voices. When he's near enough, they'll drop from the tree behind him and tickle him under his armpits, sometimes until he dies.

Rusalka. Sergey Solomko, 1928.
Sergey Solomko [Public domain], via Wikimedia Commons.

"RUSALKA" SONG BY STRIBOG

Folk metal has been described as a "mixing of traditional heavy metal with authentic folk music elements" (Boneva, "Folklore Elements"). One band who performs this music is StriboG, from Croatia. The group is named after the Slavic god of winds and storms. Their artist bio says: "The band's themes and ideologies are based on pagan Slavic mythology as it draws great inspiration from the ancient folk myths and fairy tales. StriboG's music is pervaded with classic pagan/folk rhythms and melodic yet cold atmosphere" (from: https://www.reverbnation.com/stribog).

Their song "Rusalka" appears on the "U Okovima Vjecnosti" ("In Chains of Eternity") album (2010). They have granted me permission to include the lyrics of their song here. The English translation follows.

Find them on Facebook: https://www.facebook.com/StriboG-109004042472158/

Listen to the song here: https://www.reverbnation.com/artist/downloads/311928

English Translation of "Rusalka" Lyrics by Stribog (2010)

The glittering moon shows me
The way to the river that leads to you
My thoughts are caught
In your long, green hair.

Leaves that fall in autumn
Winds are cold that bend branches
I see you at dusk
How you hide your face from me.

My vision is fulfilled
Call me with your song
Reveal your full beauty
I'm dying for you.

Green glow in the eyes
Like fire in the darkest night
The purest beauty
On the enchanted shore.

Lake vila
Rusalka
Restless soul
Rusalka.

Only your voice reaches
Through the cold wind
Which bends the branches
And while the moon hides in the clouds
I'm waiting for your appearance from the water.

And when the forest quietly calms
And when the leaves hide everything
This time calms down
You fade away ...

When the winds stop blowing
And the water turns itself into a mirror
Your dreams become visible
Drawn by my hand.

The glittering moon shows me
The way to the river that leads to you
My thoughts are caught
In your long, green hair.

You're rising from the lake
I fall on my knees
You approach me, like death, slowly,
Together we sink into a dream.

If you're brave enough to be out at night, stay away from campfires you see in the forest. These are set by Rusalki to lure you toward them while they play.[52] Even if you can't see the spirits, you'll know they're nearby from the noises and chatter resounding in the forest. Their voices sound like rustling leaves or sighing in the breeze, and you'll hear them clapping their hands.

Rusalki laugh as they tie together willow or slender birch branches so they can swing by the river. They love to perform somersaults and sing and dance in the moonlight—their enchanting voices irresistible and their laughter melodious. Some people say that merely hearing Rusalki's laughter causes death.

Sometimes, the spirits look kindly upon people and let them join in their games without causing anyone harm. If a shepherd is nearby, they may beg or entice him with flattery to play the *kaval* (a long, wooden flutelike instrument). All night long he plays, his foot tapping the ground to his own music. In the morning, he finds himself alone. One foot rests in a hollowed-out spot, the grass worn away by his own actions.

Fertility of the Land

What do you imagine when you think about mermaids? Most likely, it's their beauty and lovely voices. What you're probably unaware of—and one thing that makes Rusalki different from what you may already know about mermaids—is their relationship to the fertility of the land.

Their large breasts symbolize their nurturing ability. The water in which they dwell also adds to the overall picture of this fertility: water has been called "the feminine realm of life-giving water: amniotic fluid, menstrual blood, maternal milk, or, in folklore, the revivifying 'water of life.' "[53]

How do these spirits aid the nourishment of crops?

The answer lies in the "unused fertility" or the "potent yet not quite tapped fertility"[54] Rusalki carry with them after death. However, while Rusalki's fertility may be potent, it's not "fertile and procreative in a proper, cultural, social manner."[55] It's fertility they can bestow upon nature.

In life, the young women died before their fertility was realized, that is, before they had children, at least legitimate children. In a patriarchal society, they didn't achieve women's one main function in life— to be mothers. Their fertility, however, didn't disappear after their death. In fact, it became more powerful.

Rural people wanted—needed—to be able to access that fertility. The poor girl never got to use it, so why waste it? In much the same way that farmers believed they could "coax" spring to arrive by performing rituals, they believed that if they were nice to Rusalki and tried to understand their ways and imitate their behavior, they could coax the maidens to dole out that fertility onto the crops, land, animals, and even people. (In the section on "Rusalka Week" below, you'll learn how they imitated the spirits.)

How do Rusalki accomplish this transfer? Through their songs, caresses, dances, and swinging on tree branches. However, some researchers believe Rusalki, in performing these actions, are unaware of the benefits (or damage) their activities cause. They merely love to sing, dance, and play upon the land during the time they're free of their watery home.

Besides their beauty, you probably think about mermaids' lovely, enchanting voices. You may have heard that talking or singing to plants helps them grow; just imagine what the power of these divine creatures can do when attempting the same thing. Their voices, when not used to seduce men, sing in eternal harmony and bestow life upon the land.

Not only their voices, but Rusalki's mere touch also brings nurturing power to growing crops. But they do more than touch. They frolic among the rye, corn, and wheat fields, hanging off the stalks, making them sway as if tossed about by a strong breeze.

Rusalki Dancing to Shepherd's Kaval. Illustration by Nelinda. © Bendideia Publishing.

Even more than their touch, their dancing stimulates the soil. Peasants believed that "divine life simply 'dances' and in this very act of dancing is thought to create life."[56] The grass always grows thicker and greener where the spirits step or perform their circle dances. (See "The Power of the Circle Dance" sidebar for more information.)

Dancing alone cannot sustain the land, though; water is also necessary for successful crop growth. This moisture is produced when Rusalki comb their hair. Water flows from the long, thick strands to moisten the soil. Their green tresses are symbolic of fertility and have been called "a metaphorical image of the long green 'hair' of the flowering crops."[57]

The symbolism of swinging on trees, as well, has connections to the regeneration of life. Among young people, it was part of the courting ritual, which Rusalki mimicked.

> In Bulgaria the young men also scouted out sturdy trees from which to hang swings made from hempen ropes they had just twisted. Each marriageable girl, dressed in her best clothes so as to make a good impression on the bachelors and their mothers, and each bride in her full regalia sat down in turn on the wooden seat to be swung three times by the boys,

THE POWER OF THE CIRCLE DANCE

The name of the circle dance varies from country to country: Russian *khorovod*, Bulgarian *horo*, Serbian *kolo*, Romanian *hora*, Macedonian *oro*. Today, line and chain dances also fall under the same name as circle dances. These dances are performed at all major celebrations and social gatherings: weddings, name days, funerals, and so on. At one time, they were performed as part of betrothal customs.

Healers, young women, and girls use the circle dance in their rituals for health, fertility, and initiations. But there's more to the meaning of the dances. The names of the dances themselves indicate a circle: wheel, spinning circle, cycle. And not only a circle, but a circle to a god (*Ra* being a sun god, the equivalent of sunrise or ray). And so, the *hora*, for example, becomes a "solar circle" (Beard, "Hora românilor").

The earliest dances likely date back to 3000 B.C. or earlier, during the time the ancient Thracians occupied Eastern Europe. They were thought to be part of the rites of solar worship. Sometimes, a sacred object lay within the center of the circle, or a person playing the bagpipe stood there, signifying the solar system, with the central sun and the planets circling it. The unbroken circle would "exclude evil forces from the center or from the participants" (Barber, 361).

I talk about the horo more in my forthcoming book, *The Wanderer*. Here's an excerpt:

> The horo was a way for them to connect the material world to their spiritual life, which is encoded in the dance's rhythms. For the Thracians, among whom is Orpheus, the famous musician born in the Rhodopes, the music was what connected mankind with their spiritual reality.

continues

while the other girls sang wishes for health and a good marriage. In some areas everyone, young and old got to swing, so as not to be left out of the fun. The higher the swing went, the taller the hemp would grow.[58]

In colder, harsher northern climates, where growing seasons are short and temperatures are frigid, Rusalki aren't considered fertility spirits. You won't see groups of lovely maidens dancing among the rye and corn, because these spirits are neither lovely nor social.

Poor Imitators

Water spirits are also called nymphs. The word comes from the ancient Greek *Nýmphē*, which was used to describe not only a spirit maiden, but also meant a bride. They were "females on the verge of producing new life, just like human brides."[59] In many ways, Rusalki spirit nymphs try to mimic or complete the role they could never achieve in life—being beautiful, desirable brides. But, in the same way that they're neither completely dead nor alive, they're also neither married nor unmarried.

CIRCLE DANCE *continued*

The music of the horo has a specific rhythm. The most popular is 7/8, which we Bulgarians know as our *ruchenitza* or a rhythmic dance in pairs. Within this rhythm is the vibrating of the cosmic spheres, like the sun, which held a sacred role in Thracian beliefs and rituals. Like the sun sends out two short, then one long pulse, so does the human heart work.

The worship of the sun also shows not only in the name of the dance, but also in the footsteps of the dancers. Here's another excerpt from *The Wanderer*.

I once came across an exhibition dedicated to the horo that was on display on the streets of Veliko Tarnovo, the old capital of Bulgaria. The paintings presented in the exhibition were made from the footprints of the rhythmic horo dancers. I was shocked by the symbolism encoded in every dance. Some of the footprints resembled the fiery summer sun shining on our ancestors in the fields: the sun with its burning rays, the sun that gives light and brings everything to life.

The dance consists of participants holding the hands or waistbands of the people on each side of them, forming an unbroken circle. This represents the sacred unity of the community and the continuation of life and the seasons. They dance in the direction the sun moves, toward the left, which is the spiritual, celestial, and immortal direction, while right is earthly and mortal. Spiral dances, with their counterclockwise movement, symbolize man's ascent to heaven (Beard, "Hora românilor").

RONESA AVEELA

In their attempt to become brides or wives, Rusalki emulate the appearance of a human bride: wearing a white linen chemise and adorning their hair with a wreath woven from flowers, river grasses, and willow branches. They also imitate typical women's activities such as weaving, spinning, and, of course, sex. However, they accomplish each undertaking with poor results, because the young women died before they knew the proper way to go about these activities.

Weaving, or the Problem of Clothes

Weaving and making clothes were essential parts of a rural woman's duties.

> It should be noted that the production of textiles, one of the most ancient womanly crafts, appears in traditional patriarchal societies as means of establishing, maintaining, and evaluating order, civil, domestic, and even cosmological. The woman weaving in the home is a sign that everything and everyone is in her place.[60]

Rural girls and young women begin weaving before their marriage. If you recall, Rusalki wear tattered clothing, if anything at all. Their own wedding clothes, if they happened to have been buried in them, now are in shambles. It's no wonder, then, that Rusalki attempt to accomplish the goal of weaving and other clothes-making tasks like spinning, which they love. It's one way they can obtain something decent to wear.

As part of Rusalki's in-between lives, some people say the spirits desire to move on and fulfill what should have been theirs if they had lived. The spirits hope that performing these traditional duties will provide their undead lives with a sense of order.

And yet, because they're stuck in limbo, they fail miserably when they attempt weaving. Rusalki sneak into the bathhouse, a place where women often perform their weaving because the moist air helps them work the fibers into the linen. If women haven't said protection prayers over their work at the end of the day, Rusalki can take over the task of weaving. However, they tangle the thread and end up unweaving the material because they perform the activity backward. They may even destroy the work from frustration. When their weaving attempts fail, they'll steal the yarn and linen and bring them to adorn the waterside.

They may even sneak up on sleeping women and take their clothes and other bridal embellishments, such as embroidered dresses, white shirts, and beads to decorate their hair. It's easy for Rusalki to do this if the women have fallen asleep without first praying. How else would the women explain to everyone that they ended up naked in the forest or field after they fell asleep?

If the spirit maidens do succeed in acquiring these coveted items, you'll see yarn and material hanging on tree branches and along edges of their watery homes. The spirits, although called "unclean" dead, don't like dirty objects. They'll first wash what they've stolen, and then hang them to let them dry. If you're out and about and run across such washings, avoid stepping on them. Anyone unfortunate enough to do so soon becomes weak and lame.

If Rusalki aren't able to steal clothes, they'll call out to you from tree branches. They'll beg you to take pity on them and give them something to wear. You don't have to be extravagant and purchase an expensive outfit. They'll settle for a white chemise (shift), rags, a handkerchief, or a piece torn from your own clothing as demonstrated in the following song.

24

Captain and Seductive Rusalki. Illustration by Nelinda. © Bendideia Publishing.

By the curling birch tree
A rusalka sat,
Begging for a little tunic:
"Dear young maiden,
Stop and give me a shirt,
Even if it's a thin one,
A little white one."[61]

Even if you don't hear them calling to you, or if you're afraid to enter the forest (which you should be), you can hang clothing, as well as skeins of thread, on tree boughs for the spirits to retrieve later when they come out to dance and play at night. If you do hear them calling to you, though, be sure to do as they request. Failure to do so is likely to cause them to attack and tickle you until you die.

A question to ponder about their desire for clothing is: Are Rusalki trying to live normal lives, or are their actions "a mere camouflage to look like desirable brides"[62] in order to trap or harm men?

Sex and Intimacy

Rusalki perform their imitation perhaps the most badly when they're intimate with men they've captured. Folklorists have called this intimacy "fake and not functional."[63] For the most part, the sexuality of Rusalki is associated with their fertility: it's meant to nourish the land, not be procreative. Consequently, sex for Rusalki, they say, can never be "wild" or "unrestrained," as the girls or young women are "stranded in never ending puberty."[64]

Not all folklorists agree. Some say Rusalki express their sexuality through the tickling they're so fond of. Unfortunately, this tickling, although "playful," is eventually "tragic."[65]

Their tickling of the male victim to death is, in my opinion, their only way of expressing the sexuality as they are supposed [to] know it. Theirs is the childish, unripen sexuality of young girls who do not know how to express it properly yet—or better: they *are socially supposed not to know*, because the society needs them to be "honourable" and "chaste" before wedding, ... even though this ideal, of course, often contradicts the everyday experience. Therefore, they are supposed to know only playful tickling, whimsical bathing and jolly dancing. When all this takes an unbearable amount of time and when it is performed by numerous *rusalki* outnumbering the poor lad, it can end only as unendurable endless foreplay that eventually kills the human lover.[66]

It's this view of tickling that classifies the action as a "kind of inverted, improper sex act."[67]

Rusalki and Brides

To understand Rusalki better, you need to know more about the importance of marriage in rural, patriarchal societies. Although customs around a woman's role vary from country to country and region to region, many principles about marriage itself were similar at one time.

A woman's primary function in the community was to bear and raise children. Motherhood was "the height of femininity and the highest ideal to which any woman aspires."[68] She was expected to attend to her family's needs above her own. A woman who sought other employment (especially in urban areas) was considered to be like a Rusalka, one "who figuratively 'drowned' in her job and in her quest for emancipation."[69] Women who resisted marriage or had children outside of marriage were considered "bad." They had to either "submit to the symbolic death of the wedding" or "accept the literal death of the *rusalka*."[70]

These perceptions of the role of women still prevail in many rural areas.

In Medieval times, girls could wed as early as age 13 or 14, leaving them little opportunity during their lifetime to be unwed or, in other words, to have their freedom (*volia*). Rusalki may have been considered cursed, but they had their freedom from male "ownership." Perhaps not such a dreadful fate after all.

Many things could go wrong from the time a girl became engaged until her actual marriage ceremony, and even beyond that during the birth of her first child. Her death during those periods would ensure her fate as a Rusalka because "[t]he Slavs thought that an imprint of 'impurity' quite often remained on the young wife until giving birth to a child."[71]

And it was imperative that the girl obey her

Bulgarian opera singer Hristina Morfova as a bride.
Photographer unknown, 1926.
Archives State Agency [Public domain].

father, under whose rule she lived, especially in matters of arranged marriages. The story below tells of one girl's rebellion in that matter. It's a bit more gruesome than her simply turning into a Rusalka if she died before getting married.

> Some people say that the rusalka is a girl who was engaged and died engaged. One rich man had a daughter; she was so good, rich and beautiful. One poor young man fell in love with her, but her parents didn't want her to marry him, because he was poor. And if he was poor, then he wasn't honorable; he was unlucky. And, it looked like her father made her get engaged with some rich guy. And she didn't want to get married to that rich man so bad that she poisoned herself, while she was engaged. Well, she was buried.
>
> That poor young man went to her grave, crying and grieving after her. One night he had a dream that she came to him and told him to dig her out, so she could meet with him. Well, he went to the cemetery at twelve o'clock at night—midnight—dug her out, took her to the wheat field and hid her there.

Well, every day at noon she would come to life, and meet with him. Her hair was down, and she was dressed in white [same as at the funeral]. And they were meeting in the wheat field.

And since that time everyone was saying that rusalki live in the wheat fields.[72]

The Importance of Hair

People associate Rusalki's loose and unbound tresses with the supernatural; in much the same way, witches, who possess magical powers, leave their hair uncovered. Loose hair is in sharp contrast to the braids "proper" women wear, in addition to the kerchiefs married women cover their hair with. Among villagers, the type of braid signifies a woman's marital status. Any female daring to defy this custom is considered as pagan as the Rusalki. In fact, people may cross themselves in the woman's presence, not knowing if she is perhaps a *real* Rusalka.

But there's more to hair than social status. While a Rusalka's breasts symbolize her ability to nurture the land, her long, thick hair has its own connection to fertility.

Rusalki Swimming. Illustration by Nelinda. © Bendideia Publishing.

Whence this belief? One of the first signs of a girl's sexual maturation is the arrival of pubic hair, so people associated her new fertility with her new hair—then postulated that the hair *caused* the fertility.… "Fertility resides in hair" presently extended to female head hair, too, which is why married women in Europe were supposed to cover their hair.… The most important moment in the agrarian wedding (as opposed to the Christian one) was when the girl's single braid was combed out, divided, and rebraided into two braids that were wrapped around her head and covered forevermore with a cap.… The symbolism here is that on the wedding bed her pubic hair also will be divided—by the sexual act that will produce babies.

So the longer and thicker the girl's hair, the more suitable a bride she will be.[73]

Wedding Rituals

Like Rusalki's existence, marriage itself was a liminal state, a passage that brought a woman into her expected social position in the community. She gave up her freedom of maidenhood and was "sold" to her husband through symbolic rituals dealing with her hair.

An unwed woman wore a single braid that she might adorn with ribbons, flowers, or beads. The night before her wedding began her transition. The bride's female friends brought her to the bathhouse or *banya*[74] (steam bath room, like a sauna) where they unbraided her hair, and then proceeded to wash and comb it throughout the ritual bath, much like Rusalki constantly wash and comb their hair to keep it moist. It was believed that "the constant washing, combing and plaiting of the bride's hair may be an attempt to conjure up the fertility of the rusalka."[75]

In Eastern European folklore, the word "combing" is a reference to sex.[76] Erotic and sexual references are often indirect or euphemisms, rather than explicit mentions of coitus. Popular references indicated movements, such as yanking, beating, pounding, waving, rolling, somersaulting, dancing, and horse riding.[77] The latter activity was also standard in many pre-wedding rituals, bringing to mind Big & Rich's song, "Save a Horse [Ride a Cowboy]."[78] Tales tell of Rusalki stealing horses for joy rides; they ride the creatures to exhaustion and often to death, in the same way they tickle men until they die.[79]

> **Did you know?**
>
> A Ukrainian woman could give a suitor not the finger but a literal pumpkin to show her rejection of his offer of marriage (Rubchak, "Ukraine's Ancient Matriarch," 134).

When young women were through with their bathhouse rituals, they braided the bride's hair into a single plait for the last time. This action had them all crying, because it was the end of her *volia* or freedom from having to submit to a husband.

In other regions, instead of the bride's friends braiding her hair, the best man would cut it off the night before the wedding. They believed a Rusalka's hair contained power. Since the yet-to-be-bride was so much like these water nymphs, it was a way to "render her 'harmless' to the new husband."[80]

The next day, her wedding, the woman was well on the way to becoming part of her husband's family. She fell completely under his rule when either her father or the groom unbraided her hair and covered it with a kerchief or wreath.

In Ukraine single women wore wreaths until the wedding eve, as a talisman against the evil eye and blandishments of the devil. To ensure the neutralization of the dangerous magical powers associated with virgins (which the wearing of wreaths symbolized), if the prospective bride still had not lost her innocence, she was ritually deflowered.[81]

A bride's wedding day was one point in her life that her hair remained loose like Rusalki, as it was a liminal state between maidenhood and marriage. The difference was that a bride's hair remained covered, although unbraided, while Rusalki's flowed freely. Only after the couple entered the church could the bride's veil replace the kerchief.

After the wedding, the bride went to the groom's home, where the ritual continued. The family created two braids, which they coiled around the woman's head. She still wore her bridal veil, but when she removed it, she had to hide her hair with a kerchief or headdress. Her husband was the only person who could see her hair uncovered. Since hair symbolized fertility, this meant the only person who could have access to her "fertility" was her husband.

Giving Birth, or Death during Labor

The next important, and critical, point in a woman's life was giving birth to her first child. Among Russians and other Slavic people, the mother would give birth in the *banya* (bathhouse).[82]

In many cultures, childbirth was considered "so dangerous that it calls for a separation of the mother from her community."[83] It's dangerous because it's not only a time of creating new life, but also a time

Rusalki. Ivan Kramskoi, 1871.
[Public domain], via Wikimedia Commons.

when a woman's life was in jeopardy. Creator and creation, life and death intertwined. Both liminal states. Therefore, these two phases converging created a great sense of danger to the community. If the woman died before the child was born, she was left in a permanent state of transition, and, thus, became a Rusalka.

Funeral Customs

During a wedding, a woman is considered to ritually die.[84] In the same way, many elements of funeral rituals are reminiscent of weddings. When a woman mourns at a loved one's grave is the only other time she can have her hair unbraided.

A funeral mimics a wedding procession: bridal attendants, best man, matchmaker, and family proceed to the burial site. During the ceremony, a special wedding bread remains on top of the casket, to be broken and given to the deceased's relatives after the funeral. Unmarried people who die—both male and female—wear wedding attire. The deceased woman appears the same as a bride on the way to her wedding: with hair unbraided, a wreath on her head, and a ring on her finger. Sound familiar? Except for the ring, this is how Rusalki are attired.

People who die early, whether by their own hand or from a violent act, are said to have not died "their own death." They are not given all the special Christian burial rites, nor are they buried in sacred ground, because people believe doing so would bring drought and famine to the land. Instead, any of the following can be done to their bodies.

> [They] were literally "set aside" and buried (or just thrown carelessly) on demarcated places, such as at crossroads, on the boundary strips between fields, alongside roads, in woods and forests (or on the boundaries of forest and field). Sometimes, they were thrown into swamps or rivers. In other words, they are always buried on places distant, marginal, boundary, or otherwise liminal.[85]

Failure to perform the special burial rites meant the deceased could return to walk the earth as the unclean dead. Therefore, to prevent an unmarried, deceased girl from becoming a Rusalka, parents sometimes performed their own marriage ceremony for the girl after she died. First, she needed a fiancé. One account tells of a father who tied his engaged, but deceased daughter to a pillar. He placed a wedding ring on her finger and one on the pillar (the substitute groom), so she wouldn't become a Rusalka.[86] With this symbolic completion of her lifecycle, the potential Rusalka is appeased and can continue into the spiritual world.

Even dying before a marriageable age might not prevent that fate; with high infant mortality rates, girls could become Rusalki if they weren't baptized. It's no wonder so many wandering, unfulfilled spirits still roam the waterways and countryside today.

Another interesting funeral custom[87] is that the comb used to brush a deceased person's hair and the hair itself that remains in the comb are both discarded somewhere neither people nor animals are likely to wander. Is this the same comb Rusalki use to free water from their hair?

The purpose of many other funeral rituals is to ensure the dead person's soul leaves the house without harming anyone in the family in the process: from closing the corpse's eyes, to positioning the body, to reversing the placement of furniture to confuse the soul, and so much more.

Although the reasons behind these rituals have changed over time, people still practice many of them today.

Rusalki as Lovers

Can love exist in Rusalki's relationships with men? Some sources say "the beliefs in the spirit-lover come from the conviction that the deceased continue to have sexual needs, such as the living."[88] Literature is filled with stories of this love, but in folklore, the answer would be "seldom." This loveless relationship goes both ways.

> And, as in the case of *rusalki* towards humans, it is also very rare for them to feel love or desire for them. It seems that the emotional basis, if we can call it that, on which the *rusalki* arose in the imagination of the Eastern Slavs was not love, but fear. The *rusalki* are not the dark object of desire of unsatisfied men, in which we believe that there is a well-known difference with respect to the nymphs of classical mythology.[89]

What causes this fear is often Rusalki's association with being the unclean dead. They are cursed and therefore sinful at the same time. Stories about Rusalki willingly staying with men are told to explain how

Rusalka Embrace. Mikhail Vrubel, nineteenth century.
Mikhail Vrubel [Public domain].

their cursed souls can be saved. They can be returned to an "acceptable life" through the Church by "a cross, baptism and marriage."[90]

Once freed of their sinful nature, the spirits become human and are free to marry any men who take compassion on them, even if love isn't involved. Love wasn't a consideration for many human-to-human marriages, so it would follow that it wasn't necessary in a human-to-Rusalka relationship.

> My second uncle Maxim was a sailor on a barge on the Volga when he was young. So one morning he went to wash up and suddenly he sees there is a girl by the bridge, amazingly pretty. "Eh – ma," says my uncle, "I would go after this princess in no time. If she falls in love with me, I wouldn't mind getting married," and he was single at that time. After he said so, he feared something, like something creepy attacked his whole body. He stood and thought: where to run? And suddenly the girl spoke: "What are you, good fellow, afraid of me? If you said that you love me and want to marry me, then I won't leave you alone; take me with you!" My uncle started praying—but nothing helped; he agreed to take her with him.
>
> He lived with her on the barge for two weeks and started feeling sad. His friends noticed that he was talking to someone at night. "Who are you talking to at night? You don't look like yourself!" He told them what was the matter. They advised him to go home, and he did so. He came home, and she followed him. He took her to the storehouse and only went there to sleep with her at night. When my uncle Maxim had to leave home, the rusalka cried all locked up. Maxim's relatives noticed that someone was crying in the storehouse; they went to check it out but saw no one. They asked Maxim what kind of wonder was that? He had to tell them that the girl followed him from the barge, and he couldn't get rid of her no matter what he did: "I promised to marry her, but I'm afraid to ask your blessing." His parents answered him: "Listen, Maksimushko, if you promised to take her for yourself—then take her. And when you lie down in bed with her, put a cross on her, while she's sleeping."
>
> Uncle Maxim did everything as his mother taught him. In the morning the parents came to check on him, and saw that he wasn't alone in the storehouse; there was a naked girl there with him. They gave her a sundress and asked her: "Where are you from, girl?" She answered them: "I'm from far away, from Samara province. Mother cursed me. I went and drowned myself because of the grief I felt. But I didn't drown, just started living in the water. For three years I was a rusalka. Thanks to your son Maxim for helping me out, I will pray to God for him all my life." Soon after that uncle Maxim married her, and they lived very happy. Forty years ago, aunt Claudia died, and uncle Maxim died three years after her.[91]

Not all stories are loveless. Some, such as that of Ivan Savel'evich below, tell of the affection between a human and a Rusalka.

> A young seal-hunter who lived in the city of Arkhangel'sk, in northern Russia, and who according to one story became captivated by the unearthly beauty of a russalka and spent one long winter in her company.

While seal hunting in winter on the bleak islands of Novaya Zemlya, well within the Arctic Circle, Ivan spent many lonely nights alone in his hut playing his balalaika. One night the oil in his lamp ran out and he continued to play in the dark. As he played, he heard the sound of someone dancing inside his hut. Knowing that he was alone, he was frightened and quickly refilled and relit his lamp. The hut was empty. The following night the same thing happened. Finally he hid the lit lamp behind a thick curtain, and as soon as the sound of dancing started, he drew back the curtain to reveal a young girl.

This girl explained to Ivan that she was a russalka but because she had a human father, she was able to remain out of the water for as long as she liked, provided she was in the presence of only one person. Ivan fell hopelessly in love with the russalka, and they spent the winter together, during which time everything they ever wanted or needed magically appeared. However, when spring came Ivan had to return to his home to sell his catch. As they parted, the russalka gave him instructions on how he might find her again.

Some time later Ivan found he could not live without the russalka. Remembering what his lover had told him, he sought out her home: He climbed a tree that hung above the water, and at the stroke of midday, he dived into the water. As he reached the bottom of the river, his lover rushed out from the weeds and embraced him. Ivan stayed a long time beneath the waters of that river, but in the end he longed to return home. Remembering that anyone could be protected from the charms of the russalka by the holy cross, he made the sign and was immediately transported back home. However, having crossed himself, he could never again return to his russalka.[92]

More common are stories where a cross protects travelers from Rusalki and enables them to "tame" the spirits into being good wives, as the story below shows.

My great-grandfather went one time during Rusalia Week to strip lime-bark; and there some rusalki attacked him, but he quickly drew a cross [on the ground] and stood on this cross. After that, all the rusalki left, and only one still stayed there. My great-grandfather grabbed the rusalka by the arm and dragged her into the [magic] circle, quickly throwing a cross on her, hanging it around her neck. Then the rusalka submitted to him; after that he led her home.

The rusalka lived with my great-grandfather for a whole year, willingly carrying out all the wifely tasks, but when the next Rusalia Week came round again, the rusalka ran off again into the woods. Captured rusalki, they say, eat little—rather they feed on vapor and soon they disappear without a trace from the human dwelling.[93]

In marriage, Rusalki cease to be carefree and shameless and become dutiful, obliging wives. They lose their freedom—but regain their ability to procreate. Even though the Rusalka in the above story was compliant to the man's wishes and stayed with him for a year, no mention of love exists in the tale. She was there by compulsion. At times, even if Rusalki are content with their husbands and a married life, some word or action by the men can make the spirits long to return to their home in the water, and they will abandon both their spouse and their children.

Rusalka. Illustration © Andy Paciorek. Used with permission of the artist.

Earlier, you learned that the supernatural world of Rusalki—the water they live in, as well as the cursed places the unclean dead are buried—overlaps the "real" human world. It's perhaps this distinction between the two worlds that "contains a clue as to why the love between a rusalka and a man is so rare: because the boundary between life and death cannot be transgressed"[94] as the story below indicates.

> Rusalki in white dresses, with loose hair, fall in love with guys. They are dead. One guy came from the army; his father took him to thresh, and over there [at the edge of the field] unbaptized children were buried. The guy looked around and saw a beautiful girl. The old man started looking for him, and saw that they were sitting hugging each other and she kissed the guy. The old man started reading the Sunday Prayer, and the guy became alive, and she became dead. At first, he started to get thin [due to long meetings with the rusalka], and then recovered.[95]

On the Dark Side

Those Rusalki who do end up marrying humans are likely to kill any children they give birth to. Stories tell of Rusalki brides dismembering their human offspring. Or they may just kill the infants at birth, because the spirits have predicted that nothing good will come from the children when they grow older.[96] Even if Rusalki have children with men, and they don't murder them, the infants normally die, poisoned by their mothers' milk.

The milder-tempered southern lasses are not always innocent and helpful. Like a gang of popular high-school girls (think "Mean Girls"), they can have a cruel streak. These malicious Rusalki show contempt or aversion to humans, teasing and taunting those they encounter. They're jealous of and resent women—perhaps because they themselves never got to fulfill their own life. But men are their primary victims, attacked simply for being male.

> My son was chased by a rusalka. Last year during Rusalka week. We were in the sauna. It was 12 o'clock. He went on the hillock, and she appeared, he didn't see her face, her hands were cold—cold, and she was very tall herself. "We can take a nice walk with you here," she says. "Well, who the hell are you?" he says: "Well, you won't get away from me. I'll catch up with you." He stopped to light up a cigarette. After he started smoking, they moved forward. They reached the brickwork [bridge]. He said she was walking on one side, him on the other. After they crossed the brickwork, she said: "I don't think I can win a fight with you, but would have drowned you, if you were drunk." They reached the shopkeeper's place, and then the dog started barking, and she disappeared. There was a rusalka's pass way and pond there. So she followed him there. Yes, did not stop following. And if he was drunk, she could've drowned him.[97]

The fierceness of Rusalki's attacks depends on the location, however. Those from northern climates are more vicious—with the intent to destroy any men they meet. If it's your misfortune to run across a northern Rusalka while passing the water's edge, be quick to get away, or she'll snatch you off the path. She'll torture you in malicious ways or strangle you as she attempts to drown you.

Rusalka. Illustration © Andy Paciorek. Used with permission of the artist.

[I]t happens in the dark, at its centre is the fear of engulfing water.... The creature *points in derision* or *beckons invitingly*; the victim is dragged towards her despite himself; she arouses revulsion and at the same time is impossible to resist.[98]

Sometimes, the spirit uses trickery to pull a man under as in the account below.

A man crossed a dam in moonlight in the middle of the night and noticed a hand sticking a piece of bread out of the water. He got scared and ran away. If he took the bread out of the hand, he would be pulled under water because this was the hand of a mermaid.[99]

The spirits frequently pull their victims to the ground and tickle them to death. Such Rusalki have been described as "dead, bloodthirsty spinsters who hate humankind and just want to eradicate men by tickling them away."[100] The example below from Nikolay Gogol expresses the folkloric beliefs of his day.

At the hour when dark fades, . . . from the waves of the Dnepr the maidens who destroyed their own lives [i.e., committed suicide] come forth in flocks; hair cascades from their green heads onto their shoulders, and water, plashing noisily, runs from their long hair to the ground, while the girls shine through the water as though a glass shirt; their mouths smile wonderfully, their cheeks blaze, their eyes bewitch the soul . . . *She* would burn with love, *she* would kiss passionately. . . . Flee, Christian man! Her lips are poison, her touch cold water; she will tickle you mercilessly and drag you off into the river.[101]

Stories say Rusalki tickle men with their huge breasts. Don't laugh. Tickling can be painful, especially when prolonged. In fact, the original meaning of the Russian word for "tickle" (*shchekotat'*, щекотать) meant "to utter loud, piercing sounds, to laugh shrilly."[102]

But wait, there's even more to this torture.

While southern Rusalki's breasts are symbolic of their excessive, unused fertility, this is not the case with the northern spirits. Their black- or green-tipped nipples are made of iron and will crush their victims. They may even shove their breasts at you, forcing you to feed from their poisonous milk. As if that isn't bad enough, parents would tell their children not to go into the rye fields because Rusalki would use their breasts to crush the children and grind them in a mortar.

Instead of tickling men, Rusalki may opt to dance with them until the men are exhausted and die. The spirits may also drag men under water if they're swimming alone. The men become entangled in the Rusalki's long hair as the spirits wrap them in a deadly embrace in a "kind of erotic jacuzzi."[103] The men struggle to free themselves, but the spirits' bodies are slippery, and the men can't use them as leverage to force themselves upward. Keeping men under water the way an alligator does its victims, Rusalki wait until the men drown.

Few have escaped their grip, although the spirits do let some men go of their own free will. Insanity or illness overcomes these men, however, or they become "melancholic, mute or withdrawn from reality" until they die.[104] Special rituals can cure them of the so-called Rusalka disease if they fall under the maiden's spell. (You'll learn more about this in the "Magical Healers" section later in this book.)

Possessed. Jacek Malczewski, 1887.
Jacek Malczewski [Public domain].

It's not only tickling and drowning you have to worry about from Rusalki. Instead of being beneficial, dancing and combing their hair can produce the opposite effect. Too little attention from the spirits, and the crops wither. Too much, and crops are destroyed rather than nourished. When Rusalki dance among the stalks, they may stomp on them, smashing your harvest. They may comb their hair too long, producing a flood that will drown and rot the plants. And if angered, Rusalki withhold their blessings from crops and instead send disease and inclement weather to destroy the fields.

To prevent these actions, don't let them stay in your fields too long. After you've encouraged them to bestow their blessings during the fragile flowering and ripening stage, shoo the spirits away before they despoil the crops once they've started producing bounty. (You'll learn about these rituals in the "Rusalka Week" section later in this chapter.)

Protection from Rusalki

Before you drive Rusalki away at the end of their week among you, find ways to protect yourself from them if you happen to meet them in the forest, fields, or waterways. You've already learned that a cross or the sign of the cross will protect you. This is especially true if you're in the water or even walking over a bridge. Any action using the cross should make Rusalki powerless to harm you. If wearing a cross doesn't deter them, try pricking them with a pin. If you go swimming (even though you know you're not supposed to during Rusalka Week), put fern in your hair. This prevents you from drowning because they can't pull you down into a deadly embrace.

It's essential that you don't look the spirits in the eye. If they're persistent, following you everywhere you go, try this charm to get them to leave you alone:

> Water girl, forest girl, crazy girl! Get away, roll away, don't show up in my yard; you won't have to live here for a century, just for one week. Go into the deep river, to the high aspen. Aspen start shaking. Water girl, calm down. I accepted the law; I kissed the golden cross; I don't have to hang out with you or get married to you. Go into the woods, deep deep woods, to the forest owner. He's waiting for you; he's making a bed for you on the moss, and has laid it with green grass. He puts a deck by your headboard; you should sleep with him, and will never touch me, because I'm baptized.[105]

Better yet, here's a more elaborate ritual using a magic circle and reciting a charm that you can perform:

> To get rid of them during their attack, you need to draw a cross on the ground, and then a circle and stand in that circle. Rusalki then would not approach; they would walk and walk around the line, and then hide.
> In one of the spiritual songs, girls ask the grandmother to encircle them with the magic circle and sprinkle them with oats and hops:

> "And you, Grandma Kupriyanovna,
> Can you encircle us with the golden knife,
> Can you sprinkle us with the spirited oats?"

> Grandmother draws the line around the girls, who are in a circle, with the words:

> "Within the line are ours.
> Behind the line—not ours!"[106]

As mentioned earlier, carrying wormwood will also help, especially if Rusalki ask you a riddle. You can tuck the herb inside your clothing, or attach it to your belt. As long as it's on your person, you have a chance to escape.

Besides your body, you can also deck your homes and beds with the herb to keep the spirits away. When on household doors, wormwood prevents Rusalki from coming inside. You may wonder why it repels them. It's because the spirits are sensitive to strong odors; they abhor its heavy scent and bitter taste.

Other items that have magical powers to protect you from Rusalki are incense, a clove of garlic, lovage, hedge hyssop, hops, absinthe, and dry walnut leaves.

Be careful you don't mix up herbs and wear something that *attracts* Rusalki. Bulgarian Rusalki are especially fond of *zdravets*, a type of geranium. Depending on the variety, it can smell like lemon, rose, or even chocolate. You know how many women love chocolate. It's not wise to tempt even the undead with something that smells like this treat.

Also avoid carrying roses, parsley, or pieces of birch. You'll have all the spirits within miles milling around you, thinking you're ready and willing to be tickled. Their favorite flower that you should avoid

Plants Used for Protection Against Rusalki.

Wormwood (*Artemisia absinthium*): Franz Eugen Köhler, *Köhler's Medizinal-Pflanzen*, 1897.
Garlic (*Allium sativum*): William Woodville, *Medical Botany*, 1793.
Walnut (*Juglans regia*): Franz Eugen Köhler, *Köhler's Medizinal-Pflanzen*, 1897.
[Public domain], via Wikimedia Commons.

having on or near you at all costs (except when you're asking for a cure) is *rosen*, or burning bush. Later in this book, you'll learn more about how this can cure you with the aid of the Rusalki.

You can avoid encountering the spirits if you abide by restrictions that have been established for the week Rusalki walk on land:

- Don't go swimming, especially if you forget to wear a cross. (They'll drown you.)
- Don't bathe yourself or your children in water bodies, especially without first praying. (Again, they'll drown you.)
- Don't go outside alone, especially not to the river to fetch water. (Go anywhere near the water, and they'll drown you.)
- Don't venture into the fields or forest. (They'll tickle you or make you dance until you die.)
- Don't spy on them even from a distance. (Seeing or hearing them singing will make you go blind, mute, deaf, or insane. And watching their dances, in which they appear to "writhe and contort" themselves, will cause you to involuntarily imitate them and thus become crippled or deformed.)
- Don't step anywhere the spirits gather. (You'll get foot disease, lose your strength, or become a cripple.)
- Don't sleep near springs, forests, or in damp, cold places. (You'll lose your strength or be disfigured.)
- Don't drink from well water at night. (You'll become disfigured.)
- Children, don't clap your hands or shout in the forest. (They'll carry you off to their realm.)

- Women, don't spin, weave, sew, wash clothes, weave, or perform any other handiwork. (You'll become ill.)
- Men, don't work outside or build fences. (You'll become ill, or the Rusalki will steal your cattle and poultry.)

Rusalki have been known to enter and leave villages by walking along with the cattle. If you're a woman, to protect yourself from the spirits, try what rural women do: braid your hair before you go out, and bite the end of those braids whenever you drive cattle from and into the pasture.

If your cattle have gone missing because you didn't listen and worked in the fields and didn't bite your braids to keep Rusalki away, you'll have to give tribute to the spirits. Perform the following ritual and recite the charm below:

> Weave bast shoes, while sitting on a stump in the woods; tear up a new woman's shirt and make some rags, and, along with bread and salt, wrap it all in a clean rag, tie it up with a red ribbon and take it to an intersection in the forest. Over there, put all this on any tree, bow down to the earth, without blessing yourself, on all four sides and say:

> "I ask you, rusalki,
> Accept my gifts
> And return the cattle!"[107]

If you're young and daring, you can take a chance and venture into the fields with other brave souls to drive Rusalki away. Don't be foolish and go alone: remember, Rusalki appear in groups, so you should, too. Wave brooms and yell, "Pursue! Pursue!" as the spirits make their way through the stalks of grain. If you're fortunate, you can join the ranks of those who have seen their prey running into the woods while they sob and cry.[108] Don't let them fool you into thinking you've harmed them with your brooms; it's only their sorrow at not being able to tickle you or make you dance that's made them weep.

Appeasing Rusalki

You're not always going to be able to protect yourself from Rusalki. Sometimes, you'll be stuck outside at times you shouldn't be there. Or perhaps someone's "double dared" you to go against what has been forbidden for the week. In that case, you'll want to appease the spirits before they do anything bad to you.

Rusalki enjoy food offerings left by the riverbank. You can give them any number of different edible gifts: wheat bread and salt, cheese, butter, eggs. And don't forget about tossing them clothing and tying ribbons on the trees. The spirits will have a party, and you'll have a good chance of doing whatever it is you set out to do in their territory.

It also makes them happy if you wear something green to imitate those of their sisters who like to dress in green leaves.

If you do a kind deed for Rusalki—especially if you're kind to their children—they're likely to do something kind for you in return.

> While gathering mushrooms in the forest, a woman saw hanging from a tree a huge piece of birch bark and on it a little boy sleeping. Pitying the child, she took off her apron,

covered the sleeper with it, and moved on. Soon a rusalka—a naked woman with tousled hair—overtook her and touched her on the hand with these words: "Fight in your hands, for you!" From that time on, the woman began to work so strongly that everyone wondered where her strength came from.[109]

Don't always expect something from Rusalki, though, if you're kind to their children. The mother might not be nearby when you come across her child. Be kind regardless. All children deserve to be comforted.

The talk about rusalki's children, naked, miserable, moaning, is very common. A peasant woman from Dankov Evla Markovna told me the following:
"I was riding with my father; after passing one big fir tree, we heard a pitiable moan, as if little children were crying. Father whispered into my ear: 'These are rusalki's children crying!' We covered a spot around the tree with a kerchief, and the crying stopped."[110]

Who knows? When that child grows up, she may return the favor and not harm you if she finds you swimming alone without your cross.

You haven't come across one of their children, you say? Try this, then. Imitate their dancing while you hold a piece of linen. All the while, sing a charm to encourage the spirits to provide your desires. Tuck the material close to the part of your body that represents your goal: your heart for love, your head for knowledge, and so on. Then sing the following, while you dance clockwise:

Plants Rusalki Love.

Parsley (*Petroselinum crispum*): Franz Eugen Köhler, *Köhler's Medizinal-Pflanzen*, 1897.
Rose (*Rosa gallica*): "Les Roses" by Pierre-Joseph Redouté, 1824.
Birch (*Betula lenta*): Franz Eugen Köhler, *Köhler's Medizinal-Pflanzen*, 1897.
[Public domain], via Wikimedia Commons.

"The dance of life, the dance of power, Rusalki, join me this magic hour! To <fill in your desire> bring growth and maturity; by your power this spell is freed!"[111]

You know how Rusalki love to dance. They won't ignore your request. Be careful not to dance too long. Slip away carefully if you can, before you become exhausted. The spirits will be enjoying themselves so much, they're likely not to notice, and will dance until dawn.

Fact or Fiction?

Rusalki are not seen as often these days as they used to be. Are they a dying breed (no pun intended) like many of the races you read about in fantasy fiction? Or have they simply disappeared because the complexities of today's way of living, the destruction of the land, and political forces (see below) have driven them away?

Driven Away by Communism

Communism did much to dispel the belief in these "superstitions" as the following excerpt from *Broken Earth* demonstrates.

> The party consisted of about a dozen youths most of whom had seen service in the Red Army. They were intellectuals of the village, the leaders of the young generation. Among them were two who were especially prominent in the political life of the community.…
>
> Interesting bits of information the boys imparted to me—very interesting and very significant. None of them, not even the little ones, any longer believed in ghosts or spirits of any kind, not even in *rusalkas* (water-nymphs). It seemed hardly credible in the light of my own boyhood experiences. How we *did* dread the *rusalka*, who was supposed to be always hunting for little fellows to take back with her to the bottom of the river where she lived. And there were so many *rusalkas* at large in summer. Our fathers and mothers saw them, said so, and we, too, caught glimpses of them, so we told one another, sitting on fences with hair loosened on shoulders and with fiery eyes seeking to entice the passer-by

Rusalka and Fisherman. Jacek Malczewski, 1887.
Jacek Malczewski [Public domain].

into giving himself to them. It was all nonsense, the story of the *rusalkas*, said the boys, and they laughed heartily. There were no *rusalkas* in the world and no *domovoys* (house-goblins) and no other kind of spirits. All such beliefs came from the priests who had served the Czar and kept the muzhiks in ignorance so that they could come now and then and sprinkle water in houses and drive out evil spirits and get a box of rye or basket of eggs. Now not even children believed their dark stories of the Unclean One. I could convince myself easily enough of that by asking little boys if they cherished such beliefs. Superstition, they kept on repeating triumphantly, was dying in the village, was going the way of the landlords, the old generals and the other old forces of evil.[112]

Forum Talk

Regardless of the reason, many people no longer care to believe in the wonders and magical aspects of life that once were commonplace among rural people. Beliefs in spirits, even these doomed maidens, does still exist around the world, however. People love to comment on social media posts, explaining the unexplained with beliefs they're familiar with. A few examples follow.

- "Rusalka is pretty much respected in my family. We don't go in waters before Petrovden. We lost a lot of people because of that. They went to swim, but they never got out alive."
- "The actual date for the Rusalka is the week before the Feast of St John the Baptist, June 24. We were always told don't swim in the water until the feast because the snakes [*remember, Rusalki can appear as water creatures*] will get you. And this is from American 100% Slovaks / Rusyns stock on both sides that have been Americans for over 100 years. The story dies hard."
- "Actually a few stories on YouTube about people fishing, for example: Dad and Son were fishing maybe 40 or 50 km away from the coast and spot something in the water. Something drifting it appears to be a young woman stiff as a board just lying on her back in the water. Dad yells but no response. So he jumps in and swims to it when he reaches it there was nothing there. When he came back, the son told him, 'In just a second she sank and never re-emerged.' "[113]

A Medium Connection

One well-known medium, Madame Blavatsky (Helena Petrovna Blavatsky, 1831-1891), had a connection to the spirit world, including Rusalki. Blavatsky was born in 1831, on the night between July 30 and 31, which in the Slavic world is a day when the household spirit (Domovoi) ceases to play his tricks.[114] Blavatsky's nanny and other household servants brought her up in "an atmosphere of legends and popular fancy," and her belief in Rusalki "was developed before she had heard of anything else."[115]

On the banks of the Dnieper river, she saw a Rusalka "in every willow tree, smiling and beckoning to her." Her nurses had ingrained the idea that she was immune to the torments of the spirits. Even at the age of four, Blavatsky felt superior to others and had no fear of approaching the shores or even calling upon Rusalki to punish others. The following excerpt about her life tells about one tragic event.

In one of her walks by the river side a boy about fourteen who was dragging the child's carriage incurred her displeasure by some slight disobedience.

"I will have you tickled to death by a roussalka!" she screamed. "There's one coming down from that tree . . . here she comes . . . See, see!"

Whether the boy saw the dreaded nymph or not, he took to his heels, and, the angry commands of the nurse notwithstanding, disappeared along the sandy banks leading homeward. After much grumbling the old nurse was constrained to return home alone with her charge, determined to have "Pavlik" punished.

But the poor lad was never seen alive again. He ran away to his village, and his body was found several weeks later by fishermen, who caught him in their nets. The verdict of the police was "drowning by accident." It was thought that the lad, having sought to cross some shallow pools left from the spring inundations, had got into one of the many sand pits so easily transformed by the rapid Dnieper into whirlpools.

But the verdict of the horrified household—of the nurses and servants—pointed to no *accidental* death, but to the one that had occurred in consequence of the child having withdrawn from the boy her mighty protection, thus delivering the victim to some roussalka on the watch. The displeasure of the family at this foolish gossip was enhanced when they found the supposed culprit gravely corroborating the charge, and maintaining that it was she herself who had handed over her disobedient serf to her faithful servants the water-nymphs.[116]

Did she cause this? Or was it merely a tragic accident? Madame Blavatsky's adult life was filled with even more uncanny events that she attributed to various spirits.

Rusalka Week

Rusalka Week (Русальная неделя or *Rusalnaya nedelja*) and its various spellings is also called *vilovita nedelja* (the week of the fairies, from "vila," a word for another type of nymph or fairy), *rusalska sedmitsa* (fairy week), Rusalka Sunday, Rusalia Week, Green Yuletide, Green Holy-Days (*Zelyonïe Svyatki*), Trinity Week, Whitsuntide, and others. This is a time when the world of the living and the world of the dead "open to each other,"[117] allowing Rusalki and other spirits to wander among people. Ancient documents condemned the *Rusalnaya nedelja* celebrations, calling them pagan and demonic. (You can read more about the origins of these celebrations in the "Rusalii – Dancing for Health" section later in this book.)

Enter Rusalki

The only time Rusalki venture from their watery homes to tread upon land is during Rusalka Week. It's during this time that sowing is about to begin, and farmers petition Rusalki to scatter their unused fertility on the land so people will have successful crops.

This is a time work is taboo. Men cannot work in, or even enter, fields and vineyards. In Bulgaria, Wednesday and Friday are the most dangerous days to do any activity Rusalki have forbidden. Other places prohibit women from working the entire week—no washing of clothes or bodies, no clothes-making activities.

In the past, it was a much-needed break for rural women—more so than for men—because women's work continued through all the seasons, the process of making clothes taking up half of their day: planting and gathering flax, spinning, weaving, sewing. In the story below, a woman finds out almost too late that she shouldn't be working this week.

> A long time ago one woman told this story. During that week [Rusalka week] she went to weed the flax. And she went out to the field; she looked around and saw some girls walking. Seven girls. She said: "Girls, where are you going? Come help me to weed the flax." And then she realized that all the girls had their hair down and their faces were frowning. And then she remembered that it was Rusalka week. And it was seven rusalki walking. So she hid herself and didn't go to weed the flax. After that, she saw that the girls went to the oak and soon seven guys joined them there. And over there they had fun, were laughing, and screaming, and who knows what else they were doing. They stayed there until noon. And at noon they were gone. The girls were in white. Well, they were dressed up [as they were dressed up at the funeral] and buried, as if they were getting married. And the guys were wearing suits, that's all.[118]

Setting work aside during this week is not only a safety precaution to avoid meeting or angering Rusalki. It's also a way for you to pay tribute and respect to the spirits for providing their life-giving moisture, and therefore fertility, to the land. The spirits are focused on playing: singing, dancing, swimming, and swinging. They don't want thoughts of work to ruin the fun they have during their one week on land. When you work, it shows your disrespect toward Rusalki. You should do as they do instead: play and not work.

Rusalka in Tree. Illustration by Nelinda. © Bendideia Publishing.

Not only should you do no work during Rusalka Week, it's inadvisable to go into the forest or near the water, both places the spirit maidens frequent. If you must venture outdoors, don't leave your sleeping children alone, for fear Rusalki will kidnap them. That goes for yourself, too. Sleeping during the day—whether inside or outside—is a no-no. If Rusalki catch you, they'll grab ahold of your hands or feet and cripple you. The story below demonstrates what could happen if you forget and get caught.

> Such a story is told in a Bulgarian folk song. Maiden Dragana once fell asleep on the secretive Samodivska meadow where the sun sets and the moon rises. When she woke up, she saw several fairies standing beside and staring at her. They called out for her to go to the underworld, the afterlife, with them. The girl desperately begged them to leave her at peace as she was an only child and her parents would not bear the loss. And she said she was so young that she had even failed to prepare her wedding dowry. The fairies replied that all they wanted was the canvas of silk and cotton that she had weaved during the Mermaid Week.[119]

Heed the warning and don't fall asleep outside. You may or may not get off as easily as the girl above did, so it's best not to tempt fate—or the fairies.

The period of Rusalka Week occurs somewhere between May and mid-June, around the time of Pentecost, which is fifty days after Easter. In some locations, Rusalka Week starts on Semik, the Thursday before Pentecost, when girls summon Rusalki with their rituals; in others, it starts on Trinity Sunday or the following day. In other places, it may start on a different day. Depending on the country of origin, and even various regions within a country, some of these events occur on different days than those described below. The date is less important than the events themselves.

Rusalki are especially active during the days listed below:

- **Spassovden** or **Ascension** – forty days, or the sixth Thursday, after Easter.
- **Semik** – seventh Thursday after Easter.
- **Trinity**, **Pentecost**, **Troisten**, **Whitsunday** – seventh Sunday after Easter. (Trinity Sunday is the first Sunday after Pentecost in the Western Christian liturgical calendar, but is the same day as Pentecost in Eastern Christianity.)
- **Duhovden**, **Dukhov Day**, **Day of Souls**, **Spirit Day**, **Whit Monday**, **Pentecost Monday** – eighth Monday after Easter.

Spassovden or Ascension (Thursday)

Spassovden (or the Ascension) is a *zadushnitsa*, one of many days throughout the year associated with the dead, although not specifically those who are "unclean dead" like Rusalki. Women pour wine or water over the graves of relatives, and give food to other people visiting their deceased loved ones.

In Bulgaria, Spassovden happens forty days after Easter. The name comes from the Bulgarian word *spassenie* (спасение, "salvation"), and so it's the day of salvation of souls. It's the last of the seven "Great Thursdays," the first being Maundy Thursday (three days before Easter).

The official Orthodox holiday relates to the day Christ ascended to heaven after spending his first forty days with the apostles after he had risen from his tomb. In the same way, on Easter, God releases souls of

White Butterfly Souls. Illustration by Nelinda. © Bendideia Publishing.

the recent dead, so they can wander for forty days to the places they've known in life. Their wandering concludes on Spassovden, and the souls remain on Earth until they return to the other world on Pentecost.

In folklore, souls can appear as flies or bees, visiting flowers on trees, in meadows, and along riverbanks. If you want to hear the dead speak in their graves, all you have to do is put your ear to the ground; you'll hear them buzzing like bees. They also appear as white butterflies that arise from the water and live only on this day. Windows remain open on Spassovden so these souls aren't trapped inside homes. Another belief is that if you're quiet enough when you go to a well early in the morning and peer into the water, instead of seeing your own image, you may see the reflection of a loved one you're thinking about.

A Day of Bread and Fertility

Spassovden is also a day of bread and fertility. *Sveti Spas* or St. Spas (the Holy Savior) is the saint associated with this day, although he doesn't exist as an actual Orthodox saint. He's a made-up saint to go along with the name of the holiday. On this day, people walk around the fields to ward off drought, praying to the saint, who "unlocks the sky and the Earth to let the rain through so there may be bread throughout the year."[120]

Ritual traditions forbid both men and women from working on any of the Great Thursdays. If you work in the vineyard, no grapes will grow. If you work in the fields, no grain will ripen. On Spassovden itself, women avoid touching anything green, because it will bring hailstorms in the summer instead of rain. Every drop of rain that falls on this day is considered "a piece of gold,"[121] because it means the harvest year will be rich and fertile. On the other end of the weather spectrum, to avoid a drought, women are forbidden from doing laundry and hanging clothes outside to dry.

Visiting the Rosen

Spassovden is a time, in Bulgaria, when Rusalki return from their winter home in Zmeykovo (Dragon Village). They spread life-giving dew on the fields. This dew has an added benefit besides fertility for crops: it can heal diseases, especially the dreaded Rusalka disease, which the spirits themselves bring on people who disobey rules against working.

The night before Spassovden is a time for "impossible wishes" to come true[122]—with the help of Rusalki and their favorite flower, *rosen* (*Dictamnus albus* or burning bush), which means "dew." It grows in various places across Bulgaria and blossoms for only a short time in June.

> **Did you know?**
>
> Rusalki have magical horns from which they pour out spring rain to fertilize the land (Monaghan, 519).

According to folklore, it blooms only on the night before Spassovden, when the flower is at its most powerful state for curing people.

The spirits are known to pick the white, pink, or red blossoms this night to make wreaths for their hair. On the Sunday morning after Spassovden, Rusalki use these wreaths to sprinkle the fields with dew.

Intoxicated by the fragrance of the flowers, Rusalki become merciful to people. You must be careful not to gather the flowers for your own use until the spirits have departed. Even animals abide by this rule and don't eat the blossoms. If you do pick the flowers and take them home, Rusalki will find you and come down the chimney of your house to take the flowers away from you.

Magical Night of Healing. Illustration by Nelinda. © Bendideia Publishing.

In a ritual called "visiting the rosen" or "walking on the dewy rosen grass," sick people go to a field where this plant grows, or their relatives bring them there if they're too ill to venture out on their own. Most often, however, people go there in secret, not allowing anyone to see them arrive.

They choose a location that's close to a holy spring where a church or chapel has also been built. Magic wells with water that cures all diseases are often found in locations where Rusalki live. It's possible that the springs found near rosen fields in these sacred places are ones that connect with these magic wells. One famous place you can go to is the village of Resen, which gets its name from the flower. Or perhaps you'd rather go to Krustova Gora, Holy Trinity Cross Forest, in the Rhodope Mountains. You can also travel to the Bulgarian Lourdes, a plain near the foot of the Stara-Planina mountains, where rosen grows in abundance.

Ill people, clothed in white, wash with the sacred water, then prepare for the night ahead. They spread a white sheet on the ground to sleep on. Near where their head will lie, they place a bowl of water, a twig from a rosen bush, a lit candle or oil lamp, and a white handkerchief on which they place gifts for the spirits: a cup of honey and rolls spread with honey, shirts, towels, stockings. Before they go to sleep, the people eat a meal they've brought: bread, cake, roasted chicken, wine, *rakia* (Bulgarian brandy).

BURNING BUSH
(DICTAMNUS ALBUS)
Nat. size
PL. 61

Rosen or Burning Bush (*Dictamnus albus*).
Bois, D.; Frederick Warne (Firm); Herincq, B.;
Step, Edward; Watson, William [Public domain], 1896.

They must keep a strict silence during the night. At midnight, Rusalki arrive, bearing their queen on a chariot of human bones. They cause a whirlwind to blow over the sleeping humans, carrying with it the soft, whispered words, laughter, or songs of the spirit maidens. As the Rusalki gather flowers, they strew leaves, twigs, sand, insects, and petals over the sleeping people. Tales have been told of people feigning sleep, those who have lost a limb, hearing Rusalki say, "Restore (person's name) leg (or hand or fingers)." All who hear the spirits speak their name are destined to be cured.

In the morning before sunrise, people who could sleep through the turmoil awake and check their surroundings. The sight before them displays the fact that the spirit maidens have been present during the night.

> One person in the village of Lyaskovets said that when he took his father to the rosen field for treatment, in the evening the flowers of the dew were whole, and the next morning most of the flowers were broken, as if cut with scissors.[123]

Everyone examines the water and handkerchiefs to determine their fate. If nothing has fallen onto the cloth or into the water, it means Rusalki have chosen not to heal the person. Others are fortunate if green leaves and live insects have dropped onto the items they set out. This means they will recover. If the leaves and insects are dead, or the water and handkerchief are covered with twigs, the people will remain ill and possibly even die from their malady. Dirt left on a handkerchief is a certain sign the person will die from his disease. For those who have been left signs of a healing, they must mix their "gift" in the water and drink it slowly to ensure they'll be cured.

In other areas, people believe a sick person will be healed if he picks the rosen in the morning of Spassovden, or if he washes in the holy spring water. People also leave threads from their clothes on trees or bushes, or leave gifts by the ikon in the church. Alternatively, a person can roll in the morning dew before the sun evaporates it. It will cure him, or keep him healthy throughout the year if he isn't ill.

Women who haven't been able to conceive children go to the rosen field as well, either with close friends who aren't relatives, or with a non-related man, often a shepherd or someone from another village. Around midnight, she places a bowl of water from the holy spring by her head and lies beneath the rosen to sleep. When Rusalki pass over her and her companion at midnight, the spirits sprinkle rosen on the sleepers. If any rosen, even a small bit, floats in the bowl in the morning, then the spirits have granted the woman's wish, and she'll conceive a child. She must wash herself with the water and drink the rest sometime over the next forty days. At the Sanctuary of the Nymphs and Aphrodite in Kasnakovo, it's said that if a woman drinks from the spring water, she'll conceive a boy.

A variation of this rite says that at 2 a.m. before the rooster crows, the woman and her companion must leave the food they brought in the field for the spirits, then run home without looking back. They must make sure no one sees them return to the village. The woman will become fertile because her infertility will remain with the dew. No one can question the woman about what happened that night. If any woman who spends the night in the rosen field—even an unmarried one—has a child nine months later, it's considered "magical" and not immoral behavior.

Semik or Welcoming Rusalki (Thursday)

The rites of Semik (celebrated in Russia, Ukraine, and other countries) are devoted to Kostroma, a goddess said to be the first Rusalka (or Mavka). She falls in love with and marries Kupalo, unaware he's her brother. When they discover the truth, they both commit suicide. Kupalo jumps into a fire, and Kostroma drowns herself in a forest lake—only to turn into a Rusalka.

You read earlier about how Rusalki try to imitate young women, especially brides. During Rusalka Week, young women perform rituals to mimic Rusalki—not to attempt to become spirits, but as a way to lure Rusalki out of the forest and into the fields.

Dancing is one way they imitate Rusalki. It's a way to "honor, address, and placate the spirits."[124] The girls hope that by dancing, the spirits will join them. The two become one, the world of the dead merging with that of the living.

One young woman after another invokes Rusalki to leave their temporary forest abode and bring their fertilizing moisture to the land. An account of how they might have invoked the spirits is described below.

> Based on anecdotal reports of conversations with elders who still remembered witnessing or taking part in the Rusaliia, it is possible to imagine the scene. A young woman walks to the highest point of the village and faces the vast forests that lie beyond her cultivated

world. She is dressed in her finest clothing, replete with embroidered symbols of animals, birds, and a central motif of a stylized goddess figure in the form of a tree, the Tree of Life. She stands and sings in haunting tones, begging, urging, and enticing the water spirits to leave their wild forest world and return to the fields and gardens, bringing the gift of fertilizing rain and dew. When she tires, another woman steps up and continues the call.[125]

Curling the Birches

In addition to dancing, Semik rituals involve birch trees, which are among the first to bud in spring, and also a favorite of Rusalki. The day before the festival or at dawn the next day, people decorate their homes—all the rooms, windows, ikons, doors—with garlands made from birch branches, maple, linden, or oak. They also hang decorations on tree branches in the forest specifically for the spirits.

At one time, the primary celebration, however, took place in the forest. Here, girls of marriageable age and newly married women perform a ritual called "curling the birches," "weaving the birch tree," or "christening of the cuckoos." The latter name refers to a rite in which children who die unbaptized receive

Khorovod, Circle Dance. А. Е. Мартынов, nineteenth century.
A. E. Martynov [Public domain].

a symbolic christening, so they'll no longer remain in the form of a cuckoo and be "obliged to fly wailing through the air."[126]

The girls gather flowers and birch branches from which they'll make wreaths. As they dance into the forest to select a birch sapling, they sing:

> Don't rejoice oak trees. Don't rejoice green ones.
> Not to you are the girls coming. Not to you, the pretty ones.
> Not to you are they bringing pies, pastries, omelettes.
> Yo, Yo Semik and Trinity!
> Rejoice birches! Rejoice green ones!
> To you the girls are coming!
> To you they are bringing pies, pastries, omelettes.
> Yo, yo Semik and Trinity.[127]

When they find a birch beginning to leaf and one that has sufficient space around it so they can dance, they decorate the sapling with flowers, ribbons, beads, cloth, thread, garlands, and other adornments, or even dress it in a woman's robe. Then they knot and twist the ends of the branches to form circles, symbolic of infinity. They may even place on the sapling wreaths they've made from birch branches and flowers. These circles are meant to capture "the life force visible in the sprouting birches."[128]

The girls placate all the trees and the spirits residing in them by offering them omelettes (with the egg symbolizing life). Around their special tree, they place a meal of omelettes and pancakes that they'll share after the ceremony. Boys arrive when it's time to eat (of course) and bring plenty of beer and wine to add to the meal. Afterwards, girls and boys stroll into the woods to spend the night as couples—much to the horror of the Church.

In the past, that behavior wasn't always frowned upon. Premarital sex in some places "did not prejudice a woman's marriage prospects any more than it would have impaired those of a man."[129] Furthermore, this sexual freedom possibly dates back to an even more ancient society.

> It is possible that the *rusalka* is a remnant of an older society in which women were freer to express their sexuality. Many Slavic sources state that, with the influence of nomadic patriarchal tribes and, later, of Christianity, Slavic cultures became increasingly more patriarchal and monogamous marriage was instituted. The influence of the church may have served to break the identity of village girls with the *rusalka*, and instead, to make them enemies who compete for the same village men. It may also have served to criticize the uninhibited sexuality and sensuality which the *rusalka* continually expresses.[130]

And it's that sexuality of Rusalki that the girls attempt to imitate.

But before the meal and the arrival of the boys, the girls dance around the tree while they sing songs such as the one below.

> Curly little birch tree,
> Curly and vigorously sprouting,
> Beneath you, dear little birch, …

That is not fire that glows,
Nor poppies that bloom—
Those are beautiful maidens
Who lead the round-dance:
For you, dear little birch,
They sing all their songs.[131]

The girls kiss one another through the birch wreaths (called "crowns") and swear lifelong friendship and sisterhood (*kum*), not only with each other, but also with the birch tree.

The girls attached their crosses [worn on necklaces] to these crowns, then, taking position two by two on either side of a crown, they exchanged kisses and crosses, while singing songs the contents which called for friendship. The girls thus linked were considered friends for life.[132]

If the tree is at the edge of the forest close to the planted fields, the girls bend its tip and tie it to the ground. Since the birch is the first to foliate, it has "sacred energy" and "power of vegetation." Performing

Semik. Unknown artist, nineteenth century.
http://rosysevera.ru/grafika/estamp/pictures/359 [Public domain].

this action allows the tree to return this energy and life-giving moisture to the soil so it can be transferred to the grain fields.[133]

While the girls do this, they sing:

> Oh birch, so curly, curly and young,
> Under you, little birch, no poppy is blooming.
> Under you, little birch, no fire is burning—
> No poppy is blooming—
> Pretty maids are dancing a xorovod [circle dance],
> about you little birch, they are singing songs.[134]

If the tree is not near the field, the girls cut it down and bring it to the village the next day (after their night with the boys). The boys, however, aren't allowed to touch the tree. In some cases, everyone takes the tree to the fields and rips it into pieces to scatter it around, as a means of transferring its life-giving power to the crops.

In other cases, the girls bring the tree to the village and set it in a house chosen for this purpose, leaving it there until it's time to say farewell to the spirit maidens at the end of Rusalka Week. The girls sing and perform their circle dances around the tree.

Semik songs also praise Rusalki and ancient gods as the one below demonstrates.

> Water of death to water of life. We infuse you with the healing light. Let us honor the Rusalki's return from the watery otherworld. With each step of their sacred xorovods, they bring moisture and life to the fields. With their arboreal ascent, the trees burst into leaf and bud. We salute you, water women, and invite you and all other friendly spirits of water and woodland, to enter our sacred circle.
>
> Hail and Welcome.
>
> Let us turn our thoughts to the strengthening of the Sun king, Dahzhdbog, the celestial fire, who now moves toward the apex of his glory. Let us think of Svarovich, his divine brother of the terrestrial fire, the first fruit of wisdom plucked from the flaming tree of knowledge without whom our lives would be ever dim. Let us think of the fire which rages within the belly of our great Mother Earth. And finally let us call Swarog, the divine light which shines within and about us all.
>
> Hail and Welcome.
>
> Let us now bring our attention to the belly of our Moist mother earth, womb of all who seek entrance into this life, and when this life is done, womb of all who seek entrance to the next. May she, and the Gods of Vrij grant passage to the spirits of those we have loved who have gone before us, that they may join us in today's feasting and celebration.
>
> Hail and Welcome.
>
> The kumits'ja ceremony is performed to ensure a life-long bond between friends. Whomever you choose to kiss through the kumits'ja wreaths while we dance to raise the energy, will be your friend for life. This is not a spell to be taken lightly, so choose carefully or not at all.
>
> Let it be so.

We invite you, Gods and Goddesses of our people, Sovereigns of the sacred realms of Nav, Prav & Yav, to join us in our feasting and celebration. We invite you, O Spirits of Nature, otherworldly creatures of forest and field. Join us in love and trust in our feasting and celebration. We invite you, ancestors and loved ones who have gone before us to pass through the gates of Vij and join in our feasting and celebration with those whom they love.

Hail and Welcome.

In times of yore, our ancestors would give to the river a young girl. Her soul was said to be taken by the water women where she would join their rank. Without this offering, it was believed that the number of water women would dwindle and they would soon die off, never again to bring moisture to the vegetative world. All would wither and die.

Our offerings have changed, but not our devotion. We give you, Rusalki, this humble offering, that you may receive thanks and know that your work does not go unnoticed.

The River is Flowing.

Ancestors, loved ones, those of the land of Vij, we thank you for your presence here.

Hail and Farewell.

Rusalki, Nature Spirits, Protectors of the Mother, welcome back to our Realm, and thank You for Your presence here.

Hail and Farewell.

Shining Ones, Gods and Goddesses, Sovereigns and Creators, thank you for your presence here.

Hail and Farewell.

Moist Mother Earth, doorway to life

Two girls on Semik, 1860-1870s.
Д. О. Осипов, nineteenth century.
D.O. Osipov [Public domain].

in this world and the next, we humbly beg your forgiveness for the times we have not trod gently upon your flesh, have not felt as one with your presence. Hear us now as we give you our oath to be kinder and more responsible for your well being.

Our circle is done, our rite is over, may the Gods be your guides and the Zorya protect you.[135]

By the nineteenth century, Rusalki were less prominent in these rituals.[136] Today, even the ritual itself has been virtually eliminated, although the songs of spring remain.

Remembering the Unclean Dead

Semik is also a time to pay respect to the unclean dead, those who have died unnatural or violent deaths, and who have not received sanctified burials. Relatives bring pancakes, beer and wine, and red eggs (a pagan symbol of rebirth) to the graveside. They break the eggs and pour the alcohol over the grave. What remains is left for the spirits, in particular, Rusalki. If you're attending, don't forget to sing the song below to make sure Rusalki don't come after you for vengeance:

> Queen Rusalka, / Maiden fair, / Do not destroy the soul, / Do not cause it to be choked, / And we will make obeisance to thee.[137]

In addition to appeasing the spirits with offerings at the gravesite, you can leave them omelettes, pancakes, bread, cheese, butter, milk, or honey on riverbanks, edges of fields, at crossroads, or anywhere along a road that travels through or near a forest.

Trinity, Pentecost, Troisten, or Whitsunday (Sunday)

Pentecost is celebrated among the Orthodox fifty days after Easter. This was the day the apostles received the gift of the Holy Spirit after Christ ascended into heaven. The day also has rituals dedicated to Rusalki. If the birch tree the girls decorated in the forest on Semik has been brought into a home, the girls now remove it and bring it to a river. They ceremoniously "undress" the tree, removing all its embellishments. While they do this, the tree—that is, the Rusalka—begs them not to send her away, but the girls plan to do so regardless. They sing, as if taunting the spirit:

> I was curly, I was well-dressed, / But now I stand naked. / All my clothes have been taken away, / All my leaves have been torn away, / Your friends take me away, / Throw me in the fast river.[138]

And into the river they toss the tree. Next, the girls remove the wreaths they made while in the forest and throw them into the river after the tree Rusalka. This is a fortune-telling rite to determine who their future husband will be, or if their life will be happy or sorrowful. They sing:

> I, a young girl, am going to the quiet meadow, the quiet meadow.
> To the quiet meadow, to a little birch.
> I, a young girl, will pick a blue cornflower,
> A little blue cornflower, a cornflower.
> I, a young girl, will weave a wreath.
> I, a young girl, will go to the river.
> I will throw the wreath down the river.
> I will think about my sweetheart
> My wreath is drowning, drowning.
> My heart is aching, aching.
> My wreath will drown.
> My sweetheart will abandon me.[139]

Wreaths that float mean the girl will find love in the direction the wreath drifts. In addition to this, the wreath that glides the fastest is one that pleases their Rusalka. If you look closely, you'll see her swimming away with it. The spirit has gained a new head covering without having to make it herself.

The lucky girl whose wreath the Rusalka steals will marry first. Wreaths that sink mean the girl will die that year or the next. This possibly doesn't mean a literal death, but can indicate she'll marry, perhaps later than the other girls, and to someone in another village, because it was believed that "a newly married girl left her natal family as completely as if she had died, especially if the groom lived in another village."[140] Wreaths that float in a circle signify the girl will suffer some misfortune.

This ceremony is for unmarried girls only. If they catch any men spying, the girls dunk the offenders into the river. As an alternative to throwing the wreaths into the river, the girls might throw them into the forest and ask Rusalki for a rich husband in return.

The following poem tells of one such wreath-tossing event that doesn't quite go as planned.

THE RUSALKI

'Twas when we dwelt by the Volga's side—
Ah, bless the willows that high and wide
Above its waters grew!
I then had counted but twenty years,
And Niga, my child—your mother, my dears—
Had counted barely two.

A pleasant place was my husband's mill,
With its merry hopper that never was still,
Clacking the livelong day;
The stream went rushing and flashing past,
Till up by the wheel it was caught and cast
In foam and bells and spray.

A bowshot from the mill or more,
And midway between shore and shore,
A little island lay;
And swift and deep and dark was the tide
That around it swept on either side,
Beneath the willows gray.

Such trees they were for size and strength!
A very tree in girth and length
Was every reaching bough;
For countless years on that shady isle
Their roots had fed in the fertile soil,
Untouched by spade or plough.

Continues on next page.

Willow by the River. Stylized from photo by Nelinda. © Bendideia Publishing.

Continued from previous page.

And on this isle with willows grown,
A good Rusalki, it was known,
Had twined her secret bower;
But mortal there was none so rude
As pry upon her solitude,
And brave her spirit-power.

But often in the lonely night
The fishermen have seen her light
Shine deep within the stream;
It shone as does an early star
Ere yet its sisters wakened are,
With faint and wavering gleam:

And then their nets and lines they drew,
And joy was theirs, and back they threw
Them in the stream again;
And she drove to them the scaly flocks
From hollow banks and pools and rocks,
Like sheep to fold or pen.

And this was why, from year to year,
The neighbours all from far and near,
At pleasant Whitsuntide,
Child and mother and old grand-dame,
With offerings for Rusalki came
Down to the river side.

And so, with flowers of every hue,
In dale or dell or copse that grew,
One Whitsuntide they came,
As custom was in the days gone by—
And 'tis pity to let old customs die
That have a kindly aim.

Sweet scented blooms and sprigs of may
We twined and tied that merry day
In chaplet and in wreath,
Which in the stream the children cast,
And, singing, watched them floating past
The arching boughs beneath.

When sudden, backward from the stream
They running came with shout and scream,
And to the stream ran I,
And into it I would have sprung,
But twenty arms were round me flung
As wildly I rushed by.

Away upon the rapid wave
My child was swept, and none to save,
Far, farther from the land;
Swift, swifter she was swept away,—
But fearless still and calm she lay,
A garland in her hand.

On, on beneath the willows gray—
Oh, never till my dying day
Shall I forget the sight!
But then, while disappeared my child,
E'en then was changed my terror wild
To madness of delight.

A female form,—so dreamlike fair,
With neck and arms and bosom bare
And white as lily flower,
All from the waist down garmented
In vapour, of the colours shed
By sunlight through a shower!—

Emerging from the foliage,
Just paused upon the island's ledge
Above the dewy grass,
Then pasted the drooping boughs among
To where my child was swept along,
As summer-cloud might pass.

She raised, me bore her safe to land,
She took the garland from her hand—
Oh, more than gems or gold
Your mother, dears, has treasured it!
For 'mong her dripping curls 'twas set,
And—now my tale is told.[141]

Dukhov Day, Day of Souls, etc. or Farewell to the Rusalka (Monday)

Like Spassovden, Dukhov Day is a time for honoring deceased relatives. In the early morning, women scatter walnut leaves on graves to "make a comfortable shade for the dead."[142] They also spread walnut leaves and twigs on church floors, kneel on them, and think of their loved ones who have died. This is a way for people to get in touch with those who have died before they leave for the other world. Walnuts are a bridge between the world of the living and that of the dead, and their leaves are thought to bring the spirits peace in the afterlife. If families forget to do this, the souls must grab a handful of dirt to take with them before they can leave.

All Souls' Day. Pencho Georgiev, 1927.
Pencho Georgiev [Public domain].

Ritual Banishment

This day is also *provody rusalki* ("procession of the Rusalki," "seeing off the Rusalki," "farewell to the Rusalki," and other names). In other words, it's when Rusalki are banished. It's a time to force the spirit maidens to rein in the moisture they've been supplying the land, so that it doesn't ruin crops rather than benefit them. Up until the 1930s, when the Soviet government forbade this ritual, people performed it to drive the spirits back into the water at the end of their allotted time on land. In other areas, the tradition ended after the Second World War.

As part of the ritual, some person or object is designated to be a Rusalka. Depending on where the practice occurs, the stand-in can be a girl from the village, a rag doll, a straw or wooden figure dressed like a woman, or even an image of a horse. If people choose a village girl, she's usually tall, strong, beautiful, and of marriageable age. She wears her hair loose and dresses in a white chemise or goes naked like a Rusalka.

Whatever the representation, human or inanimate, the "Rusalka" leads a group of village girls, women, and children into a rye or other grain field. All of them wear wreaths on their hair and dress like Rusalki. They form a circle around their chosen Rusalka and sing and dance on their way to the fields. At times, the girls show the Rusalka respect and offer her clothes; at other times, they jeer at her or tease her to tickle them.

In another location, the girls don't form a circle. They hold hands while traveling through the village in twos. The first pair form an arch under which the rest pass through. Each set of two performs this action until they arrive at the field. While they make their way, they sing over and over:

> I will lead the rusalki
> Into the green rye;
> There in the green rye

Goddess in the Mulberries. Jacek Malczewski, 1888.
Jacek Malczewski [Public domain].

> The rusalki were sitting,
> Ah, my little grain-spikes,
> Like little trees [you are] . . . :
> In the even we'll have pastries,
> On the table we'll have loaves.[143]

Once in the field, they blindfold the human variation of the Rusalka, and she tries to catch and tickle people. Others try to prevent this by chasing after the Rusalka, whom they say has been stealing their grain. Some participants attempt to drive her and the other spirits away by "shouting and banging metal pots, cracking whips, [and] waving brooms and pokers."[144] The Rusalka eventually escapes among the stalks of grain, and the people shout with joy that they "escorted" the Rusalka home. They amble back to their own houses, knowing it's now safe for them to wander about both day and night without fear of attack.

Then comes the time to ceremonially dispose of the non-human variation of the Rusalka.

If she's a straw doll, they may burn her. Another option is to form two groups: the married women attack the Rusalka as they perform circle dances mimicking war, trying to tear the doll into pieces; the young, unmarried women, on the other hand, defend and protect the Rusalka. In the end, the Rusalka loses. The young women, with their hair flowing unbraided, mourn the death of the spirit maiden before they fall to the ground in a deathlike state. Meanwhile, the married women dismember the doll and throw her straw into the air much like the monkeys did to the Scarecrow in *The Wizard of Oz*. Or they may bury the pieces or take the doll to the river and throw it in. Then they return home, mourning the death of the Rusalka.

KUPALA – RUSALKI AND FIRE

Although she was driven back to the waters during Rusalka Week, the spirit also makes her presence known on the summer solstice festival of Kupala, or St. John's Day. She's not the primary focus of the festivities, but in some districts, people pay her honor on this night.

> The young unmarried women choose a Rusalka from their company, and also a little girl, who is called the Rusalka's daughter. They crown them with garlands. They also make a straw figure in the likeness of a man. Then the Rusalka with dishevelled hair casts off her clothes, or remains in a shift only, and leads the band to a lonely place singing, 'I will bring the Rusalka to the forest, but I myself will return home. I will bring the Rusalka, aye, to the dark forest, but I will return to my father's court.' They gather the dry brushwood to make a fire. Then they throw the straw figure upon it, leap round and across the flames, and sing the Kupalo songs (Stewart, 115).

A story tells about a Rusalka who put out the fire several times, much to the annoyance of the people who had lit it. They run after her, trying to beat her with clubs, until she gives up and leaves the forest (Russian Wikipedia, "Русалка." From: Зеленин Д. К. Очерки русской мифологии. — Пг.: Типография А. В. Орлова, 1916).

Other girls and women prepare a mock funeral and burial to ritually end the Rusalka's time on land. This is a way for the spirit, an embodiment of *all* Rusalki, to receive the ceremonies denied each deceased girl at her own funeral: a sending off, a consecrated burial, and a ritual lament. And since funeral and wedding customs for unmarried girls are celebrated the same, the Rusalka "symbolically got 'two in one.' "[145]

They place the doll or figure into a coffin, cover it with a cloth and flowers, and carry it to the river. Pretending to be priests, they sing, "Lord have mercy," while they wave imitation censors made from egg shells. Laughing and crying, they comb the Rusalka's hair and say their final goodbyes. They attach stones to her coffin and throw it into the river. Then they dance their circle dance.

Only then can boys join the festivities. The girls remove their wreaths and toss them to the boys, or run away. More singing and dancing follow, with both boys and girls participating.

Magical Healers

You've learned that Rusalki can be charitable and heal the sick who spend the night in a field of rosen on a specified day. At other times, they inflict Rusalka disease or sickness on people or even kill them.

What exactly *is* this Rusalka disease?

Instead of tickling their victims, Rusalki may cause them physical or mental harm. Many of the illnesses include loss of strength or weight, delirium, madness, seizures, deformity, paralysis, and becoming a cripple. It can also be fatal as the story below indicates.

> [W]hen neighbors noticed a man named Purvan preparing to go to his fields on Friday of Rusalia Week, they said, "Aren't you afraid of the rusalki, Be Purvanè?" He retorted, "I'm not afraid of women," and left. In the evening, some people from another village who had passed his fields came to his house and told the residents they had better go get Purvan, for he lay paralyzed, in no condition to get home on his own. He remained ill for three months—no medicine could help him—and finally he died.[146]

On a positive note, Rusalka disease is not contagious, and you can prevent it. Simply avoid the following, which will all offend the spirit maidens.

- Disobeying Rusalka Week rules about working.
- Trying to catch a glimpse of them.
- Forgetting to give them clothing when they beg it from you.
- Stepping on cloth drying by the riverside.
- Stepping on any place where Rusalki gather: springs, meadows, riverbanks, and others.
- Not fulfilling a vow.
- Urinating under the eaves at night. (Perhaps this rule developed because ancestors at one time were buried there.)

Did you know?

"Rusalka syndrome" is a rare disease where a newborn's limbs are "glued" to his body (Bulgarian Wikipedia, "Русалка").

Your safest bet to avoid getting Rusalka disease is to stay inside for the week! Stock up on necessities the way you would if severe weather was approaching. Get a few luxuries, and snuggle up with a good book. The week will be over before you realize it.

Rusalii – Dancing for Health

Diseases Rusalki cause are not to be trifled with. To rid a person of this type of illness requires various means to scare away the spirits and drive out the illness: incantations and loud noises, such as rattling cans, ringing bells, whistling, and singing. The best solution, though, is to pay the *rusalii* to heal you, and you'll get all those methods at once.

Who or what are the *rusalii*?

Ritual Healing. Illustration by Nelinda. © Bendideia Publishing.

The word refers to a group of men who travel from village to village, healing those inflicted with Rusalka disease and possessed of unclean forces. The name is associated with the rituals or festivities celebrated as well. The rituals have mostly died out today, but are still performed for show.

These *rusalia* or *rusalii* celebrations, as they were called, have been recorded as far back as the late Middle Ages. In the twelfth century, legal scholar Theodoros Balsamon wrote about popular fairs called "*rousalia*" that occurred after Easter.[147] And in the thirteenth century, a Bulgarian archbishop mentioned the name in a homily.[148]

Rusalii festivals take place three times a year: around the spring equinox (Rusalka Week), the summer solstice (Midsummer's Day or St. John's Day), which is celebrated in northern Bulgaria, and the winter solstice (the "Dirty Days," the twelve days from Christmas to Epiphany), which is celebrated in southern Bulgaria. During the cold months, the men drive away *karakondjuli* (night spirits), *talasumi* (evil spirits), and *zmeyove* (dragons). In the warmer months, it's Rusalki and Samodivi (woodland nymphs) they focus on.

The spring rusalii, which has "a military flavor," is performed to cure the sick and drive away disease;[149] the ceremonies also are dedicated to fertility and Rusalki, who bring that fertility. The spring rusalii is when Rusalki begin "to dance their way out of the wild into the world of farmer and shepherd."[150]

The word "rusalii" has possible roots in the Roman *Rosalia* (*dies rosae* or *rosatio*),[151] a spring festival for the departed, that became popular among the Romanized Thracians. This, in turn, likely comes from the Greek Ρουσάλια (*Ronsália*) for "feast of roses."[152] Ancient Romans celebrated this day primarily in May, but festivities also occurred until mid-July in different locations.

This ritual was "a mixture of carnival, magic and burial customs,"[153] celebrated as a memorial for ancestors, *parentalia*.[154] It was common practice to strew garlands of roses and sometimes violets over graves, since flowers were "traditional symbols of rejuvenation, rebirth, and memory." The red and purple colors of these particular flowers were "felt to evoke the color of blood as a form of propitiation."[155] Celebrators held banquets and participated in races, competitions, and other games.[156] (See the sidebar "Roses for the Dead" for additional information.)

The Church condemned the practice as being pagan and immoral. In a document from 1551, the festivities were described as a time when "men and women and [unwed] girls come together for excitement at night and for immoral talk and demonical songs and for dancing and for jumping and for deeds against God."[157]

Group Dynamics

During these festivities, a group of men called *rusalii* (*rousalii* or *rusaltsi*) or *kalushari* (*kaloushari*) visit surrounding villages throughout Bulgaria and perform rites to cure sick people. The names of the groups vary depending on their location.

> The term *rousalia* occurs in old Bulgarian manuscripts, where it is loosely applied to *kuker* dances and other rites in which buffoonery plays a part, and which were condemned by the mediaeval Church. The alternative term—*kalushar*—is, in fact, Romanian (*calusar*), and ethnographers believe that the rites associated with them were introduced into northern Bulgaria between the sixteenth and eighteenth centuries by settlers of Romanian origin.[158]

ROSES FOR THE DEAD

In today's society, roses symbolize love. Think of how many people spend countless dollars to send their sweetheart a dozen roses on Valentine's day. But the rose in earlier times was associated with death. In Greek mythology, the rose sprang from the blood of Adonis.

You've learned that roses played a part in the Roman Rosalia, from which the Slavic Rusalia is thought to originate. On days dedicated to the dead, people strew flowers, often roses, over the graves. Some writers have said the pagan Slav believed their Otherworld was a field of roses (Johnson, 184).

> The rose represents the greatest, though but a momentary, fulness of life; and
> for the sake of the former quality, it is thirsted for, like wine and blood, by
> the pining shadows in the realms of the dead (Hehn, 192).

Roses have also been known to *cause* death. Not infection from their stinging thorns, but suffocation from reclining in a mass of the petals. An emperor of Heliogabalus carpeted the palace rooms with roses and other flowers, and "his guests were so deeply imbedded in flowers while reclining at table, that some of them, being probably heavy with wine, were unable to rise, and died of suffocation" (Hehn, 193).

The Roses of Heliogabalus. Lawrence Alma-Tadema, 1888.
[Public domain], via Wikimedia Commons.

Each group consists of an odd number of men, quite often seven: the leader, called a *vataf* or *vatafin*, with the rest of the men being paired like buddies, each new *rusalets* or *kalushar* (singular term) assigned to older, more experienced men for training and mentoring. A musician also joins the team as they travel. The vatafin's position is one he inherits from his father. He alone has the power to drive away Rusalki and other harmful spirits.

Each year, the vatafin chooses those he wishes to be in the band. Quite often, the men come from a select circle of families who have participated in the rusalii ceremonies for many generations and have passed down to their sons the necessary skills to participate. Once becoming members, during Rusalka Week, the men spend all their time together—including sleeping—forsaking their homes and families.

Not all the men from select families are accepted, however. Each one has to meet certain physical and psychological requirements before he is initiated into the group: he must be "honest, cooperative, kind-hearted, physically strong and healthy, [and an] agile dancer."[159] He must also be susceptible to suggestions that will put him into a trance, have the ability to withstand austere situations, and most importantly—be someone who can keep a secret. He can't be a womanizer, thief, drunkard, or glutton.

When sworn in as a member of the group, each man kisses the banner and the leader's hand or his ceremonial staff, and vows to keep the secrets of the group. He then receives his own staff, which he'll own until he's too old to dance with the group. At this point, a ceremony is performed to transfer ownership of the staff, quite often to the man's son. However, the vatafin guards the staffs in his home from generation to generation.

These staffs are three to four feet long, made of various types of wood: cherry, ash, sycamore, maple, or dogwood. The tips are pointed, covered with iron to support the dancers' weight, and decorated with colorful items and metal that rattles.

The tools of their trade include the flag, herbs, a bowl of vinegar and garlic, their staffs, and silent water.

- **Flag**: Only the vatafin can touch the flag or the pole. The other men won't even stand in its shadow because its magic is so powerful. Music is an essential part of the rituals for contacting the spirit world, so while the vatafin sews herbs into each of the four corners, the band's musician plays a *kaval* (shepherd's pipe, a long, wooden flutelike instrument), *gaida* (goatskin bagpipe), *zurla* or *zurna* (double-reeded wooden wind instrument), or *tupan* (drum). The vatafin attaches more magical herbs to the top of the pole: including wormwood, garlic, rosen, and iris.
- **Herbs**: The vatafin collects the curative herbs known for their antiseptic and cleansing abilities. Only the vatafin knows the correct spells for treating each ailment. Among the herbs are chamomile, garlic (to repel evil spirits), rosen (Rusalki's flower), wormwood (to make the dancers strong), and wheat (symbolic of brotherhood).[160] They are attached to the flag, along the men's belts, and on the dish with the silent water. The herbs become twice as powerful after the men perform their dances.
- **Staff**: This item is symbolic of the World Tree, a tree that connects all dimensions—heavens, earth, underworld—and the creatures residing in each. The staff is the implement that entices the illness or evil spirit to leave the sick person's body. Inside is a hollow spot, filled with magical herbs. In northern Bulgaria, they use a wooden sword instead of a staff.
- **Water**: The men use "silent water," which is water that comes from a sacred, healing spring that is obtained in ritual silence. Others have called it "untouched" or "unbroken" water, having obtained

it before anyone else has broken the surface of the water that day. Ancient ancestors believed that water had a memory,[161] so the purpose of "silence" is to ensure the water doesn't "hear" any words except those that will restore a sick person's health. If they can collect the water on a sunny day, it'll be even more powerful. In addition, the music performed at the healing ritual gives the water positive charges, strengthening it even more.

The men have to observe strict rules and taboos throughout the time they band together.

- Remain silent: cannot talk to or greet anyone they meet, even friends and family. Only the vatafin can speak.
- Must immediately and without question follow all the vatafin's commands.
- Can't pray, enter a church, make the sign of the cross, or bless food.
- Can't wade through water; they either have to jump over a stream or cross it on a bridge or in carts. Water is the place where Rusalki and numerous other spirits reside, and the men risk being harmed by them if they get too close.
- Can't have sex during their membership in the group because celibacy is a "prerequisite for ritual potency" that allows them to "summon up the magic power to bring fertility to all."[162]
- Must be on their best behavior and not "get drunk, steal, speak shameful things, [or] quarrel with anyone."[163]

These may seem like odd restrictions, but they have a purpose.

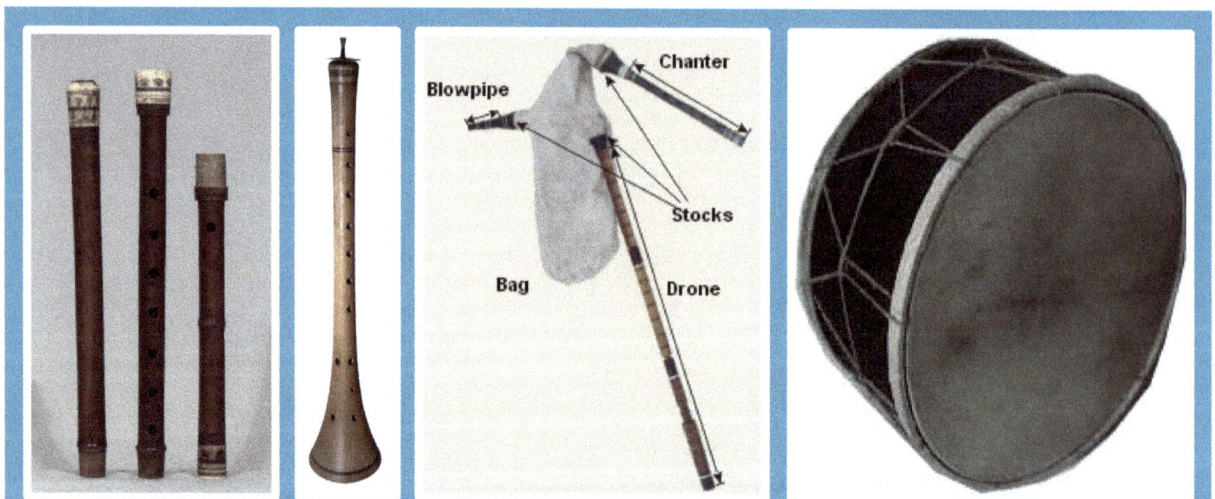

Rusalii Musical Instruments.

Kaval: Sketchee at en.wikipedia [Public domain].
Zurla: The original uploader was Bjankuloski06 at Macedonian Wikipedia.
  [CC BY-SA 2.0 (https://creativecommons.org/licenses/by-sa/2.0)]
Gaida: Boychrist at Bulgarian Wikipedia [Public domain].
Tupan: Arent [Public domain].
[Public domain], via Wikimedia Commons.

Those bans signify the unusual, borderline state in which they were found—between the human and the yonder world. In this important zone of transition they were able to confront the creatures causing the illness and to defeat them thus helping the sick ones to survive and recover.[164]

A Traveling Band

The men march from village to village, dancing around houses and through fields to bring health, luck, and fertility to people and the land. The dances are fast, with much twisting, jumping, and feet pounding the ground. Wherever they pass, it's believed that "crops and fruit ripen and no one gets rusalka sickness, for 'the rusalki are content.' "[165] However, the brotherhood won't dance in a village where other bands have danced. (You can watch an amateur Bulgarian kalushari performance in this video: https://m.youtube.com/watch?v=Fx0UU9-Y2rA. A professional, theatrical Rusalii dance gives you a different perspective in this video: https://www.youtube.com/watch?v=akdV40CDeOc.)

They dress in "holiday national costume, with white kilts and two red scarves tied crossways over their chests."[166] They carry swords or staffs (their colorful, noisy sticks). Medicinal herbs in the form of a wreath or nosegay decorate their hats, and iron spurs, small bells, and other noise makers adorn their leggings and leather sandals (which they are forbidden to remove during their time together). These adornments rattle when the men dance. The vatafin carries both the pot with vinegar and garlic and the white linen flag with herbs attached to it. The musician beats on a tupan, or plays a zurla or zurna, kaval, or gaida as he follows along.

The men perform ritual dances to music, not only to cure people of Rusalka disease, but also to cleanse homes of lurking illnesses and to ensure the fertility of gardens, fields, and vineyards. They wrestle with "demonic creatures,"[167] not physical ones, but spiritual ones from the underworld. Through their rituals, the men banish the evil hold these spirits have on sick people.

Some dances take place in the village square, some on the streets, while others are in private homes. A pair of men cross swords "for health" on the foreheads of sick people as they weave their way through the dance line. They also cross swords on hearths and doorways and at crossroads, wells, springs, and other sites thought to be imbued with magic.[168]

A Private Ceremony

Many people seek to hire the dancers for a special healing at their homes and pay with money or goods. However, the vatafin doesn't accept every case—only those he's certain Rusalki caused.

At a private residence, the men dance not for luck or fertility, but to cure a person. The ritual begins with the sick person lying on a rug or blanket. The vatafin fills a new earthenware jar with silent water and magical herbs, covers it, and places it next to the patient. The leader also fills a bowl with vinegar and garlic.

The vatafin holds the flag in his right hand and the bowl with garlic and vinegar in his left, while the other men form a circle around the sick person—from oldest to youngest, with the oldest man leading them. While their musician plays a gentle tune on a kaval, gaida, or zurna, the men dance from right to left, imitating the direction of the sun, which is considered a good, healthy direction. The tempo and speed of the music become faster and wilder as the dancing progresses. Eventually, the men dance in place for a time and lean back on their staffs.

All the while, the men enter a trancelike state. They suddenly pick up the blanket, tossing the sick person into the air, and then lay him back down. They move aside as the vatafin waves his banner over the patient, blows in four directions, sprinkles him with vinegar, gives the sick person a drink from the bowl, and whispers incantations into his ear.

When the vatafin has finished, the men again dance around the patient three times, shouting as they jump over the sick person. Then they shout and dance even faster around the jar of water, while the accompanying musician plays a special melody called Florichicka-ta.[169] The vatafin or the oldest man smashes the water jar so hard with his staff that the liquid splashes everyone: sick man and dancers alike. The breaking of the jar means the Rusalki's infectious hold over the man has also been broken.

The sick person is now cured. He rises, jumps, and dances along with his healers.

But the ceremony isn't complete. The water that splashed against the dancers causes one or more of them to fall unconscious onto the floor as if the illness has been transferred to them.

One man described the situation as follows:

> When we go round the invalid, I feel like I'm becoming mesmerized bit by bit. When I approach the vatafin and sip from the vinegar and he stares me in the eyes, I get dizzy;

Rusalii, Serbian Tradition. Photographer unknown, 1901.
virtuelnimuzejdunava.rs [Public domain].

when he hangs the flag over my eyes, I feel that everything gets dim . . . like when there's a mist. When we begin to go round the pot—already I remember nothing, not even what the vatafin does—as though someone were carrying me. When they hit and break the pot and it shatters and the water sprays out—then I go limp, my legs fail me, and I fall. After that I remember nothing.[170]

This loss of consciousness enables the dancer's soul to access the spirit world and plead with Rusalki to forgive the sick person his wrongdoing and remove the illness. If the disease is easy to get rid of, only one man falls because it indicates Rusalki are only a little angry. If the disease is severe, it'll be more difficult to remove. To entreat Rusalki, two or three men must fall. The healing fails if no men fall, signifying Rusalki are unwilling to have the healers enter their realm.

After the healers fall, the remaining dancers repeat the above ritual—but in the reverse direction, from left to right, against the sun—so the fallen men will recover and return from the spirit world. If they remain unconscious for too long, the spirit realm will keep them captive, and they will die. Dancing in reverse is "the most efficient way to retrieve souls from the spirit realm,"[171] where everything is reversed. In addition, the vatafin gives the fallen men water to drink that has different herbs than those given to the sick person.

Sometimes, even the dancers can't heal a sick person as the story below demonstrates where Baba Pechovitsa worked on the Wednesday of Rusalka Week.

[S]he went crazy, and the madness lasted three years, until she died. They went to the churches and monasteries, to the Rusaltsi and the sorceresses, but nothing helped. They even tried [the herb] dittany—again, nothing worked. "They [the rusalki] hit her hard—they were very angry!" concluded [her friend] Baba Marija.[172]

Going Home

At the conclusion of their week of healing, the men return to their leader's home. Outside, they dance around the banner one final time, before the vatafin gathers up all the staves and equipment and puts them away until the next year. The men's final act together is to have a feast and divide the money and gifts they received from the people they treated.

Being a member of the rusalii could be dangerous. Many bands traveled from village to village. They tried to avoid one another, but sometimes they crossed paths. When this happened, they had to fight, often to the death. Wherever each man died, that's where he would be buried without a funeral. Even though this custom died out by the end of the nineteenth century, those places are still known as "*rusalii* cemeteries."[173]

Călușari – Playing a Fool

The *călușari* (also called *rusalci*) of Romania are another group of men who heal and bring fertility to the land with their frenzied dances (called *călușer*, *căluș*, *călușar*, *călucean*, or *călușean*).[174] The "artistry of the performers and the beauty of their attire" was mentioned in 1572 at an emperor's coronation.[175]

Their name comes from the word *căluș*, which means "a little horse," and the suffix *ar* makes the entire name become "the little horse dancers."[176] The men imitate horses by neighing and galloping as part of their routine, and the red sashes across their chests act like harnesses. (You can see this in this video of Romanian călușari: https://www.youtube.com/watch?v=xcHufgrCSKU.) Once, long ago, a horse was possibly part of their fertility rituals, as this creature protected vegetation, animals, and people from illness.

Now, however, only a carved horse's head the first dancer carries is represented in the rituals. The fertility aspect has been lost, while the focus remains on health.

Origins of the Călușari

Various Latin, Greek, and Thracian theories attempt to determine the origins of the călușari.

- **Latin**: This is the most popular, and four theories fall into this category.
    1) *From the Salii, twelve "leaping priests" of the war god, Mars.* These youths derive their name from the Latin word *salio*, which means to "leap or jump," which attests to the athletic jumping in their ceremonial performance. Dressed as warriors in "an embroidered tunic, a breastplate, a short red cloak (*paludamentum*), a sword, and a spiked headdress," they traveled around Rome in March, singing and dancing, under the leadership of a *vates*.[177]
    2) *From the dance representing the abduction of the Sabine women.* In the early days of Rome, under the leadership of Romulus, men requested brides from the neighboring Sabines. Through trickery, these early Romans "seized" (from the Latin *raptio*) the women during a festival. This so-called "Rape of the Sabines" is now believed not to have been a sexual assault. Rather, some people say Romulus went to each woman and coaxed her into accepting Roman husbands with promises of "free choice" and "civic and property rights."[178] In the same way, the călușari "lure women with all kinds of objects considered to have magic powers." They also shout, "Get her!"[179]
    3) *From the Latin holiday of Rosalia.* This has already been discussed earlier as the origins of the rituals performed in Bulgaria.
    4) *From the Latin* collusium/collusii. This refers to a secret society of men and also a dance group, "whose members share a secret and a state of complicity."[180]
- **Greek**: *From the Cretan priests' (*curetes *and* korybantes*) ritual dance.* These were "armed and crested dancers" who worshipped Cybele to the beat of drums and the stamping of their feet. It was considered "a male coming-of-age initiation ritual." The men were also considered magicians and seers.[181]
- **Thracian**: *From dances dedicated to the goddess Pyrrha and the Thracian* kolabrismos *dance.* This was a circle dance, *kolo*, that was part of the worship of the sun, performed at the solstices and equinoxes.[182]

Group Dynamics

Like their Bulgarian counterparts, the group consists of an uneven number of men (between seven and eleven), all of whom must undergo special rites before they can become members. It's important that they're able to withstand the rigors of the dance, which involves performing somersaults, high jumps, and fast-paced steps.

They practice in secret in the woods where the fairies live, to ensure the supernatural powers choose the men they wish to join the group.

> [T]he dancers' [believed] in the existence of a supernatural power who watched their dances and assisted their jumps and, moreover, the belief that one who was not able to keep

pace with his dance companions fell to the ground in a state of dizziness as an indication of the fact that he was not to the divinity's liking, which entailed his immediate removal from the group.[183]

The călușari also have an additional group member who's not present among the Bulgarian rusalii (although he is among the *kukeri*, another group that drives away evil spirits):[184] the "Fool," "Dirty One," "Masked," or "Mute," who's allowed to speak only rarely. He's a comic figure, dressed in rags or humorous attire and wearing a leather mask, goat beard, or a stork mask, the beaks of which he can move with a string. He carries a stick with a hare's skin tied to the tip, and he wields a whip, sword, hatchet, or bow and arrows to drive away evil spirits. A pouch of healing herbs is tied to the front of his clothing.

Once the men make the decision to join—and are accepted into the group—they perform an initiation ceremony.

[T]he young men gathered in a circle, entreating Irodeasa (Herodiada), the călușari's protectrix, to support and help them. The vătaf sprayed the dancers with water and ordered them to raise their iron-knobbed clubs above their heads and strike them against one

Romanian Students Blaj in Călușari Costumes. Leopold Adler, between 1900 and 1920.
Leopold Adler [Public domain].

another three times, looking westwards first and then eastwards; this signified a mysterious sign indicating those who were part of the călușari society. With this completed, the dancers were ordered to return home and never look back, to remember that they were duty bound, and had to remain so, in good and evil, to appeal to Irodeasa for help before starting dances, and not to forget to sacrifice the first morsel or glass of beverage to their goddess by throwing them under the table.[185]

The men have to remain a member for nine years. To renege on the commitment means the fairies can torment them thereafter. Unlike the Bulgarian healers, the călușari don't set aside all the ordinances of the Church. After they're initiated, they become blood brothers and recite the Lord's Prayer.[186]

In some locations, they are bound to the brotherhood in other ways.

[T]he vătaf used to measure the height of the dancers on a red thread and bind it together with the apotropaic plants on the flag, or he would make a sign on the very pole of the flag, kept in vertical position, indicating the height of each călușar. This was considered as a pledge of everlasting commitment to secrecy and obedience given to their protectrix. After taking the oath, the călușari pass under the flag, or through a gate formed by either the flag pole and the Mute's body, or by the flag pole and the Mute's sword held aloft to form an arch. This is the moment the profane world is left behind and the dancer enters the sacred world.[187]

A Traveling Band

Much like the healers in Bulgaria, the călușari dance mostly for show these days. The men travel from village to village during the week around Pentecost, when the fairies are most active. They visit every home along the way to cure people of the *luat de Rusalii* ("taken by the fairies") and to drive away evil fairies who want to bring ruin or harm to the land and people.

The villagers vie with each other in inviting the Călușari to come and dance in their yards, because they believe that he who receives them will not get ill and will have good luck.[188]

The fairies they chase away go by different names, *rusalii* (that is, Rusalki) being one of them. Often, to avoid calling them by their name for fear of summoning the fairies, people use euphemisms: the beautiful ones, the white ones, the merciful ones, the glorious, the ladies, the powerful, the field's daughters, the forest's daughters, the courageous ones, the laborious, and more.[189]

At one time, the main ritual was to symbolically kill, then resurrect the Fool, imitating spring, in which nature comes alive again after its winter death. The Fool, therefore, is a representation of the Sun god, who brings life back to the land.

[W]e can understand the important role of the fool as the leader or captain of the dancers and as "the powerful medicine man who is making the potent magic to ensure that darkness will be followed by light." The fact that the fool often appears in old clothes and as a clown does not disprove the theory, because we have many proofs of the frequent degeneration of the figures in popular plays, like the God of the ancient religions who becomes the devil or the clown with the coming of the new.[190]

The fairies watch the dancers wherever they go, so the men must observe strict rules to avoid succumbing to the fairy disease. They must always sleep under church eaves so the fairies can't cripple them. (Another source says they must keep away from churches or holy items, in the same way the Bulgarian healers do.) Whenever they cross bodies of water, they turn around to see if a fairy is following them. Like the children's game of "Red Light, Green Light" ("Grandmother's Footsteps" in the UK),[191] the men keep an eye on the fairies to make sure they never get too close.

However, in order to acquire the power they need to heal the fairy sickness, the men must "venture beyond their normal human space. They must face the liminal space by going to the boundaries that separate human habitation from non-human."[192] And so, they go to where the fairies are: the waterways, forests, and hills, and chase them away by firing a gun three times.

Two Călușari. Costică Axinte.
Costică Axinte [Public domain].

79

When they've finished their touring, the călușari don't return the implements of their trade to their leader's home. Instead, they "break," "undo," or "bury" the flag and other possessions in silence in an isolated place to provide secrecy. In some locations, they throw the flag into the water when their dancing is done, and then "they run away without looking back so as not to be made ill by the fairies."[193] They return from their hiding places when their leader whistles. Finally, they "get together, shake hands, and greet one another as if they hadn't ever met before, then take their own ways home in complete silence, lest the fairies chase them."[194]

Relationship to Fairies

What makes this group of healers even more interesting is their connection to—or more accurately, *personification of*—the Romanian fairies, whose diseases the men cure.

First, and most easily identifiable, is the way they dress. The fairies wear the white attire of a bride, have flower wreaths in their hair, and sport bells around their ankles. Likewise, the men wear wreaths of flowers on their heads, with long, bright-colored ribbons dangling behind. They cover their faces with veils of white linen, and bells, as well as spurs, jingle around the men's ankles.

The veils serve another purpose, that of concealing the identity of the men. In the past, anyone who attempted to uncover their faces would be killed, such was the secrecy of the membership.

Iele, Romanian Fairies. Illustration by Dmitry Yakhovsky. © Bendideia Publishing.

Their clothing consists of long, white shirts over white, loose pants, which in an eighteenth-century document was described as a "feminine costume."[195] Red belts cross their chests and wrap around their waists. White signifies "purity and chastity," while red is a symbol of "maximum vitality" that provides the men confidence they need to protect people against evil spirits.[196]

Second, the uneven number of men in the group, which is often listed as nine, matches the number of fairies commonly referred to in Romanian folklore. Unlike the Slavic version of the fairies, who are described as being in groups with no specific number of maidens specified, Romanian fairies gather in groups of three, seven, nine, or eleven. The male dancers take on the name of each of the fairies.

Third, the călușari imitate the circle dance of the fairies. The men's quick, lively steps make them appear to fly through the air like the whirlwind that transports the fairies.

Fourth, both men and fairies have magical powers to cause illness and to cure these illnesses as well. According to the fairies, humankind has stolen this knowledge from them.

What illnesses do the călușari cause? If you recall, people believed that stepping where the fairies have trod will make people unwell. The same is true of the călușari; they avoid stepping in their companions' footsteps as they travel to avert the danger of becoming ill.

They also have a connection to the sun, with images of the sun, moon, and stars displayed around the horse's neck. They dance only during daylight hours, and their dance steps imitate the movement of stars around the sun and moon.

Rusalki – Fairy-Seers or Healing Angels

Throughout southeastern Europe, select women (and a few men) are healers who work alone, rather than in a group, and they often live in isolated areas. They are called by various names, some of which are the same as the fairies with whom they communicate: *rusalii* or *rusalki* (and other spelling variations), *vili* or *samovili* (Serbian and others), *samodivi* (Bulgarian), and other names. In addition, they may be called "*vilarkas* ('the ones from the fairies'), *padalicas* ('the ones who fall'), *vilenicas* ('the ones from the fairies'),"[197] and more.

Many of these women possess a natural-born psychic ability of clairvoyance and healing. Others are taught this skill from a relative, often passed down from grandmother to granddaughter. A smaller number of healers are even more distinguished. This latter group can communicate with the fairies who have "chosen" them and "infected"[198] or "gifted" them this ability—as far back as when they were a child. These chosen ones often suffer from a physical impairment that makes them "more suitable for an otherwise solitary profession."[199]

The fairies may kidnap the child and bring her temporarily to the fairy world. Or, in order to bring a child to them, the fairies inflict her with a severe case of the fairy sickness (Rusalka disease) to the point the child is near death. This is the time when the child first comes into contact with the fairies in their realm. When the mother brings the girl to a fairy-seer[200] for a cure, the woman diagnoses that the problem is a charm or spell put on the child because the fairies have "chosen" her to became their "sister," that is, to become a clairvoyant and learn the healing arts.

But gifts from fairies, like magic, come with a price. And that price is the child won't be healed of her own infirmities unless she undergoes an initiation when she becomes an adult—and is thereafter obliged to convey messages from the fairies and practice the healing arts. To refuse to do so after being healed infuriates the fairies, who will physically punish the fairy-seer—causing bruises on her body and preventing her from moving or speaking for a period of time. At worse, it means the illness will return and quite often be fatal.

The initiation and subsequent communications with the fairies happen in the liminal, in-between land, often called the "upper world," where the fairies reside. The women find themselves climbing a mountain or even a tree (often a pear tree), where their initiation begins. From there, the fairies take the women on a journey where they have a sense of flying above the mountains or falling into an abyss. Women who have participated have described the initiation as "ecstatic" and "festive." They are alone with the fairies, and all of them sing songs and dance.

Fairy-seers are not limited to practicing during Rusalka Week. Healing happens throughout the year, although communication with the fairies usually occurs only on a few specific holy days during the year. The fairies tell the women when they'll speak to them next.

This communication is performed through trances at a specific time of day: early morning or late afternoon. There must be absolute silence before the woman begins. Each fairy-seer acquires this state in different ways: dancing, singing, and reciting charms or prayers are among the common methods. She may also wear specific clothing as a sort of charm. However, it's essential the fairy-seer's body is clean, and she's not menstruating.

While in these trances, the fairy-seers are unaware of what's happening in their earthly surroundings. Instead, they are in the fairy world where they can see, speak to, and hear the fairies, who often appear as

RITUAL FOR ENTERING THE OTHERWORLD

If you'd like to try to reach out to the fairies or other spirits (since the fairies may not be receptive to you if they haven't called you), this is one way you can attune your mind and soul to enter into communication with them.

Find a sapling that can support your weight and (for the sake of your comfort) has very few branches. Lean your back against the sapling and begin to bounce gently, back and forth.

Close your eyes. Relax, and let all thoughts leave your mind. Let awareness of the physical world disappear.

When you are completely relaxed, clear of all thoughts and still bouncing gently back and forth, allow your clarified consciousness to drop into your heart center. Rest there for a moment, still bouncing.

… [I]magine an extra pair of arms attached to your heart center. These are your energy arms or spirit arms. Move them gently, gracefully back and forth as you bounce.

Now reach out with your energy arms. Feel them growing, expanding, reaching out forever to embrace the Otherworld and all its inhabitants (Johnson, 141-142).

three women: all beautiful, young, and long-haired, and dressed in either white or black. The fairies have names they go by as well: "Ilona, Helena, Elena, Diana, Sinziana, Maria, *Muma*, *Majka Prečasa* ('the honorable/the most clean Mother')."[201] These are the spirits of women caught in a parallel world between life and death, whom you've come to know as Rusalki, but who go by other names depending on country, region, or culture.

The women healers see the future, events the fairies wish for them to communicate to those who have gathered for guidance. The observers have come not only to know what's going to happen to them or their village, but also to receive messages from their deceased relatives, messages the fairies deliver to the fairy-seers.

> During the trance different emotional states are expressed: the communicator is crying, begging, or ecstatically happy. The emotional states are also "messages" about what the individual witnesses in the creature world or they anticipate information that is transmitted to the world of the living.[202]

And the people have come for healing, for the fairies impart their special knowledge to the fairy-seers, telling them both what ails each person and how to rid him or her of the affliction. Often, the illness—whether physical or emotional—is the fairy sickness, which the fairies have caused themselves, because a person has offended them in any of the ways you've read about earlier in this book: a common reason being the person has trespassed on places special to the fairies. Unlike other illnesses, fairy sickness can be cured only through the magic of a fairy-seer.

The illnesses that people seek relief from have three root causes: spells, evil charms, or *strava*, "fright" (defined as a "sudden intense feeling of fear").[203] *Strava* is often caused by a near-death experience, which opens the door to the upper world of the fairies; its symptoms are typically like post-traumatic stress disorder, and has physical or psychological effects. *Strava* "first affects the spirit of an individual and shows itself later physically." Or, in other words, "first it consumes the soul, and then it destroys the body."[204] Symptoms include high fever and nightmares in small children, while adults suffer nervousness, headaches, intestinal problems, and sterility in women.

Another way a fairy-seer can tell if a person suffers from *strava* is to measure his limbs with a rope or string. If one limb is shorter than the other; this means someone has cast an evil spell on the person, and the spell has "misbalanced" the body, making one limb shorter.

The illness may be "natural," resulting from something within our environment, or it can be a hex an evil person puts on you. Worse still, it can be more than a disease or state of mind; it can be a creature from the upper world that the fairies send to possess a human body as punishment for some misdeed. The fairy-seer is able to distinguish the cause and determine a cure. If it's left untreated, the fairy-seer says "the fright becomes alive" (*oživela je strava*), that is, it worsens and completely consumes the ill person, preventing him from living a normal life. The fairy-seer must "chase out" the *strava*.

Treatment of *strava* varies. The following are a few techniques used.

- *Casting spoons*. The fairy-seer tosses spoons on a table. From the position the spoons land, she can tell if *strava* possesses the patient and what causes it.
- *Melting the fear* or *casting bullets*. The fairy-seer melts a piece of lead, then pours cold water over it. It scatters into various figures, which tell her what the cause of the *strava* is. The person must

throw the lead over his shoulder while reciting an incantation, then leave without looking back. I talk about my own experience with this method when I was a child in Bulgaria. The healer performed the ritual for my cousin. You can read about it in my forthcoming book *The Wanderer*.

- *Throwing coals*. Similar to the above, but the healer tosses burning coals into water.
- *Casting matches*. The fairy-seer throws a lit match into water to "see" if the illness is from a fairy, a spell, or a natural cause. If it's from the fairies, they will communicate with the healer how to treat the individual.

You can read about a couple of these fairy-seers below.

Ivanka

In the spring and summer of 2015, Vivod observed the practices of two fairy-seers in Serbia. For one of them, a fairy-seer named Ivanka (born 1956),[205] she captured the event in a video, which you can view here: http://www.imdb.com/video/wab/vi796439833/. The video lacks subtitles for what Ivanka says, but key points of what's happening are indicated in English.

Ivanka was initiated as a fairy-seer when she was twenty or twenty-one, at the same time, her first husband "disappeared." Perhaps his disappearance was the work of the fairies, so that she could become their "sister"; Ivanka didn't specify what happened.

Her initiation happened in a pear tree, where her mother-in-law found her "singing in a stupefied state oblivious to her surroundings."[206] At first, she hid in a haystack to avoid the fairies, but they had no trouble finding her. They punished her by "taking away her voice, paralyzing her or beating her," leaving her body black and blue.[207] Afterward, they brought her to the top of a pear tree, or sometimes a cherry tree, where she received their messages.

Most often, she doesn't receive messages in a tree. The following describes her ritual.

> The ritual of trance starts at dawn. Ivanka avoids working in the stables on the farm in order to stay clean. The creatures abhor filthy, unclean clothes, people, and places. She also washes herself, avoids speaking (the fairies prohibit her from speaking before the ritual) and she dresses in light-colored clothes. She leaves the house and stands in the yard facing east, then she closes her eyes. In her right hand she holds three branched basil (Lat. *Occimum basilicum*) that she continues holding during her trance and during consultations. She also has to be "clean" (not menstruating) and so too the women who attend the ritual or who come to consult her three sisters through her mediation.[208]

She induces a trancelike state by dancing, shouting, whistling, and singing a certain song:

> In a field covered with flowers I climb, climb, with my sisters on the Krš up, up.
> In a field covered with flowers I go down with my sisters to the pear tree; my sisters make me climb the pear tree.
> And they are young, my sisters.
> In a field covered with flowers I climb, I climb with my sisters on the Krš up, up.[209]

An assistant leads Ivanka into her house when she's completely "taken" or possessed by the fairies. Visitors come, first asking about the future for themselves or their family. When all have passed through, they each return, bringing with them flowers and candles, a candle for each person they want to ask about. They inquire about what their deceased relatives request of them; responses may be "a visit to the grave site, flowers, candles or a commemoration bringing new clothes or a favorite food and drink to the dead at their graves."[210]

In certain areas, these rituals were performed publicly rather than in nighttime secrecy; the dead were offered gifts and their favorite tunes were played for them in order to entice them back for conversations. The village men danced around the entranced mediums; when the séance was over and the dead had departed, one of the men sprayed a concoction of river water and herbs into the faces of the women in order to awaken them.[211]

Ivanka (left); Radmilla (right). Illustrations by Dmitry Yakhovsky.
© Bendideia Publishing.

From the time she was initiated until she reached the age of sixty, Ivanka had been in communication with three fairies, whom she called Sinziana, Maria, and Majka Prečasa. When she turned sixty, she claimed she could continue to heal, but could no longer receive messages from the fairies, because they communicated with females between the ages of six and sixty only.

Radmila

In 2005, when Vivod visited Radmila, the woman was about sixty-five years old.[212] With the help of the fairies, she "sees" not only an individual's past, present, and future, but also the causes of the person's illness. Radmila was chosen by the fairies at an early age. When she was four, she was seriously ill, "almost dead," she says, with a high fever that caused her to lose weight because she couldn't eat properly. Nightmares plagued her. When doctors were unable to diagnose or cure the problem, Radmila's mother brought her to a popular fairy-seer, a *vilovita*, one who could communicate with the fairies called *vili* (singular: *vila*). The old woman pronounced that Radmila suffered from *bolesna od vila* ("ill from the fairies"), the fairy sickness. A cure was possible, she told the mother, but she said, "In exchange, when Radmila grows up, she will start to cure other people, otherwise the fairy-illness will come back."[213]

Radmila did become a fairy-seer when she reached adulthood, first healing neighborhood children, then relatives, until she branched out to heal others who came to her. Like Ivanka, she rebelled from time to time, with the result being the fairies punished her. Many of the ill people she treated suffered from *strava* (fright) mentioned earlier, rather than the fairy sickness.

She has seen many cases where the fairies send humans the fairy illness because people pollute the canal that runs through her village and destroy the rivers and mountains. Even though many fairies are called "unclean dead," they themselves do not like "the dirt, the garbage and the unclean places."[214] The pollution and "dirty" humans have also been driving the fairies away, so Radmila sees fewer and fewer of them.

Rusalki in Literature

The image of Rusalki in literature varies from that of the spirits in folklore (popular oral traditions). In fiction, they're seen more as sexual creatures, longing for love or revenge, their nurturing aspect as fertility goddesses long forgotten. Many of the stories were influenced by Hans Christian Andersen's *The Little Mermaid*. (You can find the original story, not the Disney version, in the Appendix.) Perhaps like me, you've never envisioned this story to be sexual, but one article about a passage in *The Little Mermaid* (quoted below) says the "vaginal and phallic images are threatening."

> All the trees and bushes were polyps, half animal and half plant; they looked like hundred-headed snakes growing out of the sand, the branches were long slimy arms, with tentacles like wriggling worms, every joint of which, from the root to the outermost tip, was in constant motion. They wound themselves tightly round whatever they could lay hold of and never let it escape. The little mermaid standing outside was quite frightened, her heart beat fast with terror.
>
> There is little wonder: she sees there the still entwined remains of some of the forest's victims.
>
> Then she came to a large opening in the wood where the ground was all slimy, and where some huge fat water snakes were gamboling about. (Andersen, "The Little Mermaid," 130, 132.)[215]

In literature, Rusalki's sexuality has run the gamut from girlish innocence to womanly eroticism, including also incestuous relationships and lesbianism. Authors offer their own interpretations based on political climate and life choices. Much literature about Rusalki from the great Russian writers (such as Pushkin, some of whose works are provided below) deals with the beauty, treachery, and wretchedness of Rusalki.

The theme of the lovelorn maiden committing suicide by drowning and becoming a Rusalka was popular in both literature and opera during the collapse of the feudalistic period. Dvorak's opera based on Pushkin's *Rusalka* play is a classic example of this. Quite often, noblemen seduced or raped female serfs, then left them pregnant. Scholars claim Pushkin's *Rusalka* was autobiographical, a result of him getting Ol'ga Kalashnikova, his peasant mistress, pregnant. This occurred around the same time he started jotting down ideas about the play. Others disagree, saying Ol'ga didn't drown herself, and so the story isn't about her.[216]

The practice of incest may have contributed to other literature about Rusalki, in particular the concept of *snokhodchestvo*, in which "the father of the groom would have sexual intercourse ('*snoshenie*') with his new daughter-in-law ('*snokha*') before his son."[217] In these stories, this reality is portrayed through the Vodnik (male water spirit), who is sometimes the father of Rusalki and other times the husband. But in all the stories, he's their lord and is often seen chasing after the women, frequently without catching them.

To be called a Rusalka when referring to one's sexuality in literature or reality was considered an insult, because the spirit behaves the opposite of how a good girl should. She expresses "aggressive" sexual behavior toward men, which, although often considered acceptable for males, is deemed abnormal or repulsive for women. On the other hand, some compare a Rusalka to a lesbian because, like author Zinaida

Gippius, the spirit (and author) "preferred to live with her own sex and was unable to consummate heterosexual relations, posing a mortal danger to her male admirers."[218]

You can discover some of these themes about Rusalki in the following stories included in this book:

- "An Unbaptized Spirit," Whishaw, *The Romance of the Woods*, published in 1895.
- "Rusalka" short poem, Pushkin, published in 1819.
- *Rusalka* unfinished play, Pushkin, published in 1837.
- *Rusalka* opera, Dvorak, first performed in 1901.
- An excerpt from *A Hero of Our Time*, Lermontov, 1840, translation published in 1916.
- Excerpts from *Sacred Blood*, Gippius, published in 1901.
- "Ballad" poem, Gippius, published in 1903.
- Excerpt from an untitled and as-yet unpublished modern story.
- Excerpt from *Mystical Emona: Soul's Journey*, Aveela, published in 2014.

An Unbaptized Spirit

The following story is found in Frederick Whishaw's *The Romance of the Woods*. It's a story about an infant who died unbaptized and was doomed to become a Rusalka. The author omitted the source of the tale. It may have been from stories he collected, or it may have come from others who did much folkloric research. Nonetheless, it's a look at what people in that era believed would happen.

"An Unbaptized Spirit" (1895)

There was grief in the house of Pavel Shirkof, a peasant of the village of Chudyesin, near Perm, beneath the shadow of the dark Urals. Pavel was unlike most of his kind, for his ideas of happiness were not as theirs, bounded by the narrow limits of the interior of the kabak or drinking-shop. Pavel was gifted with an earnestness of disposition rare enough among men of his standing; he took life seriously, and had been a good husband to his wife. He had married but a short year ago, and now, alas! the buxom girl of twelve months since lay, a young mother, sighing out the last moments of her stricken life. Unattended by doctor or nurse, far from all skilled assistance, and watched only by her terrified and ignorant though loving husband, the poor wife tossed upon her so-called bed, while her tiny child lay helpless and neglected upon a nest of old potato-sacks and coats and rags in the corner by the stove—a thing of feeble, struggling existence, as near to its end had Pavel known it, as it was to its beginning, and this was but a matter of half-an-hour or so. The baby lay and wailed unnoticed, for her poor father had his dying wife to attend to, and the sick woman, but half conscious, had not as yet caught that sound so dear to every mother's ear—her own child's voice. But suddenly she paused in the restless side-to-side movements of her head upon the pillow, and appeared to listen.

"Pavel," she said, and her pale cheek flushed, "it is the child. Let me see it before I die. Hold it near me. Let me take it in my arms!" Pavel brought the little wailing thing and laid it in the mother's arms, which scarcely had strength to clasp themselves round their precious burden.

A beautiful smile went, like a sunset, over poor dying Doonya's face—the last gleam before nightfall; then she looked anxiously at the tiny bundle at her breast. "Pavel, my poor man," she said, "the child has death in its face; it will accompany me into the Unknown; we shall both leave you together, my soul. God comfort you at this time of tribulation! But now you shall do her the only service you can ever render her. Fetch the good priest from Volkova; take Shoora, the best horse, and the lightest cart, and fetch him quickly, my Pavel, for the child must be baptized."

But Pavel refused to leave his wife in her present condition. The child must wait, he said; and in case of emergency any one could pronounce the baptismal formula. He would do it himself. Meanwhile, what was the child to him, body or soul, in comparison with his beloved Doonya?

A very few minutes after this the soul of Doonya passed peacefully away, and poor Pavel was a widower. In his anguish of mind during that saddest hour, he had no thought for the tiny bundle of sickly humanity lying neglected upon its bed of rags and sacking. No neighbours were at hand. All were at work in the fields. For none had known of poor Doonya's sudden and immediate need of their services. When at length Pavel remembered to look at the child, therefore, it was cold and dead, and might have been so for an hour for all he knew. Pavel was not so ignorant as to be unaware that the fate of a child dying unbaptized is most melancholy. He knew, as every Slavonic peasant knows, that the unbaptized soul, whether of child or grown person, is doomed to wander over earth and sea and air for seven long years, seeking for some one sufficiently pure of spirit to hear its spirit-voice appealing to be baptized. If such an one should hear it and pronounce the orthodox formula, all would be well with the soul, and it might depart in peace into those blessed realms where waiting souls, as Christians believe, rest until the great day of their resurrection. If, however, none should hear the wanderer (and, alas! how few are those qualified to catch the tone of a spirit-voice!), and the seven years should expire, then that poor unbaptized soul must lose its soulship, and descend among the mortal rusalki, or water nymphs, to be a rusalka for the remainder of her life, cut off for ever from the blessed privileges of Christianity. Then Pavel was overcome with sudden remorse, and, in the hope that the soul of little Liuba (for so the parents had agreed to call her) was still within hearing, he pronounced aloud the words, "Liuba, I baptize thee in the name of the Father, and of the Son, and of the Holy Ghost." But, alas! it was too late. The little neglected soul had fled away in its distress and despair, and was already far from the place of its birth, wandering over sea and land, and crying aloud to every human being whom it saw: "Have pity, Christian brother (or sister). Hear my cry and baptize me, or my soulship is lost, lost!"

***

When the spirit of little Liuba first left the tiny body in which it had commenced its career, and fled away, it knew not whither to direct its flight. One central idea was all the consciousness it possessed as yet, and this was the knowledge—half hope and half despair—which is given to each infant unbaptized soul for its heritage, namely, that it has been deprived by misfortune of something which should have been its dearest possession, the sweet privilege of Christian baptism, and that it must wander and weep and entreat until such time as it shall find a baptized Christian into whose own pure soul the cry of the wandering spirit may enter; from him it may then receive the precious gift which is its own by right, but of which it had been unfortunately deprived.

So Liuba's infant soul fled wailing over valley and hill and sea, and was far away when her widowed father pronounced the baptismal formula over the poor little wasted body which had once been her earthly tenement. Liuba knew nothing of the fate predestinated for those whose seven years expire and find them still without the pale of blessedness; all this she should learn in good time; at present she only knew that she must wander and chant her monotonous sorrowful prayer that she might be heard and baptized.

Rusalki. Witold Pruszkowski, 1877.
[Public domain], via Wikimedia Commons.

Red-shirted peasants were busy at work in the fields, together with gaily-clad women and a few children. It was the time of the cutting of the corn, and there was much laughter and merriness, while each peasant did as much work as he felt was good for him, which was not much; the women worked harder than the men and sang in a light-hearted manner as they laboured. The men were glad to allow the women to work as hard as they were willing to; it saved them much trouble.

"Brothers and sisters—Christian people," wailed the child-spirit, "baptize me and save my soul alive!" But not one of all the chattering, toiling throng could hear the spirit-voice, for the sounds of the world were loud in their ears and no other voice could reach them by reason of the noises which deafened them. So Liuba left them and fled away over hill and dale, wailing and weeping, for she had experienced her first taste of failure and disappointment; and by-and-by she came to the banks of a large river, and here she rested herself upon the shore, strange and lost and lonely. It was a beautiful sunny morning in August, and little Liuba could not resist the charm of the sunshine and the sparkle of the clear water about her; she saw it with delight, and the rustle of the leaves and the songs and twittering of the happy birds amid the leaflets overhead filled her with wondrous joy and content. "How beautiful it all is," she cried; "if only it were to be always like this I should not so much mind my misfortune."

To Liuba's surprise, at the sound of her voice a very beautiful form suddenly appeared rising out of the water. The shape was that of a human girl, but indistinct, and with wavy outlines that quivered and shifted, instead of the fixed lines of a human body. Masses of golden flowing hair fell over bosom and shoulders and lay floating upon the ripples of the water, of which it seemed to form a part; and though it had proceeded from the stream and still lay upon the surface of the river, yet the hair was not wet and draggled but wavy and dry and lovely to look upon. Liuba looked at the new-comer with admiration and joy. "How beautiful you are!" she cried, "and you have heard my voice and will baptize me!"

The beautiful creature laughed aloud, and the sound of her voice was like the flowing of shallow waters over the rapids.

"Oh, no!" she cried, "I cannot baptize you, and I would not if I could! You must be very young or you would know that I am a river-spirit, a rusalka, such as you yourself will be one day, unless you find some one to baptize you, which is very unlikely. I can hear your voice for I am a spirit, but mortal men cannot distinguish your speech, and if they hear anything they say, 'Listen to the whispering of the wind in the tree-top!' or, 'Do you hear how the breeze sighs this evening among the reeds in the stream?' Do you not know that you have but seven years in which to perform your hopeless task, and that after that you are at liberty to come down among us here in the cool waters? It were far better to save yourself these years of disappointment and toiling and to become one of us at once."

But the soul of Liuba thirsted for baptism as the new-born plant longs for the touch of the sun-god, and she was not satisfied with the words of the rusalka.

"But who are you? and are you baptized? and what do you do down there in the cool waters?" she asked. The rusalka looked grave for an instant, and then quickly laughed once more.

"No," she said, "we are not baptized; we are spirits now, but when the world comes to an end and the rivers are poured out and dried up, we shall exist no longer. We are the Water Folk, and our ancestors fell with Lucifer from heaven; at which time we took up our abode here, instead of following our captain to his home. As for what we do, we dance and sport amid the shining stones and caves, and chase the brilliant fishes, and scare the greedy otters; we fascinate silly humans, and when they follow us into the waves we strangle them or torture them to death because we hate them."

"Why do you hate them?" asked Liuba.

"Because they have souls and we have none; you will know why in seven years. And now, good-bye till then, for my sisters await me yonder; they are ready for the dance, while I tarry chattering here." With these words the beautiful nymph seemed to fade from the sight, growing every instant more and more indistinct. Liuba saw her wave her arms and heard her silvery laugh, and then she quite disappeared. From the spot where she had stood upon the bank a tiny stream of crystal water trickled through the grass and flowers and found its way back to the parent river.

"How terrible!" said Liuba. "Oh, how I hope I shall never be a rusalka!" and a great rush of longing came over the little bankrupt soul for that baptism of which it knew nothing save its own great need and desire for the gift, and away she floated once more over woods, meadows, and rivers, wailing and crying, "Oh, who will baptize me, baptize me! Christian men, have pity upon a soul that wanders and weeps, and baptize me!"

But the merchant was too busy over his money-making, or too preoccupied with his money-losing to have a thought to spare for a lost soul. And the ships riding upon the bosom of the sea, many of which Liuba passed in her flight, were filled with sailors who thought of their dear wives and children at home on shore, and of the loved cliffs of their native country, but not of the poor bereft spirit passing in distress and beseeching over the deck of their vessel. Now and again one would say to his comrade, "What sound was that amid the rigging like the sighing of wind and the whirring of the wings of a bird that flies from land to land?" and the other would reply: "I heard no sound, and it is too dark to follow the flight of a bird to-night." Even the worshippers in the churches were unable to hear the spirit-voice; they were busy praying for themselves or for their dear ones; some thought of worldly matters in spite of themselves, some were sad for their sins, some were full of petty jealousies because of the grand clothes of their fellow-worshippers, or of pride for their own; none heard the wailing spirit-voice, and Liuba, the saddest soul in all that churchful of souls, went weeping upon her journey, ever weeping and ever beseeching, but never obtaining that sweet gift for which she longed with a longing that increased with each day and with every disappointment.

Once, when she had wandered thus for months enough to make two whole years, Liuba met with an adventure. Passing over the streets of a large city she was surprised to hear a voice, which at first she took for an echo of hers, for it spoke the same words, and the tone was that of distress and entreaty, as sorrowful as her own. Then she saw that the sound proceeded from a little form like hers, which slowly and sadly winged its way through the dusky air, close above the roofs of the human habitations below, and ever as it went it chanted its melancholy refrain: "Christian men and women, hear my voice, and baptize me ere it is too late, and my soulship is lost, lost!" Liuba accosted the little wandering soul, which was, she found, sadder even than herself because it had less of hope. This soul was that of a little human boy who had died unbaptized nearly seven years ago. For six long years and as many months it had wandered, entreating for baptism and finding none that could hear its voice; now there remained but a few months wherein to gain the blessed privilege, and hope had grown faint and weak. Liuba's companion had been over the world, he said, and over it a second time; but all in vain—none would hear him. He had met many lost souls like himself, and all were sad and disappointed; and for some, he knew, the term had expired and they had fallen to the status of water-spirits. Some had taken the form of cuckoos, and in the shape of that bird had wandered over the world crying "cuckoo" instead of the usual entreaty for baptism, because there are many, he said, upon the earth, who believe that each unbaptized soul assumes the form and voice of this bird in order to be seen and heard by Christian men. Those who believe thus are in the habit of pronouncing the formula of baptism over each cuckoo whose voice they hear, in the hope of thus saving some lost human soul.

"And are some saved in this way," asked Liuba.

"I have heard so from others," said the newcomer, "but I know not whether it is true. For myself, I have been content to preserve my own likeness and voice, for surely, surely some day, though the time is now short, I shall yet be heard and saved!"

So Liuba and her companion journeyed together henceforth, and together they chanted their monotonous song, which none of all the Christian men and women they saw might hear: "Brothers, Christians, hear us and baptize us, or our soulship is lost!"

Then there came a sad day when the elder wanderer knew that his time for hoping was past, and that his soulship was indeed lost for ever. By the bank of a lovely river he and Liuba parted, and Liuba wept bitterly, and said: "Farewell, poor lost brother, in pity and love I greet you a last time, and even as your lot is so shall mine be; for, alas, there remain but a few more years!" But the other said, "Nay, hope on, Liuba, for, perhaps, by the mercy of the Highest, you may yet be saved." Then he drooped his wings and plunged beneath the waters, and when the cool element touched him he forgot for ever that he had belonged to a higher race of beings, and went among the river-spirits, and was with them and of them, and knew of nothing better.

But Liuba wandered on and on, and wearied not of wrestling with Christian men and women for that which they alone could give her if they would. Once—a year from the end of her term—she passed through a church in which prayers were continually offered for those who die unbaptized, and in which the form of baptism is gone through annually once for the benefit of these, in case one should be within hearing; but the service was just finished as Liuba passed over the church, and she was too late to hear those longed-for words which should give her the priceless boon she desired. In another place she came where a certain good man pronounced every morning and every evening the baptismal formula, in case some poor wandering soul should be passing within hearing and should hear and live. But though she saw him, she knew not of his benevolent daily action, and passed on unaware; neither did he hear her spirit-voice, for his soul was full of many worldly matters, and when at evening he performed the pious rite which was his daily custom, Liuba was far away.

And it happened that a few months before the expiration of her time, Liuba passed once again by that stream where, on her first day of wandering, she had seen the river-spirit; and now again, as she rested upon the bank of the stream, that beautiful nymph-form rose, glistening and undulating, from the waters, and waved her arms and laughed and beckoned to Liuba, and said, "Aha! little lost soul, a few more days or weeks and you are ours. We shall be kind to you, never fear, and you shall dance and sport your time away instead of wandering and whining over land and sea, and all for the sake of something which may not be worth the finding! And you shall learn to captivate the hated human beings who would not listen to your voice, and you shall entice them down and strangle them—strangle them!" But Liuba fled away in horror and dread, and would not listen to what the rusalka had to say. But her last few months were at hand, and the poor wanderer toiled on, beseeching and entreating wherever she went, and weeping and wailing more pitifully as hope receded further and further.

***

Far away in the east of Europe there is a great city which is full of large shops, and immense houses, and busy streets, and of rich and poor, and of good and evil, as is every other large city everywhere. It was Christmas eve, and the last hour of work had come for bank and shop and factory. After this there should be holiday-time for all. The factory hands poured in a great stream from the open doors of a cotton-mill— pale men and women, happy enough in the prospect of a day or two to be spent far away from the stuffiness and the heat and the toil of the mill. All chatted and laughed and made plans, and told one another of what they would do at Christmas and on Boxing Day. And many went away to dance and to sing and enjoy themselves; and some went to the inns and public-houses, and were rowdily happy in their own way; and many went to the brilliant shops and bought materials for their Christmas dinner or presents for their friends. And one man of all the crowd did not join those who were bent on merrymaking. Yet he, too, was full of plans of happiness for the season. He was not rich, this man, but he spent little, and the wages of the factory were good; and each year he contrived to save a sum of money in preparation for that which he had in his mind for Christmas time. He had brought his savings with him this evening—a fair sum for a man in his position—and with the money he proceeded from shop to shop, buying here a pot of sweet flowers, there a book, here a doll, and there a toy, until his large basket was full and as heavy as he could carry. Then he went to the children's hospital, where for seven years his kind face had been well known; and here he was received with acclamation by the little suffering inmates, for they knew well the meaning of his appearance in company with the basket; and there were some who had been in that building, alas! for years, and had learned to consider the visit of this man and his basket as an established thing, as certain and as regular as Christmas itself. Many little hearts beat higher with joy when Paul Shirkof's round was finished and the basket was empty, and Paul's own heart was joyful and happy indeed as he returned to his home that night and knelt to say his Christmas prayer. His was no conventional prayer, nor did he pray in the words of any formula; but he thought of the Christ-child born as on this night in its helplessness and innocence, and he prayed for simplicity and for innocence, that his heart might be as the heart of a child, and his spirit pure, so that he might discern God in all His works.

And even as he prayed there was borne in upon him—though he could see nothing—the sound of the voice of a tiny child, and it said—entreating and wailing—"Oh, Christian man, pity me; hear my voice and baptize me, or my soulship is lost!"

And a great fear fell upon the man, so that he could scarcely frame words to ask:

"Who are you that address me?" Then the answer came: "An unbaptized soul—Liuba; baptize me before it is too late, and save me!"

And the man delayed no longer, but made the sign of the Cross and said, "I baptize thee in the name of the Father, and of the Son, and of the Holy Ghost, Amen." Then at the words the soul of Liuba rejoiced with a great joy, and departed, whither I know not; but this is certain, that it wandered no longer wailing over land and sea, for it was henceforth at rest for ever, and, by Divine mercy, in possession of that sweet privilege which for a while had been lost to it.

And the father knew not that he had baptized his own child's soul; but he shall know it one day, perhaps, when those who are pure in spirit shall see God.[219]

"Rusalka" – Short poem by Pushkin

Alexander Sergeyevich Pushkin (1799-1837), a cultured, but poor Russian nobleman born in Moscow, was a beloved poet, novelist, and playwright. His first adventure into writing was a poem he wrote when he was fifteen. He's been called "Russia's greatest poet and the founder of modern Russian literature" by being "the first to use everyday speech in his poetry, fusing Old Slavonic with vernacular Russian."[220]

His life was full of disappointments: exiled by the emperor because of his writings on social reform and atheism, he was later restored, but the emperor censored his works. He was unable to "make any trip, participate in any journal, or publish—or even publicly read—any of his works" without permission. His wife was openly courted by the man who married his wife's sister. This led Pushkin to challenge his brother-in-law to a dual, a fight he lost when he was hit by a bullet in his hip that went into his abdomen. He died two days later.

His poem about a Rusalka was published in 1819. It has an air of mystique: "its mysterious atmosphere intensified by uncertainty as to whether the rusalka submerges the mesmerized anchorite or whether he voluntarily plunges into 'her' lake."[221]

To go along with this poem is a short, animated video that Aleksandr Petrov (born 1957) loosely based on the monk's story: https://www.youtube.com/watch?v=Js6biCftfks. Looked at from a Christian perspective, it's a story about self-sacrifice and atonement of sins. However, there's more to it than that. It clearly demonstrates the Slavic folkloric aspect of a Rusalka's revenge and the fact that she can't be at peace and move to the other side until she's been avenged.

It's also been suggested that the video reflects the "circularity of time" in that "[t]he old monk sees in the novice his own image from long time ago. He is just entering the cycle of life, this novice, and the old monk wants to protect him."[222]

The poem has been described as follows:

> Pushkin's "Rusalka" poem frames the destructive force of female sexuality within a tale of pagan and Christian realms colliding. Just as the rusalka entices the priest into the lake, the poem itself pulls the Christian 'saint's life' genre into the alien waters of a pagan myth. The journey of a mind into God is abruptly ended at the banks of a misty lake.[223]

If you're confused about the video, here's a summation of it:

> As the novice starts to respond at the love games of *rusalka*, the hermit has a flashback, the remembrance of his sins of youth. He realizes that the girl in the river is his own love that he betrayed long time ago (*an interesting detail: the sledge from today's hut appears also in the flashback; to say nothing about the fox who runs at the beginning of the movie, a witness of this circularity of time, of this endless repetition of sin and repentance*).
>
> The monk falls asleep while praying and in his dream he ascends Jacob's Ladder to find advice from Heaven. The Blessed Virgin is handing him the Lamb of God, and the monk realizes that he got the Stigmata of Jesus: the heavenly advice is to offer himself to sacrifice in order to save the novice. And that's what he's doing: going to the river, throwing himself inside the waters to save the novice, dying, together with the *rusalka*, who is now revenged. The novice remains alone, taking care of two graves: monk and *rusalka* have finally found their solace.[224]

"Rusalka" (Pushkin, 1819)

In lakeside leafy groves a friar
Escaped the world; out there he passed
His summer days in constant prayer,
Deep studies and eternal fast.
Already with a humble shovel
The elder dug himself a grave,
And calling saints to bless his hovel,
Death—nothing other—did he crave.

So once upon a falling night he
Bowed down beside his drooping shack
And meekly prayed to the Almighty.
The grove was turning slowly black;
Above the lake the mist was lifting;
Through milky clouds across the sky
A ruddy moon was softly drifting,
When water drew the friar's eye—

He looks; his heart is full of trouble,
Of fear he cannot quite explain;
He sees the waves rise more than double
And suddenly grow calm again.
Then, white as first snow of the highlands,
Light-footed as nocturnal shade,
There comes ashore and sits in silence

Upon the bank a naked maid.

She looks at him and brushes gently
The hair and water off her arms.
He shakes with fear and looks intently
At her seductive, luscious charms.
With eager hand she waves and beckons,
Nods quickly, smiling from afar,
And shoots within two flashing seconds
Into still water like a star.

The glum old man slept not an instant
All night. All day not once he prayed;
Before his eyes still hung and glistened
The wondrous girl's persistent shade.
The grove puts on the gown of nightfall;
The moon walks on the cloudy floor;
And there's the maiden—young, delightful,
Reclining on the spellbound shore.

She looks at him, her hair she brushes,
Smiles, sends him kisses sweet and wild,
Plays with the waves—caresses, splashes—
Now laughs, now whimpers like a child,
Moans tenderly, calls louder, louder…
"Here, monk, here, monk! To me, to me!"
Then vanishes in limpid water,
And all is silent instantly…

On the third day the ardent hermit
Was sitting on the shore, in love,
Awaiting the voluptuous mermaid,
As shade was lying on the grove.
Night ceded to the sun's emergence;
By then the monk had disappeared.
It's said a crowd of local urchins
Saw floating there a wet gray beard.[225]

Rusalka – Unfinished Play by Pushkin

Between 1826 and 1832, Pushkin worked on a play he referred to as Mel'nik' (The Miller).
It was first published in his journal, *Sovremennik*, in 1837. Pushkin never finished this play because he was killed in a duel when he was thirty-seven.

In this story, a prince abandons his peasant mistress to marry a noblewoman, despite the fact he discovers she's pregnant. The distraught girl drowns herself and becomes a Rusalka. The story ends when the prince meets his lover's daughter, also a Rusalka.

Many authors have added a conclusion to the story. Whether or not they have any resemblance to what Pushkin would have written if he had lived, we'll never know unless new documents come to light. However, they give you an idea of how the story *might* have ended. You can read a few of these "endings" after Pushkin's play and decide for yourself.

An interesting interpretation of the short video you watched about the monk and the Rusalka indicates the two poems may be related. Perhaps Pushkin did connect the two in his mind. It's something to think about.

> The movie of Aleksandr Petrov unifies somehow the stories from the two poems. The old monk is the prince who in his youth betrayed his love. He hopes now to find solace through prayers and mortification.[226]

Rusalka (Pushkin, 1837)

The bank of the Dnieper. A mill.
The MILLER, *his* DAUGHTER.

MILLER
Eh, you are all the same, you giddy maids,
All foolish, scatterbrained. When fortune sends you
A man of rank, an enviable prize,
It's your plain duty to attach him fast.
And how? By sober, virtuous behavior,
Now strict, now yielding, blowing hot and cold
Upon his passion. Sometimes—just in passing—
A hint at marriage; last, but most important,
To guard your maidenhead, that priceless treasure,
Which, like the spoken word, once it is given
May not be taken back. Or, if there is
No hope of honest wedlock, marriage bells,
Then, even so, and at the least, you should
Get some advantage for your family,
Some slight advancement from it; why, just think,
The old song says: "He will not love me ever
Or seek to please me!" But dear me no, you have
No thought to use your opportunities!
It's not the time, you say, and lose your heads;
You're happy to fulfil his every wish

For nothing, happy to hang upon the neck
Of your true love all day, but your true love
Is here today and gone tomorrow; you—
Left empty-handed; eh, what fools you are.
Haven't I said to you a hundred times:
Now, daughter, you take care, do not be
A fool, don't miss your chances, girl,
Don't let the prince slip through your fingers, do not
Despoil yourself for nothing. To what end?
Now you may sit and cry your pretty eyes out
For ever. Tears won't bring him back.

DAUGHTER

But what
Should make you think that he no longer loves me?

MILLER

What do you mean? But what? How many times
A week used he to visit our poor mill?
Eh? Every blessed day, and sometimes twice
A day—then he began to come more seldom,
More seldom still—and now it's nine whole days
Since he was here. Well, what say you to that?

DAUGHTER

He's busy: do you think he has no duties?
He's not a miller—may not stand and let
The water work for him. He often says
That his work is the hardest in the world.

MILLER

A likely tale. Why, when do Princes work?
What is their work? To hunt the fox, the hare,
To feast, to roister, to browbeat their neighbors,
And to seduce poor ninnies such as you.
He has to work himself; poor, ill-used fellow!
The water works for me, indeed! ... I know
No peace by night or day; always alert!
Now here, now there some new repair is needed,
Now rot, now leaks. If only you had managed
To ask the Prince for just a little money
To put the mill straight, that would have been
something.

DAUGHTER
Ah!

MILLER
What is it?

DAUGHTER
I hear the sound of hoof-beats!
His horse's .... It is he!

MILLER
Look you, Daughter,
Remember my advice, do not forget.

DAUGHTER
He, here he is.

Enter PRINCE. *The groom leads away his horse.*

PRINCE
Good morrow, dearest heart.
Good morrow, Miller.

MILLER
Most gracious Prince,
You're welcome. It has been a long, long time
Since we last had a sight of your bright eyes.
I must be off to find you some refreshment.

Exit.

DAUGHTER
Ah, at long last you have remembered me!
Thought you not shame to torture me so long
With empty, cruel anxiety and waiting?
If you had known what thoughts came to my mind!
With what dread fears I harassed my poor heart!
Sometimes I'd think your horse had bolted with you
Into some quagmire, over some steep cliff,
Or that a bear had killed you in the forest,
That you were ill, that you no longer loved me—
But glory be to God! You're live and well,
And love me still, just as before, my Prince,

Am I not right?

PRINCE
Just as before, my angel.
No, better than before—

SHE
But you are sad.
What is the matter, love?

PRINCE
Do I seem sad?
You have imagined it. No, no, I'm merry
As always at the sight of you, sweet.

SHE
No,
When you are merry, you come running to me
And cry while still far off: "Where is my sweetheart,
What is she doing?" Then you kiss me, then
You ask me questions: "Am I glad to see you?
And did I think you would be here so early?"
But now—you listen to me and say nothing,
You do not hug me, do not kiss my eyes;
For sure, you have some worry. What is it?
Is it, perhaps, that you are angry with me?

PRINCE
Indeed, it is unworthy to pretend.
You have guessed right! My heart is heavy now
With sorrow—sorrow which you cannot charm
Away with fond caress or tenderness,
Cannot assuage and cannot even share—

SHE
But it is hurtful to me not to grieve
One grief with you—tell me your secret, Prince.
If you permit it—I shall weep, if not—
No tear of mine shall fall to vex your heart.

PRINCE
Why should I drag it out? The sooner said
The better. Dearest, you must know that in

This world there is no lasting bliss; nor rank,
Nor beauty, neither strength, nor riches—nothing
Can shelter us from the blind strokes of Fortune.
And we—is it not true, my little sweetheart?—
We had much happiness together. I,
At least, was happy with you, in your love,
And now, whatever may befall me more,
Wherever I may be, I shall remember
You, my dear love; in losing you I lose
A treasure nothing ever will replace.

SHE
I do not yet quite understand your words,
But I am frightened. Fate holds some threat for us,
Prepares some doom unguessed at, unforeseen.
Not—separation?

PRINCE
You have read the riddle.
Fate wills that we should part.

SHE
But who should part us?
Can I not follow you wherever you
May go, on foot if need be? I'll go dressed
As a young boy. I'll serve you well and truly
Upon the road, or in the field, at war—
I have no fear of war—if only I
May see you and be near you. No, I will not
Believe it! Either you put me to some test
Or you arc teasing me—some empty joke.

PRINCE
No, no, today I have no mind for jokes,
Nor do I need to put you to the test;
Neither am I to ride away to war
Or to far countries. I remain at home,
And yet must part with you, my love, for ever.

SHE
Wait now, I understand it, everything.
You are to wed?

The PRINCE *is silent.*

You are to wed!

PRINCE
I must.
Put yourself in my place, poor child. A prince
May not obey his heart as young girls may—
He is not free, but chooses in accordance
With calculations made by others for
The good of others. … Time and God will comfort
Your sadness; don't forget me; take this headband
In memory of me—I'll put it on.
And I have brought this necklace, too—
Come, take it—this too. I promised it
To your good father. See you give it to him.

He presses a bag of gold into her hand.

Farewell—

SHE
One moment. There is something I should.
I have forgotten....

PRINCE
Think.

SHE
For you I would
Do anything ... no, that's not it.... Wait, wait—
It cannot be, you could not leave me now
For ever.... No. All that's beside the point....
Ah! I have it now: Today your child
Moved for the first time underneath my heart.

PRINCE
Unhappy maid! What can we do? Look after
Yourself if only for his sake; I will not
Abandon either you or your poor child.
In time, may be, I'll even come myself
To visit you. Be comforted. Don't cry.
Come, let me hold you in my arms once more.

On his way out.

Oof! That is that.... A great load off my mind.
I thought there'd be a storm, but things went off
Quite peaceably.

Exit. SHE *remains motionless.*

MILLER
entering
May I invite you. Prince,
To step inside the millhouse ... where's he gone?
Tell me, where is our Prince? bah, bah, bah! What
A headband! All a-glittering with gems,
It shines like fire! And pearls, too!... Well,
I must say
That is a royal gift. Ah, benefactor I
And what is that? A bag! Not money, is it?
Why are you standing there not answering,
Without a word to say? Or are you crazed
With joy at such an unexpected windfall,
Or are you struck with lock-jaw?

DAUGHTER
No, I'll not
Believe it, it cannot be. I loved him so.
Or is he a wild beast? Or is his heart
Untame and—shaggy?

MILLER
What do you mean, girl?

DAUGHTER
Tell me, my father, what I could have done
To anger him? In one short week is all
My beauty gone? Perhaps he is enchanted
By some vile potion?

MILLER
What makes you say so?

DAUGHTER
My father, he is gone.—There, there he gallops!

And I was mad enough to let him go,
I did not clutch his cloak, I did not leap
To grasp his horse's reigns and swing on them!
He might at least have hewn my hands in anger
Hacking them from the wrists, his stallion might
Have trampled me to death beneath his hooves.

MILLER
Have you gone mad?

DAUGHTER
But you don't understand....
A prince may not obey his heart as young
Girls may. He is not free to choose ... but he
Is free, it seems, to lure, swear oaths and weep,
To promise: I will take you, sweet, to live
In my fair castle, in a secret solar,
And I shall clothe you in brocades and velvet....
But he is free to teach poor maids to rise
At midnight and come running at his whistle
To sit behind the mill till break of day—
His princely heart is touched by our small woes,
He lends a willing ear to them—and then:
Farewell now, sweetheart, go your ways in peace,
And love who takes your fancy.

MILLER
Ah, so that's it.

DAUGHTER
But who's to be his bride? For who, I wonder,
Has he exchanged me? Ah, I shall find out,
I'll find the heartless wench, and tell her straight:
You leave the Prince alone, I tell you, two she-wolves
Don't hunt in the same valley.

MILLER
Silly slut!
If it's the Prince's will to take a bride
Then who's to stop him? Serve you right, I say.
Have I not told you all along....

DAUGHTER

He could
Take leave of me like a good, kindly man
And give me presents—what d'you think of that!—
And money! Buying himself off. That's it!
He thought to gag me with his gold and silver,
So that no ill repute of him might reach
His youthful princess in her innocence.
Ah yes, I was forgetting; he commanded
To give this bag of coins to you for all
Your kindness to him, that you let your daughter
Trail after him like any drab and set
No strict guard on her virtue.... You will be
The gainer by my ruin.

Hands him the bag.

FATHER
weeping
My poor, grey hairs!
What have I lived to hear! Shame, shame on you
So bitterly to taunt your aged father.
You are my only child, all that I have,
The only comfort of my feeble age.
I could not help but spoil you, could I now?
The Lord has punished me for lack of firmness
In my parental duty.

DAUGHTER

Ah, I stifle!
A cold snake clings about my neck and squeezes!...
The snake! He has entwined a snake about me,
Not ropes of pearls!...

She tears the pearls from her neck.

MILLER

Think what you're doing!

DAUGHTER

So! and so!
I would tear you to pieces, heartless snake,
Accursed thief of my beloved's heart!

MILLER
You're raving, daughter, raving.

DAUGHTER
taking off the headband
Here's my crown,
A crown of shame! This is the bridal crown
The devil put upon my head when I
Turned me from all that I had once held dear.
Our bridal's over—perish, then, my crown!

She throws the headband into the Dnieper.

Now all is over....

Throws herself into the river.

THE OLD MAN
falling to the ground
Oh, horror, horror!

THE PRINCE'S PALACE
A wedding. The BRIDE *and* BRIDEGROOM *sit at table.*
GUESTS. A CHOIR OF YOUNG GIRLS.

MATCHMAKER
We've made a merry wedding of it, truly.
Your health, then, Prince, and your young bride's,
Our Princess!
God grant you long and happy days together,
And us—good fare and frequent at your table.
Why, lovely maidens, have you fallen silent?
Or have you sung all your sweet songs already?
Or are your white throats dry from too much singing?

CHOIR
Matchmaker, matchmaker
Stupid old matchmaker!
Went to fetch the bride
Missed the way inside,
Out behind the hut
Emptied out a butt
Of beer upon the cabbage-patch

Then fell into the garbage-ditch,
Bowed down to the gate-posts,
"Gate-posts, gentle gate-posts,
Show me pray the way
To fetch the bride today."
Matchmaker, make a guess!
Matchmaker, where's your purse?
In the purse the money's turning
For to treat fair maidens burning.

MATCHMAKER
You rascals, what a song to choose!
There, there, lay off the matchmaker!

Gives the girls money.

A SINGLE VOICE
Where pebbles lie and yellow sands are sifting,
Very swiftly hastened the river.
In the swift river two small fish were swimming,
Two fishes, two small, little roaches.
And have you heard the news, little sister,
The news of what happened in our river?
How that yesterday a fair maid died by drowning,
How she drowned herself and dying cursed her lover?

MATCHMAKER
My beauties! What a song to sing just now!
It's not a wedding song, it's most unfitting,
Who chose that song? Eh?—Who chose it?

THE GIRLS
Not I—
Not I—it wasn't us....

MATCHMAKER
Who sang it then?

Whispering and confusion among THE GIRLS.

PRINCE
I know who.

He leaves the table and quietly issues instruction to the GROOM.

Find the miller's daughter, get her
Away from here—and quickly. Then find out
Who dared admit her.

The GROOM *walks up to the girls.*

PRINCE
sitting down, to himself
She may well have come
Prepared to kick up such a shindy
I shall not know where to put myself for shame.

GROOM
I could not find her, Prince, amongst the others.

PRINCE
Go. Look again. I know she's there. Her voice
It was that sung that song.

A GUEST
What splendid mead!
It goes straight to the head—and to the legs—
A pity that it's bitter: sweeten it for us.

The bride and bridegroom kiss. A faint cry rings out.

PRINCE
It's she! That was her jealous cry.

To the GROOM.

Well,
Found her?

GROOM
I cannot find her anywhere.

PRINCE
You fool.

BEST MAN
rising
Is it not time the bride and groom retired
While at the door we shower them with hops?

All rise.

MATCHMAKER
High time, indeed, come, serve the cockerel.

The bride and bridegroom are served with roast cockerel, then showered with hops and conducted to their bedroom.

MATCHMAKER
Sweet Princess, do not cry, don't be afraid,
Do as he says.

The bride and bridegroom retire to their bedroom, the guests all take their leave, except for the MATCHMAKER *and the* BEST MAN.

BEST MAN
Where is my cup? All night
I have to ride around beneath their windows,
A drop of wine to fortify myself'd
Not come amiss.

MATCHMAKER
pouring him a cup
Here, drink this.

BEST MAN
Oof! I thank you.
It all went off quite well, I think, don't you?
The wedding feast was fine—

MATCHMAKER
Yes, God be praised,
All went off well, but one thing was not well.

BEST MAN
Why, what?

MATCHMAKER
It was an evil omen that
They sang that weird song, most unfit for bridals.

BEST MAN
Those wretched girls—they simply can't be trusted
Not to get up to tricks. Who ever heard
Of such a thing! To trouble royal weddings—
On purpose, too.... But I must to my horse,
Good night, good gossip.

Exit.

MATCHMAKER
My heart's not easy in me!
This marriage was not made in a good hour.

SOLAR
Seven years later.
The PRINCESS *and her* NURSE.

PRINCESS
Hark—I hear trumpets! No, not yet returned.
Ah, nanny dear, when he was courting me
He never left my side, day after day,
It seemed he could not sate his eyes on me.
He married me, and everything was changed.
Now he wakes me up at crack of dawn
And, as I wake, he's ordering his horse;
Then he rides off, the Lord knows where, till nightfall.
When he comes home he scarcely has a word
Of tenderness for me. He scarce bestows
An absent pat upon my fair, white face.

NURSE
My Little Princess, man is like a rooster:
Cock-a-doo-doo! Flip-flap and off he flies.
A woman, like the modest broody hen,
Must keep her nest and hatch her clutch of chicks.
While he is out to win you he will sit,
Take neither food nor drink, but sit and stare.
Yet once he's married—he's so much to do:
The neighbors must be visited,

He must ride out a-hawking with his falcons,
And then—the Devil's in him—he is off to war.
He's here and there—and everywhere, save home.

PRINCESS
What do you think? Has he perhaps some secret,
Some hidden paramour?—

NURSE
A sin to say so, love:
Where would he find a fair exchange for you?
You have it all: you're wise and beautiful
And gentle in your ways. Why, only think:
Where could he find the match of such as you, Princess?

PRINCESS
If God would hear my prayers, send
Me children. Then I would have the means
To conquer his affection ail anew—
Ah, see, the courtyard's full of huntsmen. He
Is home at last, Why can't I see him, though?

Enter a HUNTSMAN.

Where is the Prince?

HUNTSMAN
He ordered us to leave him
And ride for home.

PRINCESS
But where is he?

HUNTSMAN
Alone
He lingered in the woods that fringe the Dnieper.

PRINCESS
And you dared leave the Prince alone, without
Attendance; what assiduous servants!
Go back at once, this instant, at the gallop,
Tell him that it was I who sent you to him.

Exit the HUNTSMAN.

Ah, gracious heaven! In the woods at night
The haunt of desperate men, wild animals,
And evil spirits—danger everywhere.
Quick, light the candle, here before the icon.

NURSE
At once, my love, at once....

THE DNIEPER. NIGHT.

WATER-NYMPHS
A merry procession
From deep in the stream
The moon draws us upward
To bask in her beam.
River floor and water leaving,
Merrily at dead of night,
Glassy surface head-first cleaving
We arise to seek the light.
Hear our voices calling, teasing,
Vibrant through the upper air;
Shaken dry on free winds wreathing,
See our green and dripping hair.

A NYMPH
Sisters, listen, hearken, hush!
In the dark wood something stirs....

ANOTHER
See, between the moon and us
Someone walks upon the earth.

They hide.

PRINCE
How well I know these melancholy places!
I recognize each landmark—there's the mill!
It's fall'n into disuse, a heap of ruins;
The merry sound of turning wheels is silent;
The millstone grinds no more—the old man's dead,
It seems. He did not mourn his hapless daughter

Long. A path wound there.... It's overgrown.
For many years no one has come this way.
There was a garden here with a high fence.
Could it have grown into this riot of thicket?
Ah, here's the fatal oak, here's where she stood,
And held me in her arms, all drooping, silent—
Was it all so indeed?...

He goes up to the tree, a shower of leaves falls on him.

What does this mean?
The leaves turned pale before my eyes, curled round on
Themselves and rustling fell like ashes all
About me. Now the tree stands black and bare
Most like a thing accursed.

An OLD MAN *enters, ragged, half-naked.*

OLD MAN
Good-day to you,
My son-in-law.

PRINCE
And who are you?

OLD MAN
A raven,
I live here.

PRINCE
Could it be? The miller!

OLD MAN
Not what
I'd call a miller! I have sold my mill
To poltergeists behind the stove, and giv'n the money
To water-nymphs for keeping, to my daughter,
The wisest of 'em. Now it's buried deep
Down in the Dnieper sand. A one-eyed fish
Keeps guard on it.

PRINCE
He's mad, unhappy man,

His thoughts are scattered like a storm-spent cloud.

OLD MAN
You're late. You should have come to us last night—
We had a feast and waited long for you.

PRINCE
Who waited for me?

OLD MAN
Who? My lass, who else?
You know I look at all that through my fingers,
You may do as you like: and she may sit
All night with you, till cockcrow, if you wish,
And mum's the word for me.

PRINCE
Unhappy miller!

OLD MAN
I am no miller, man. I've told you who I am.
A raven, not a miller. Very strange
It was! When she (remember?) flung herself
Into the river, I ran after her
And meant to leap from the same rock, but then
I suddenly felt two strong wings had grown
From 'neath my armpits, and they bore me up
Suspended in the air. And from that day
To this I have been flying about and, now
And then, I peck at carrion—a dead cow, say—
Or perch on graves and caw.

THE PRINCE
The pity of it!
Who cares for you, old man?

OLD MAN
Now that's a thought!
I need to be took care of. Getting old
I am and always up to tricks. But I
Must thank my stars I have the water-babe,
She looks to me.

PRINCE
The who?

OLD MAN
My grandchild.

PRINCE
No.
I can't make head or tail of what he says:
Old man, here in the wood you'll die of hunger
Or some beast will devour you. Would you not
Come home with me to live?

OLD MAN
With you? No! Thank you!
You'll lure me in and then, as like as not,
You'll strangle me with pearls. Here I'm alive
And fed and free. I will not go with you.

Exit.

PRINCE
And this is all my doing. Terrible.
To lose one's wits. To die were easier.
We look upon a corpse with due respect,
We pray for him. And death makes all men equal.
A man who's lost his reason is a man
No more, and speech a worthless gift to him,
For he controls not words; a brother he to beasts
And to his fellowmen—a laughing stock;
All folk are free to mock him, no one may judge him,
Not even God! Poor man! The sight of him
Has woke the torments of remorse in me!

HUNTER
Here, here he is. I thought we'd never find him!

PRINCE
Why are you here?

HUNTER
The Princess sent us, Sire.
She was afraid for you.

PRINCE
Insufferable
Solicitude. Or am I a small child
Who may not walk a step without a nanny?

Exit. The WATER-NYMPHS *rise up from the river.*

WATER-NYMPHS
Sisters, shall we overtake them
Lapping round them as they ride,
Scare their horses, spray and shake them,
Whistling, laughing at their side?
No, too late. The forest darkens
And the deep grows colder yet.
To first cockcrow we must hearken,
Look and see, the moon has set.

ONE
Let us tarry here, sweet sister.

ANOTHER
Nay—for we must go, must go,
Summoned by the stern Tsaritsa
Who awaits us down below.

AT THE BOTTOM OF THE DNIEPER
Water-Nymphs' Palace.
The WATER-NYMPHS *sit spinning around their* TSARITSA.

TSARITSA
The sun has set, so leave your spinning, sisters.
The moon beams like a pillar through the deep.
Enough, swim up to sport beneath the sky,
But see that you molest no living soul:
Tonight you may not tickle passers-by,
Nor snag the fisherman's wide-spreading net
With grass or weed, nor lure the little child
With tales of fishes down beneath the water....

Enter the WATER-BABE.

Where have you been?

Rusalka and Daughter. I. Volkov (Illustration of Pushkin's poem), 1899.
I. Volkov [Public domain], через Викисклад.

DAUGHTER
I've been out on the land
To visit grandfather. He begs me always
To gather up the money that he threw
Into the water to us long ago
And give it back to him. I looked and looked;
Though what this money is I do not know,
But anyway I brought him from the depths
A handful of bright shells, all different colors,
And he was very pleased.

TSARITSA
The crazy miser!
Now listen, daughter, and attend—this once
I put my trust in you. Tonight a man will come
Down to the river's bank. You will watch out
For him and go to meet him. He is kin
To us—your father, child.

DAUGHTER
The same one who
Abandoned you to wed a mortal woman?

TSARITSA
The same; greet him with tenderness, and tell
Him all you know from me about your birth,
And tell him too what has become of me.
If he should ask you whether I've forgot him
Or not, you may say I remember him
And love him, and invite him to my home.
Now—have you understood me, daughter?

WATER-BABE
I understand.

TSARITSA
Then go.

Alone.

Since that fell hour
When, crazed with grief, I leapt into the water,
A desperate, rejected, simple girl,

And woke again beneath the Dnieper-river,
A waterspirit, cold of heart and potent,
Full seven long years have passed....
And every day I scheme and plan for vengeance.
At last, today, it seems, my hour is come.

THE BANK

PRINCE

Unwillingly to these sad banks I come
Drawn by some unknown power—I know not why.
For me each stick and stone speaks of the past.
Retells the sad but well-beloved tale
Of my young days, my fair and carefree youth.
Here, once upon a time, love waited for me—
Freehearted, ardent love—ah, what a madman
I was to let such joy slip through my fingers,
Renounce such happiness—for I was happy....
How sorrowful, how sorrowful these thoughts.
That meeting yesterday has brought them back.
The poor, mad father! He is terrible.
Perhaps it may be that today I'll meet him
Again and he'll consent to leave the forest
And come to live with us....

The WATER-BABE *emerges on the river-bank.*

What's this I see!
Say, pretty child, whence came you?[227]

~~~

This is where Pushkin's tale ends. Notes found about the conclusion of the play are sparse—six lines to be exact, one for each scene: "Miller and his daughter," "Wedding," "Princess and Nurse," "Rusalki," "Prince, old man and Rusalochka," "Huntsmen."[228] So, from this, it's evident he planned to have the final scene include the hunter.

But what happened between the prince and the Rusalochka (Little Mermaid) after he meets her? Read on to discover various interpretations.

Nabokov's Ending (1942)

What follows is Vladimir Vladimirovich Nabokov's (1899-1977) ending to the story, written in 1942. In summary: "Nabokov presents a sceptical Prince who tries to bribe Rusalochka into leaving him alone, but the little girl insists he will die unless he follows her into her underwater kingdom."[229]

The Rusalka and prince *are* reunited—but perhaps not in the way you may think. A commentary about his ending says:

> And we can ask ourselves: is the rusalka looking for revenge, or just for being again together with her lover? It is this ambiguity that marks the genius of great writers.[230]

Nabokov's Ending (1942)

LITLE RUSALKA
From the terem[231]

THE PRINCE
Where is your terem? All the other terems are far away from here.

LITLE RUSALKA
It is in the river.

THE PRINCE
This is how in childhood we strive to compare our being
With a dream about some secret world.
And what is your name?

LITLE RUSALKA
Call me Little Rusalka.

THE PRINCE
I see that you are skilled in bizarre things,
But I'm a superstitious listener
And wonders are not a good idea for a child
Near the ruins at night. Here is a
Silver coin for you. You can go now.

LITLE RUSALKA
I would've taken it to my grandfather but it is hard to
Catch him. He waved his wings and disappeared.

THE PRINCE
Who—disappeared?

LITLE RUSALKA
Raven.

THE PRINCE
Stop babbling.
Why are you looking at me so gently?
Tell me.... No, I am deceived by the shadow of the leaves and
The game of the moon. Tell me ... your mother
In the woods probably was picking the berries
And you got lost by the end of the night ... or got to the
Swampy shore.... No, not that. Tell me
Are you a fisherman's daughter, the youngest one,
Aren't you? He is waiting for you; he is calling you.
Go to him.

LITLE RUSALKA
Here I come, father.

THE PRINCE
Help me God!

LITLE RUSALKA
So are you afraid of me?
I can't believe this. Mother told me
That you are strong, friendly and brave,
That you can sing better than nightingale in the night,
That you can run faster than the forest doe.
In the river Dnieper she is our queen;
"But,—she says, turning into a rusalka,—
I still love him, still smile,
As back in the days when I ran to meet him,
Forgetting my scarf, behind the mill at night."

THE PRINCE
Yes, I remember that cute voice
And this is all madness—
And I will die....

LITLE RUSALKA
You will die if you are not going to
Visit us. Only a human is
Afraid of death and obsession,
But you're not a human. You are ours, since

The time you left my mother you are longing for her.
In a dark bottom you will find your motherland
Where life flows, without bothering your soul.
You wanted it. Give me a hand. See
The moon glides like scales and there—

THE PRINCE

Her eyes shine clearly through the water
Her shaking hand are reaching out to me!
Lead me, I'm scared, my daughter....

Disappears in the river Dnepr.

RUSALKI

sing
Pop up, play
And wave the wave.
To the river wedding
We call the moon.
Swinging slower and slower,
The foggy groom
Sank to the bottom
And completely quieted down.
And now so carefully,
To the bottom
To the blue forehead
The moon reaches out.
And laughs softly
Leaning towards him
Queen Rusalka is
In her terem.

They hide. Pushkin shrugs.

Dargomyzhsky's *Rusalka* Opera (1856)

Russian composer Alexander Sergeyevich Dargomyzhsky (1813-1869) created his *Rusalka* opera between 1848 and 1855, which he based on Pushkin's play. The opera, however, which premiered on May 4, 1856, wasn't well received until 1865. Even so, it's considered the most successful of the endings to Pushkin's play.

Dargomyzhsky experimented with various versions of his libretto, but in the end, returned to be "as faithful as possible" to Pushkin's unfinished play.[232] Unlike the play, the cast in the opera have proper names, rather than simply being

professions, ranks, and family-clan relationships as in Pushkin's play. The Miller's daughter is Natasha. Instead of a nurse, the companion to the princess is an orphan called Ol'ga. Instead of returning to the river bank seven years later as happens in Pushkin's play, in Dargomyzhsky's libretto, this takes place twelve years later. At this time, "Rusalochka has had time to grow up and is now dangerously close to the age when she can be herself seduced."[233] In the scene where the hunter tells the princess that the prince has remained at the river bank, the princess and Ol'ga hurry off to find him, instead of remaining at home.

The summation of the final scene is below. You can skip it if you want to read the libretto that follows instead.

> More women arrive on the shore (Ol'ga and the Princess), but the focus inexorably turns toward the traumatized Prince, who is mesmerized by Rusalochka, his child. The Princess—loving, deceived, hurt and proud—looks on in disbelief. Although an archetype of the 'rival', in her grief the Princess is not opposed to, but fused with, the Miller's Daughter. Ol'ga tries to intervene. But the Prince, as his culpability becomes ever clearer, is pulled inexorably toward the river's bottom.... As in the royal Wedding of Act I, a woman's voice from nowhere rises up—this time not to punish him with stories of her drowning, but to call him home ('I wait for you as before [...] We will be inseparable'). As the Prince begins to follow Rusalka's voice, the Princess begs him ever more frantically to leave with her. But the Raven-Miller, fantastical patriarch of the first abused family, appears on the bank to protect the 'bridegroom' from these interlopers from the palace. Everywhere the Prince looks, he sees someone he has betrayed. The banks of the Dnepr are the banks of the Real.
>
> ... Rusalki whisper and laugh above the waves. As the Prince is led to the river, the Princess falls unconscious on the shore. Just before the curtain falls, the corpse of the Prince is deposited silently at the feet of the Rusalka-tsaritsa.[234]

You can listen to the music of all four acts of the opera here:

Act I: https://www.ucis.pitt.edu/opera/ROB/rusa/rusalka1.mp3
Act II: https://www.ucis.pitt.edu/opera/ROB/rusa/rusalka2.mp3
Act III: https://www.ucis.pitt.edu/opera/ROB/rusa/rusalka2.mp3
Act IV: https://www.ucis.pitt.edu/opera/ROB/rusa/rusalka4.mp3

Rusalka Opera (Dargomyzhsky, 1856)

Translated from the Russian from http://home.tiscali.cz:8080/ist987/libreta/rusalka.html.

LITTLE RUSALKA
I was sent to you
By my mother on purpose.

PRINCE
By your mother, but who is she?

LITTLE RUSALKA
She is the one that once
You loved ... and left!

PRINCE
How is it possible
Is she alive and remembers me?

LITTLE RUSALKA
Not only remembers, but loves, as before;
Now she is the queen of the Dnieper waters.
And she told me to call you to my tower.
Ah, if only you knew how cool and fun it is out there.
She ordered me to tell you that she will certainly be waiting for you.

PRINCE
kisses the LITTLE RUSALKA
Lovely child!
But what is wrong with me?
How fast my heart is beating!
Tell me where is she?

LITTLE RUSALKA
And if you want, I will take you.

PRINCE
Take me, take me now!

He wants to go. PRINCESS *and* OL'GA *show up from behind the mill.*

PRINCESS
Stop!

PRINCE
Princess! Why are you here?

PRINCESS
with hardness
To catch you cheating!

PRINCE
Am I a child?
Or not free
In my deeds?

PRINCESS
Prince, have mercy and listen to me.
Many years already in grave misery
Day and night I languish.
Where are the oaths, assurances,
Where are the vows of your unchanging love?
In fierce and lonely sadness,
Tortured with jealousy
I am dragging my young days.
Ah, believe me, I have no more strength
To bear the love scorns.
So I decided to prove your faithlessness
Here on the spot.
Oh, believe me, I had no more strength
to stand the jealousy torture!

PRINCE
Does anyone have the right to follow me here?
Am I a child?
Or do I have to give you the report
For my actions?
I won't let you follow me, no!

OL'GA
Prince, let me say a word too
And justify the princess!
It hurts me to see her suffer,
Take pity on your wife, Prince.
Remember the oaths, assurances
And vows of your unchanging love.
Remember the happiness of past days
The peaceful bliss of old days!
Seeing her suffering hurts me.
Ah, have pity on her
Believe me, believe me, Prince,
You will find the joy and happiness with her!

LITTLE RUSALKA
Come on, Prince.
And if you don't believe me,
A familiar voice may remind
You about my mother. Listen.

RUSALKA'S VOICE
behind the scenes
My Prince! You, dear Prince, I call you.
I still languish with the same passion for you.
Come to my tower.
I'm still waiting for you,
And we will be inseparable
Forever with you.
Come, Prince, come!

OL'GA
What does this voice mean?
The fear freezes my soul!

PRINCESS
Where does this voice come from?
My blood is burning with jealousy!

PRINCE
Oh, sweet to my heart voice
Will help to reborn my past love!
Inimical power is calling me!

He takes the LITTLE RUSALKA *by the hand.*

LITTLE RUSALKA
Come on, Prince!

PRINCESS AND OL'GA
I beg you
Prince, return home
They are up to no good, calling you to follow them.

LITTLE RUSALKA
Do not listen to them, let's go!

Feodor Chaliapin as Miller in *Rusalka*. Photographer unknown, 6 October 1910.
http://visualrian.ru/search/32/75702.html [Public domain], via Wikimedia Commons.

PRINCESS AND OL'GA

Ah, take pity on us, Prince.
Let's get home!

PRINCE

Blood boils in my chest!
Ah, take me, take me now!
Natasha! Love for you again
Burning in my heart!

PRINCESS AND OL'GA

You are so pale, you are upset, oh, have mercy.
Believe us, let's hurry back to the tower!

MILLER *runs in and pushes the* PRINCESS *and* OL'GA, *as if he is trying to protect the* PRINCE.

Oh my God! You will protect us from trouble!

MILLER

Get away! Leave me alone, I'm the raven here and the boss!

Pointing to the PRINCE.

He is our groom; we will not let you take him!
Today is a wedding, and I invite you to the feast.

OL'GA

Fear is bothering my soul,
And my heart is trembling humbly.
My breath freezes, the word is powerless;
The soul is ready to change.
Here, in this boondocks, so late at night,
Away from home, who will protect us
From the evil people's attacks?
Prince, do not leave, do not leave us, I beg.
You are bewitched by the inimical power.
Let's leave right now, hurry.
Believe me, they are up to no good, calling you to follow them!

PRINCESS

Fear is bothering my soul,
And my heart is trembling humbly.
I have no strength to catch my breath ...

Here, in this boondocks, so late at night,
Who can give protection, protection to us?
Prince, do not leave, do not leave us, I beg.
You are bewitched by the inimical power.
Let's leave right now!
Believe me, they are up to no good, calling you to follow them!

PRINCE

My soul strives for her again
Familiar dreams again
Familiar love excites my heart.
I have to go to her, to that magical land.
Inimical power is calling me.
Leave me, leave me alone, I have to
Fulfill my vow!

MILLER

Yes, he is ours, we will not give him back.
Today he should marry my daughter.
I invite you to the wedding party.
We are happy to see guests.
And we will have fun.
We will congratulate the couple and drink
To their health.
He is our groom; today I am
Inviting all of you to the wedding.
We invite you to the joyful feast.
Today everyone is invited!

To the PRINCE.

Let's go! Let's go!
They are waiting for you!

The PRINCESS *and* OL'GA *in despair. The* PRINCE *is completely unconscious. The* MILLER *and the* LITTLE MERMAID *carry him to the river. The* LITTLE MERMAID *rushes into the river; after her, the* MILLER *pushes the* PRINCE *into the water and runs away. The* PRINCESS *falls unconscious.* OL'GA *tries to revive her.*

RUSALKI
in water
Ha ha ha!
Now he will not leave us!

HUNTERS
running in
Here! Here someone's voice called for help!
What is it? The Princess herself is here and unconscious!
Do you hear! That's the laughter of the damned rusalki!
Oh! Something evil had happened here; we must find the Prince!

In front of the proscenium, below, rises a cloud that covers the whole scene. When it disappears a view of the underwater part of the Dnieper opens up in the luxurious atmosphere of the underwater kingdom. The moon shines through the water. The scene is lit up by the blue light. The RUSALKI are standing in a living picture, in the middle is the queen. A group of RUSALKI shows up from the top; they are swimming and carrying the PRINCE's body to bring it to the feet of their queen.

A Forgery?

In 1897, sixty years after Pushkin's death, a Russian scholarly periodical published the final scenes to the *Rusalka* play of what were supposedly Pushkin's own words. Dmitrii Zuev, fourteen years old at the time, said he wrote them down in November 1836, two months before Pushkin died, as the poet recited them in the home of Eduard Ivanovich Guber. Although nothing of the sort was found in Pushkin's papers, his friends "confirmed that in the months preceding the fatal duel, Pushkin was indeed telling his friends about his 'lyrical drama' Rusalka and especially about its end."[235]

Others believed it was a forgery. Why, they questioned, did Zuev write down only the final 228 lines that were later discovered missing from Pushkin's play, and not the entire play? In addition to this, the new lines of the play did not scan the way the existing ones did (but somewhat matched an older style Pushkin had used), and they had too much "aggressive detail," talk, and backstory.

The lines themselves are not readily available, but are summarized below:

Zuev's transcript begins where Pushkin's final draft ends, the Prince's question: 'Where did you come from, you marvellous child?' Rusalochka has no problem answering. She is a chatty little girl who supplies pre-histories and motivations. She describes her mother's plight, enduring love and instructions to 'kiss and caress' the man on shore. The Prince, fascinated, takes the little girl's hand and kisses her. At that moment the mad Miller bursts in: 'are you thinking to ruin my granddaughter too? I'll pluck out your heart, peck out your eyes and bring them as a gift to my daughter'. He throws himself on the Prince....

Scene seven: the frightened Rusalochka calls out to her mother for help. The Miller's Daughter (for thus is she identified, not as Rusalka) rises out of the water to curse her father the Miller and drive him off. Then she turns to the Prince, relating how for years she had thirsted for vengeance but now, seeing him, she forgives him everything, loves him as before, and desires his embrace. 'But my kiss is death', she adds. 'Farewell, flee, be happy with your young wife, forget me.' The Prince refuses to leave: 'I haven't the strength to live without you, without our child.'

Scene eight opens on the huntsmen and a chorus of rusalki. The Prince has vanished. Rusalki sing in the trees. A new character, 'The Favourite of the Prince' ('Liubimets kniazia'), appears among the hunters sent by the Princess. His purpose is to elicit, and then to discredit as a pagan fairy-tale, the story of the drowning and surviving of the Miller's Daughter. One of the hunters hears from the river the distant voice of the Prince, then of a child, then an old man's threat, then a woman's voice. The Favourite is fed up with these stunts. Little Rusalochka again appears on shore, this time bringing a wedding ring that the Prince wished returned to the Princess (with a request to pray for him—but, says Rusalochka, 'I don't know what praying is'). The favourite, sensing the presence of the unclean force everywhere, orders the little girl seized. But Rusalochka slips back under the waves, as the Miller's corpse washes up on shore. The huntsmen flee.

In the final *scene nine*, the royal chambers, the Princess relates to her Nurse a terrible dream. She was dressing herself in rich jewels for her wedding, then entered the church where choirs sang and candles and gold glistened, when at the sanctifying moment, the floor beneath her turned translucent and through its icy mirror she saw her Prince marrying another woman, a beautiful water creature: 'I uttered a cry! […] and awoke.' At that moment the huntsmen rush in with the ring. Seeing it, the Princess collapses dead in the arms of her Nurse. The Nurse's final plea: 'Accept her into the angelic host, Almighty!'[236]

A Silent Film

As a final example of Pushkin's play, you can watch a 1910 old silent-film re-enactment of the poem, by Vasily Goncharov and Aleksandr Khanzhonkov:

https://www.youtube.com/watch?v=ViMEzISLej4.

It's highly dramatic as silent films were known to be.

Rusalka – Opera by Dvořák

Antonín Leopold Dvořák (1841-1904) was a Czech composer. Dvořák wanted his operas to reflect Czech national spirit. *Rusalka* was his ninth opera, but perhaps one of the most famous and well-received. Poet Jaroslav Kvapil (1868-1950) wrote the libretto, basing it on stories by Karel Jaromír Erben. Much like Andersen's *The Little Mermaid*, the mermaid in this story falls in love with a prince, but must lose her voice before she can have the opportunity to meet him as a living being. However, this tale retains the folk element of the Rusalka, especially her duality.

One of the typical traits of Dvorak's compositional style is also applied in *Rusalka*, namely the art of contrast: completely different means of expression are used to depict two opposing worlds (human and supernatural); the scenes featuring the carefree, playful wood nymphs are set apart from the emotional dialogue between Rusalka and the Water Sprite or the Witch; and, using dissimilar vocal lines, the composer creates an effective contrast between the ethereal Rusalka and the fiery Foreign Princess. In this way, Dvorak—perhaps subconsciously—reinforces Kvapil's intentions to portray the impossibility of uniting two distinct worlds and the destiny of an individual who, for disrupting the natural order of things, is expelled from both.[237]

One of the opera's most famous tunes is "Song to the Moon." The moon evokes romantic notions, and has been a symbol of women's sexuality since ancient times. Goddesses such as Artemis/Diana (Greek/Roman mythology) and Bendis (Thracian mythology) are deities of the moon. In this song, the lovelorn Rusalka "sings of unsatisfied passion," and her seductive voice, which is used to enchant men for her sexual pleasure, is "virtually co-synonymous with her sexuality."[238]

You can watch the full opera here: https://www.youtube.com/watch?v=kobTXKUBe3w.[239]

Or, if you prefer, you can listen to only the famous "Song to the Moon" here: https://www.youtube.com/watch?v=UwVYFpY3VL4.[240]

Rusalka Opera (Dvorak, 1901)

This version has been modified from the one found on Open Arias website, and used with their permission: https://www.opera-arias.com/dvorak/rusalka/libretto/english/.

A CT ONE
A glade at the edge of the lake, surrounded by forests in which, situated on the shore of the lake, stands JEŽIBABA's cottage. Moonlit night. On an old willow tree reclining towards the lake sits RUSALKA, deep in thought.

FOREST NYMPHS
dancing in the glade
Ho, ho, ho,
The moon stands over the water!
She curiously peers into the depths,
Flowing over the stones to the bottom.
Vodnik nods his head,
His old green head.
Ho, ho, ho,
Who is coming through the night?
Vodnik, the moon rises,
Through your window she peeps,
Soon she will break in,
Into your silvery chamber!
Ho, ho, ho,
The moon roams over the water!
A breeze dances across the lake,
Vodnik awakens,
Vodnik, the water-clown,
Ho, ho, ho.
Bubbles rise from the bottom.

The VODNIK emerges and wipes off his eyes.

Ho, ho, ho,
Vodnik's above the water!
Vodnik wants to get married,
Which of you wants to foam the water,
Comb the grandfather's hair, change places,
With Vodnik's wife?
Ho, ho, ho…

They dance around the VODNIK.

VODNIK
A warm welcome, forest dwellers, to the lake!
What, are you noisy ladies sad there?
I have unseen splendors on the bottom
And golden fish by the bagful.
I can rush through the reeds,
I just stretch out my hand,
Seizing a lady,
I grab her by the feet,
I'll drag her down to us!

He clumsily tries to catch one of the FOREST NYMPHS.

FOREST NYMPHS
Vodnik, come on, hey,
Try to catch us!
The one you catch, dear man,
Will give you a nice kiss,
But your woman, ha, ha, ha,
Will pull your ears!
So catch us!

They disperse.

VODNIK
Urchins, all of them!
Look how madly they run!
Up, down, across the field,
Well, they're young!

RUSALKA
Vodnik, my dear daddy!

VODNIK

What the heck, child!
What are you doing,
Drying my nets in the moonlight?

RUSALKA

Vodnik, dear daddy,
Until the water foams,
Stay with me a while,
So I won't be sad!

VODNIK

Why are you sad?

RUSALKA

I'll tell you everything!

VODNIK

And down below, too?

RUSALKA

So sad I suffocate!

VODNIK

Down, where there's dancing?
Not possible, tell me!

RUSALKA

I want to leave you,
Leave the deep waters,
To be human,
And live in the golden sunshine!
I want to leave you,
Leave the deep waters.

VODNIK

Can I trust my own ears?
To become human? A mortal being?

RUSALKA

You told me these strange tales yourself,
That they have a soul that we don't have,
And the soul of people goes to heaven,

When one dies and vanishes into nothing!

VODNIK
As long as waves cradle you,
Don't wish for a soul, no, it's full of sin!

RUSALKA
And full of love!

VODNIK
By the ancient waters,
Don't tell me, child, you love a man?

RUSALKA
He often comes here
And steps into my embrace;
Throws his clothes on the shore
And bathes in my arms.
But I'm only a wave,
He can't see my being.
Oh, I know that I'd first have to be human,
To embrace him and hold him in my arms,
So he would embrace me himself
And kiss me passionately!

VODNIK
Child, night after night
Your sisters will cry for you!
There's no help
If a man can entice you in his power!

RUSALKA
Vodnik, dearest,
He has to be able to see me,
Tell me, tell me, daddy,
What am I supposed to do?

VODNIK
Lost forever,
Lost to humans!
No sense to lure you down below to play.
Call Ježibaba,
Poor pale Rusalka!...

He submerges.

Alas! Alas! Alas!

Disappears under the water.

RUSALKA (*Song to the Moon*)
Moon in the deep sky,
Your light sees far,
You wander over the wide world,
And peer into people's dwellings.
Moon, stay for a while,
Tell me, where is my love?
Tell him, silvery moon,
My arms embrace him,
So that at least for a moment,
He'll remember me in his dreams.
Shine for him in a faraway place,
Tell him who's waiting for him here!
If his human soul dreams about me,
Let him awake with that memory!
Moon, don't disappear!

The moon hides behind a cloud.

The water is cold!

She trembles with anxiety.

Ježibaba! Ježibaba!

VODNIK
under the water
Poor, pale Rusalka!
Alas! Alas! Alas!

RUSALKA
with urgency
Ježibaba! Ježibaba!

JEŽIBABA
coming out of her cottage, looks around
Wailing, sobbing, lamenting,

Who's waking me before dawn?

RUSALKA
Ježibaba, give me a potion,
To take the water magic away from me!

JEŽIBABA
I hear something, smell something,
Speak up and tell me who are you?

RUSALKA
I'm Rusalka, a water nymph,
Give me a potion, auntie dear!

JEŽIBABA
If you're a nymph, appear quickly,
Show yourself, beautiful child!

RUSALKA
I'm held captive by the waves,
Tangled in water lilies.

JEŽIBABA
Tear yourself away, step out, hop,
Hurry to my cottage!
Let her go, little wave, let her come to me,
Let her feet touch the ground!

RUSALKA *jumps down and moves with difficulty to the witch.*

Little feet, carry her, little feet, hold her up!
See how her legs can walk!

RUSALKA
falls at Ježibaba's feet
Ježibaba! Help!
Your centuries-old wisdom knows everything,
You've solved nature's mysteries,
On dark nights you dream about people,
You understand the ancient elements.
The poisons of the earth, the rays of the moon,
You can concoct thousands of potions,
You can join together, you can tear apart,

You can kill, you can create.
Human into monster, monster into human
You can transform them with your age-ole wisdom.
You make the Rusalki tremble at night,
For human woes you prepare strange cures,
For us and for people
In a world far away
You are an element of nature yourself,
You are human.
An eternity with death is your dowry,
Help me, miraculous woman!
Help me!

JEŽIBABA
I know that, such wishes everyone brings to us!
But listen, listen closely,
Before you try the potion:
You have pearls, you have beauty,
If I help you, what will you give me?

RUSALKA
Take everything I have,
But make me human!

JEŽIBABA
And nothing more? Nothing more at all?
Is that why you came here crying?
The water bores you already,
And you hunger for a human body,
For loving, for playing
For kisses and sweetness.
I know that, such wishes everyone brings to us!

RUSALKA
Your wisdom knows everything,
Give me a human body, a human soul!

JEŽIBABA
I'll give them to you, I will, by the devil, I will!
But you have to give me
Your transparent watery dress.
And if you don't find love in the world,
You must live an outcast, cursed by the undersea world.

If you lose that love,
Which you now crave,
The curse of the powers of the water
Will drag you back into its depths.
And before you get what you desire, you'll have to suffer:
To all human ears, you'll remain mute!
Do you want to be mute, do you,
For the one you love?

RUSALKA
If I can know his love,
Gladly, believe me, I'll become silent for him.

JEŽIBABA
Keep him and know this:
If you return cursed to the Vodnik's realm,
You will also destroy your lover,
He'll become a victim forever,
Of your eternal curse!

RUSALKA
A pure soul, a pure human soul,
My love will overcome all spells!

JEŽIBABA
Come on then, come quickly,
Come with me into my cottage.
We'll brew poisons in the fireplace,
Rusalka will drink them,
But then she'll be mute,
Abracadabra!

They enter the cottage and a red glow pours out of its window. A stream of sparks bursts out of the chimney. In a while we hear the brew seething in the kettle. These sounds mingle with JEŽIBABA's incantations. The FOREST NYMPHS come running out of the woods and frightened peep in through the window.

Abracadabra,
White mist rises from the meadows!
A drop of dragon's blood,
Ten drops of bile,
The warm heart of a bird,
The kettle's already hissing.
Jump, my tomcat, jump and jump,

Stir the brew in the kettle!
Abracadabra,
Don't be afraid of greater torments!
This is your human dowry,
And you have to drink it,
Drinking this brew
Will make your tongue wooden.
Jump, my tomcat, hey, hey,
Pour the brew down her throat!
Abracadabra,
But now not a word!

The hissing sound from the cottage weakens. The FOREST NYMPHS *have dispersed. The sky clears and horns are heard from the distance. Morning glow appears over the lake.*

VODNIK
from the depths
Poor, pale Rusalka!
Alas! Alas! Alas!

The horns become more distinct. The hunters are approaching. We hear the song of the HUNTER.

HUNTER
from the distance
A young hunter rode, rode and rode,
He saw a white doe in the forest.
She had deep eyes,
Will my arrow strike her down?
Oh, young hunter, hurry on,
Don't shoot the white doe,
Keep away from her body!
Will my arrow strike her down?

The horns are sounded again.

PRINCE
emerges from the woods, bow in hand
Here she appeared and disappeared again!
Over the hill and down the dale, through the forest and fields,
This strange creature that roams around
And here the trail has vanished completely!
And with mysterious waves,
These waters lure me into their arms,

As if my hunting passion
Could be cooled in their embrace.
My step stumbles, I feel strange,
My weapon falls from my tired hand.
The hunt has just begun, yet I'm tired of it,
Strange magic has captured me again!

HUNTER
approaching
That was no doe, hunter, stop!
God protect your soul!
Your heart is sad,
Who did your arrow strike?

The hunters emerge from the woods.

PRINCE
Stop hunting, go back to the castle.
Strange magic is roaming the forest,
Stranger magic in my heart.
Go home, I want to be alone!

The hunters depart. The PRINCE *sits down on the shore of the lake, but when he looks up he sees* RUSALKA *standing before him.* RUSALKA *has left the cottage. She is barefoot and clad in a gray garment of a destitute child. Her beautiful golden hair streams down along her body. She is mute.*

The PRINCE *jumps up.*

Beautiful vision, so sweet,
Are you a human or a fairy tale?
Have you come to protect the rare game,
That I saw in the dim forest?
Have you come to beg for her,
Sister of the white doe?
Or you yourself, coming toward me,
Do you want to be a hunter's prey?

Unable to speak, RUSALKA *stretches out her hands toward him.*

Does a secret seal your lips,
Your tongue forever silent?
If your lips are silent, God knows
I'll kiss an answer from them!

The answer to the mysteries,
That lured me here,
That called me here,
Over thorns, over rocks,
To be here finally on this blissful day,
Child, to be suddenly enchanted by your eyes.
What's hidden in your heart,
If you love me, show me!

RUSALKA *throws herself into his arms.*

CHOIR OF RUSALKI
under the water
Sisters, one of us is missing!

RUSALKA *listens frightened.*

Sister dear, where did you go?

RUSALKA *trembles for indecision and fright.*

VODNIK
under the water
Over the hills, over the hills,
Valleys and forests!

CHOIR OF RUSALKI
Sister dear, where are you?

RUSALKA *clings to the* PRINCE.

PRINCE
I know you're magic that will pass,
And melt into mist,
But until our time is over,
Oh, my fairy tale, don't run away!
My hunting is finished, why think about it?
You are my most precious doe,
You're a golden star shining in the dark night,
My fairy tale, come with me!

He takes RUSALKA away.

Rusalki Emerge from the Water. Konstantin Egorovich Makovsky, 1879.
Konstantin Egorovich Makovsky [Public domain].

ACT TWO

A park surrounding the PRINCE'*s castle. In the background a gallery and the banquet hall. In the foreground a lake under old trees. Late afternoon, dusk and later night.*

GAMEKEEPER
comes in with the SERVANT
Well then, dear boy,
Tell me,
What kind of festivities
Are taking place in the palace today?
Guests are in the banquet hall
Work is happening in the kitchen,

On the tables and shelves
Are all kinds of utensils!

SERVANT
We're in a hurry,
Dear Uncle Vaněk,
From evening to dawn,
The work doesn't stop!
Think about it, think about it,
Have you ever heard such a thing, Uncle?
The prince found in the forest
A strange creature,
And it seems, can you believe,
He may marry her!
He found her in your forests,
In your deep forests.
But wherever he got her,
I'd be afraid of her, Uncle!
The girl is mute,
She doesn't have a drop of blood,
She walks like she's stunned!
That would be a fine bride!

GAMEKEEPER
Is it really true,
What is spoken everywhere?
My poor, dear boy,
It seems that it is!
May the Lord God protect us,
I'm an old hunter,
But I believe that in this love,
There's some strange magic!
My forest is haunted
By sinister powers,
Through the forest strange creatures
Walk around at midnight.
If the soul is weak in the body,
Ježibaba will bewitch it,
At the bank of the lake
The Vodnik
Can easily
Drag you to the bottom!
And whoever sees the forest nymphs,

Without a shirt, without a skirt,
Will be crazed with love.
The Lord God be with us
And deliver us from evil!

SERVANT
with anxiety
Uncle, I'm scared!

GAMEKEEPER
Well, no wonder!
May the Lord God have mercy
On your sinful soul!

SERVANT
Our prince used to be so handsome,
How he's changed now!
He's not as he used to be, no,
He wanders like in a trance,
The old woman Háta says prayers,
Offering them day after day.
And the priest, when he heard about it,
Came to warn the prince.
But the prince said, no and no,
The girl's going to stay here!

GAMEKEEPER
That's why there are guests here!
That's why the pantry is so empty!
That's why I hurried to bring
A lot of game for the palace!

SERVANT
Fortunately, though,
Nothing may come of it,
And another woman
May spoil his plans!
Old woman Háta says,
How the prince is fickle,
She says his love is already fading,
That he has another in mind,
That some foreign princess,
Has now caught his eye.

GAMEKEEPER
God be praised, God be praised,
Keep him in good health!
If I were the prince, straight away,
I'd drive away the strange girl,
Before she entangled me in hell,
Let the beggar get out of here!

SERVANT
suddenly
Ugh, here comes the prince leading that monster!

He runs away.

GAMEKEEPER
I won't wait for her either!

He runs in an opposite direction. RUSALKA, *beautifully attired, but always sad and pale, is coming with the* PRINCE.

PRINCE
You've been by my side for a week,
Like a vision from a fairy tale you seem to be,
I search your eyes in vain,
To understand your mystery!
Will I only find in marriage,
The love I've been seeking for so long,
That your blood will burn with passion,
And be my wife completely?
Why is your embrace so cold,
Why are you afraid of passion?
Why do I feel you shake with anxiety
When I hold you in my arms?
And in vain I suppress a sad feeling,
I cannot escape from your arms,
However cold, timid you are,
I must have you, possess you completely!

FOREIGN PRINCESS
comes through the gallery, sees the PRINCE *and* RUSALKA
No, it's not love, it's a feeling of anger,
That another one is where I want to be,
And that I'm not supposed to have him,

May the happiness for both of them die completely!

She comes forward.

I wonder if the prince will remember for a moment,
That though he's a lover he's also the host?
Should all your guests silently contemplate,
That happiness the world bestows on you?

She stands between the PRINCE *and* RUSALKA.

PRINCE
startles as soon as he sees the PRINCESS
Oh, your reproach is timely indeed,
And I gladly endure it coming from your lips,
Even the bridegroom, lovely princess,
Is above all only your servant!

FOREIGN PRINCESS
regarding RUSALKA
And your love, lady of your heart,
Hasn't rebuked you with a single word?

RUSALKA *regards her with pain and anger.*

Or does she have so much tenderness in her gaze,
That she speaks to you only with her eyes?

PRINCE
embarrassed
But her eyes forgot to say,
That the host became negligent.
Let him now quickly compensate, if you consent,
For his momentary neglect.

Offers the PRINCESS *his hand.* RUSALKA *steps forward and firmly takes hold of it.*

Why are you embarrassed,
And why are you trembling so much?
Hurry to your room
And get ready for the ball!

He takes the PRINCESS *away.*

FOREIGN PRINCESS
departing, to RUSALKA
Oh, dress yourself in a superb gown,
I have his courtesy,
But you have his heart!

RUSALKA *stares after them as if she would like to restrain the* PRINCE *from going, but then, sad and heart-broken, she departs through the gallery. Dusk sets in, night falls and later appears the moon. In the hall festive music is heard and lights are lighted. Festive milling is seen in the background, guests are arriving and forming circles. Later singing and dancing.*

VODNIK
emerges from the lake and looks into the gaily animated hall
Alas! Alas!
Poor, pale Rusalka,
Enchanted by the splendor of the world!
Alas!
The whole world will not give you, no indeed,
What blossoms in my water empire!
You could be a human a hundred times,
Bounded by a connection to eternity.
Though a man loved you a hundred times,
You can't attract him forever!
Poor, pale Rusalka,
Captured by the magic of human worldliness!
Everywhere your sisters seek you,
Wanting in vain to embrace you!
When you return to your sisters,
You'll only be a source of death,
You'll return sick of life,
Eternally cursed because you've failed!
Poor, pale Rusalka,
Enchanted by the splendor of the world!

CHORUS
heard from the hall
White flowers on the road,
Everywhere on the road bloomed,
A boy rode and rode to see his bride,
And the day smiled so brightly.
Don't wait, boy, hurry along,
You'll grow into a man soon,
When you go back this way,

The blooms will be red roses.
The flowers will be white first,
Wilted in the sun's heat,
But those fiery roses,
Adorn the wedding bed!

Now and then the PRINCE *appears among the guests, courting the* FOREIGN PRINCESS *and neglecting* RUSALKA.

VODNIK
Poor, pale Rusalka,
Enchanted by the splendor of the world!
Alas!
On the waters a white water lily dreams,
It will be your sad companion,
For your wedding bed,
Red roses do not bloom!

RUSALKA, *desperate, runs from the hall and flies through the park to the lake.*

Rusalka, you know me, I'm here!

RUSALKA
suddenly regaining speech
Vodnik, daddy dear!

VODNIK
Have I come to your palace,
To see you mourning so soon?

RUSALKA
Daddy, Vodnik, save me,
A terrible anxiety has seized me!
Alas, I've betrayed you,
Alas, the misery of those who know humans!
Alas! Alas!
Another woman's beauty has captured him,
Passionate, human beauty
And he doesn't know me again,
Rusalka from the waters!

VODNIK
He rejected you, the one who loved you?

Now you must, you must persevere!

RUSALKA
Oh, it's useless, it's useless,
And emptiness is in my heart,
Useless are all my charms,
If I'm only half human!
Oh, it's useless, he doesn't know me again,
Rusalka from the waters!
Passion burns in her eyes,
That cursed human passion!
Cold water bore me,
And I don't, I don't have that passion!
Cursed by you, lost to him,
A faint echo of the ancient elements.
I can't be a woman or a nymph,
I can't die, I can't live!
I can't die, I can't live!

The PRINCE *and the* FOREIGN PRINCESS *come out of the banquet hall.*

See them, see? They're here again!
Daddy, save me, save me!

FOREIGN PRINCESS
accompanied by the PRINCE
A strange glow is burning in your eyes
And I listen to you confused.
You are growing more ardent and sweet,
Oh, prince, what does that mean?
Where has your chosen one fled,
The one without speech and without a name,
Where has she fled when she ought to see,
That the prince has completely changed?

PRINCE
Where did she go? Dear God knows!
But you are guilty of my change.
And this summer night won't reveal
That I was captured by other spells!
Oh, call it a whim,
That I loved another for a while,
And be a blazing fire,

Where until now the light of the moon burned white!

FOREIGN PRINCESS
When my fire burns you,
And scared all your passions,
When I leave you far away,
What will you do with the shine of the moon?
When you're embraced by the lovely arms
Of your silent, sleeping beauty,
What will warm your passion?
Oh, pity, pity for that passion!

PRINCE
full of passion
And if the whole world,
Wanted to condemn by longing,
You are the red blossom,
Even if it bloomed for only a moment!
Only now do I realize,
Why my body was dying,
When it wanted love
To heal!

FOREIGN PRINCESS
Oh, only now do I realize,
That suddenly I'm being courted,
The groom, it seems, doesn't know himself,
Whether he courts me or another!

PRINCE
suddenly embraces the FOREIGN PRINCESS
What remains of that love
In whose snares I became entangled?
I'll gladly throw off all bonds,
So I could love you!

RUSALKA, *desperate, runs out of her hiding-place and throws herself into the* PRINCE*'s arms.*

Your shoulders are freezing,
you white beauty, white and cold!

He pushes RUSALKA *away.*

VODNIK
appears in full moonlight and shouts
Hurry into another's arms, hurry,
You can't escape this one's embrace!

He drags RUSALKA into the lake.

PRINCE
stupefied and not understanding anything
From the embrace of a mysterious power,
 Save me!

He falls to the FOREIGN PRINCESS's feet.

FOREIGN PRINCESS
in an outburst of laughter
Into the nameless abyss of hell,
Hurry after your chosen one!

She departs.

CT THREE

The glade on the shore of a lake. Night is descending, the sky is overcast, yet later evening glow appears and finally, there is a moonlit night. RUSALKA sits above the lake where she sat previously. She is all white and pale. Her hair has turned ashen, her eyes are extinguished.

RUSALKA
Insensitive watery power,
You've dragged me back into the depths,
Why in this cold, hopeless,
Don't I die? Why don't I die?
Deprived of my youth,
Without the joy of my sisters,
Condemned for my love
I grieve in the cold currents.
Having lost my sweet charm,
Cursed by my beloved,
In vain I long to return to my sisters,
In vain I long for the world.
Where are you, the magic of summer nights
When water lilies bloomed?

Why in this cold, hopeless,
Don't I die? Why don't I die?

JEŽIBABA
comes out of her cottage
Ah, ah, you've come back already?
Well, you didn't stay there long!
And how pale your face is
And how you mourn all alone!
Didn't the kisses taste sweet
And didn't a human bed warm you?

RUSALKA
Oh, alas, dear auntie,
All betrayed me, I lost everything!

JEŽIBABA
Short was your loving,
Long will be your moaning,
After kissing a man's lips,
Your fasting will be endless, eternal!
A man is a man, outcast by the elements,
Long ago his roots were severed from the earth,
Alas, who wanted to know his love,
The one whose betrayal has now condemned her!

RUSALKA
Wise auntie, auntie, tell me,
Is there no hope for me?

JEŽIBABA
Your lover condemns you,
Ceased to love you,
And now Ježibaba
Is to help you again?
After worldly pleasures,
Little daughter,
You'd like to return to your sisters now?
Well, I have advice,
I have good advice,
But whether you'll listen,
The devil knows himself!
With human blood

You must wash away the elements of the curse
For the love you wanted to have
In a human embrace.
You'll be what you were before,
Before the world disappointed you,
But only the warmth of human blood
Can heal you.
All anguish will forsake you.
You'll be happy right away,
If your hand kills hm,
The one who deceived you,
Who seduced you!

RUSALKA
frightened
Ježibaba, alas, what are you saying?

JEŽIBABA
offers her a knife
Take this knife and promise,
That you'll obey!

RUSALKA
throws the knife into the lake
You horrify me; leave me!
I'd rather suffer eternally in anguish,
I want to feel my curse forever,
All my rejected love,
My despair, I want to see everything,
But he must be happy!

JEŽIBABA
bursting into wild laughter
Into a deceitful human life
Your desires lured you,
And now you don't have the strength,
To shed human blood?
Man is only human,
Until he's dipped his hand in another's blood,
Incited by a passion for blood,
He is drunk with his neighbor's blood.
And you wanted to be human
And impress a man with passion?

You empty water bubble,
A moonlit, pale good-for-nothing,
Go, suffer from ages to ages,
And dry up with longing
For your man!

She hobbles back to her cottage.

RUSALKA
Torn from life in deep solitude,
No companions, without sisters I must live.
Beloved, I know, I know,
I'll never see you again,
Oh, woe is me a hundred times!

She submerges in the lake.

CHORUS OF RUSALKI
under water
You went into the world,
You fled our games,
Little sister cursed,
Don't come down to us!
You are banned from our dance,
You whom a man has embraced,
We'll scatter, we'll scatter,
If you approach us!
Fear blows out of your sadness
Into our joyful games,
With the will-o'-the-wisps in swamps
You should play at night!
Lure people with your light,
Wait now at the crossroads,
With your little blue light
Lead them to their graves!
At the graves and crossroads
You'll find other sisters dancing,
To the dance of the water sisters
Don't come back!

Silence. Evening glows in the west.

GAMEKEEPER
brings along the SERVANT
You're scared? Don't be silly,
Others used to come here!
Knock and say nicely,
What they told you to say at home:
The prince is tormented,
That he's lost his senses,
A cursed creature from hell,
Came to the palace,
And that the old woman Háta begs
Ježibaba for advice!

SERVANT
refusing
My legs are lame,
I can't see clearly,
For the living God,
Uncle, go there alone!

GAMEKEEPER
How many times I've passed this way,
During the dark hours of night,
You're a real coward,
That you're afraid of an old woman!

SERVANT
Once when you were visiting us,
You yourself scared me, Uncle,
Don't be surprised now, Uncle,
That I'm afraid in the forest!

GAMEKEEPER
Idle talk, idle talk,
Sometimes I overstate things.
But now get to it quickly,
To get an answer!
Come on, hey, knock,
And ask the old hag for advice!

SERVANT
I would surely chatter,
I'm so scared,

Better for you to ask her
About it yourself!

GAMEKEEPER
I'd be ashamed,
to be your father!
But to show you,
I'm not afraid!
Ježibaba, Ježibaba! Hello, hello!

JEŽIBABA
comes out of the cottage
Who's making noises? Who's calling?

The SERVANT *hides behind the* GAMEKEEPER.

GAMEKEEPER
Old Háta sends us to you,
Ježibaba, for advice!

JEŽIBABA
For that advice, for a bit of reason,
Does she send me this boy to munch on?

She touches the SERVANT.

As soon as the poor boy eats
He'll make a nice roast!

SERVANT
defends himself desperately
Let me out of this place!
Uncle, she wants to eat me!

JEŽIBABA
shaking with laughter
Ha, ha, you little scrap,
Stupid creature,
I should eat you,
Pure roast!
For the hell of it, I'll let your cursed lineage grow!
Now tell me quickly,
What you have to tell me.

SERVANT
with anxiety
Our prince is gravely, gravely ill,
She's bewitched his heart
Like a sorceress.
He brought her to the palace, gave her everything,
Like his own life he loved her.
She would have become his wife,
But the beautiful sorceress had no wedding.
When the prince was thoroughly confused,
The unfaithful enchantress disappeared.
The whole palace is spellbound
To this day,
The devil himself took the enchantress
And carried her off to hell!

VODNIK
suddenly emerges from the lake
Who took her away?
Whom did she betray?
Cursed breeds,
That sends you here!
Miserable creatures!
He betrayed her,
Put a curse on her!

GAMEKEEPER
takes to his heels
Vodnik!

SERVANT
follows close after him
Uncle! My God, Uncle!

VODNIK
in a frightful voice
I'll avenge her, avenge,
As far as my realm reaches!

JEŽIBABA
Ha, ha, ha, ha!

She hobbles back to her cottage. The evening glow vanished, night has fallen and the moon is rising. FOREST NYMPHS *dance in the glade.*

1ST FOREST NYMPH
dancing
I have, golden hair I have,
Fireflies fly around them,
My white hand has untied my hair,
The moon combs them with its silver rays,
I have, I have, golden hair I have!

2ND FOREST NYMPH
dancing
I have, white feet I have,
I ran through the glade,
I ran barefoot,
And the dew washed them,
The moon dressed them in golden slippers!

3RD FOREST NYMPH
dancing, together with the others
I have, a beautiful body I have,
In the glade at night
It shines with its loveliness.
Wherever I run, there my lovely body
The moon clothes in silver and gold!

FOREST NYMPHS
Let's dance, sisters, let's dance,
Into the gentle night breeze,
In a moment he'll call from the reeds
The green Vodnik.

Seeing the VODNIK.

Here he is, here he is,
Already mending his nets,
Already here, already!
Dancing around him.

Vodnik, hey, hey,
Come on, try to catch us!
The one you catch, dear man,

Will give you a nice kiss.
But your woman, Vodnik,
Ha, ha, ha, Vodnik,
Will pull your ears!
Vodnik, hey, hey,
Come on, try to catch us!

VODNIK
sadly
Don't tease me coyly,
Dear golden-haired children,
Our native water
Has become clouded with human grief.

FOREST NYMPHS
stand still
What's ruining our fun joke?
Tell us, dear man, tell us!

VODNIK
Deep down at the bottom
Rejected by her sisters,
Poor, pale Rusalka!
Alas, oh alas!

He submerges. The moon hides behind clouds.

1ST FOREST NYMPH
I feel a tear in my eyes,
The cold suddenly blows on me.

2ND FOREST NYMPH
In the gray clouds
The moon has hidden.

3RD FOREST NYMPH
Darkness oppresses my head,
Sisters, sisters, let's flee!
They disperse.

PRINCE
like a madman runs out of the forest
My white doe!

Fairy tale! Mute vision!
My grieving, my constant searching
Will it never end?
Day after day I hunt for you
Breathless I seek you in the forest,
When night approaches, I sense you in it,
I catch you in the moonlit mist,
I'm looking for you all over the earth.
Fairy tale, come back to me!

He stops.

It happened here,
Speak, silent forests!
Sweet vision, beloved, where are you?
My white doe! Where are you?
With everything I have in my dead heart,
I entreat heaven and earth,
I entreat God and the demon,
Come to me, come to me, where are you?
My love!

The moon emerges from the clouds.

RUSALKA
appears in the moonlight above the lake
My love, do you recognize me, do you?
My love, do you still remember?

PRINCE
startled
If you are long since dead, destroy me,
If you're still alive, save me, save me!

RUSALKA
Neither alive nor dead, neither woman nor nymph,
Cursed, I wander under a spell,
I dreamed in vain for a moment in your arms
About my poor love, my poor, wretched love.
I was once your lover,
But now I am your death!

PRINCE

I can't live anywhere without you,
Can you, can you forgive me?

RUSALKA

Why did you call me into your arms,
Why did your lips lie?
Now I'm a moonlit vision,
Destined to forever torment you!
Now I lure you in the darkness of the night,
My womanhood has been dishonored,
And with the will-o'-the-wisps on the water
I'll lead you into the depths.
Why did you call me into your arms,
Why did your lips lie?
You were looking for passion, I know, I know,
You were looking for a passion that I didn't have,
And now if I kiss you,
You are lost, you are lost completely.

PRINCE

staggering toward her
Kiss me, kiss me, give me peace,
I don't want to return to the world of rejoicing,
Kiss me until I die!

RUSALKA

And you gave me, my dearest, so much,
Why did you, my dearest, betray me?
Do you know, love, do you know,
From my embrace you'll never return,
Your doom
Awaits you in my embrace.

PRINCE

I want to give you everything,
Kiss me, kiss me a thousand times!
I don't want to go back, let me die,
Kiss me, kiss me, give me peace,
I don't want to go back, let me die,
I have no thought, no thought of going back!

Rusalka and Prince. Illustration by Nelinda. © Bendideia Publishing.

RUSALKA

embraces him and kisses him
My love will freeze all emotions,
I have to destroy you,
I have to take you in my arms!

PRINCE

Kiss me, kiss me, give me peace!
Your kisses will redeem my sin!
I die happy,
I die happy in your embrace!

He dies.

VODNIK

deep under the water
In vain he'll die in your arms,
In vain are all sacrifices,
Poor, pale Rusalka! Alas!

RUSALKA

kisses the dead PRINCE *for the last time*
For your love, for your beauty,
For your fickle human passion,
For all my cursed fate,
Human soul, God have mercy on you![241]

A Hero of Our Time – Novel by Lermontov

Mikhail Yurevich Lermontov (1814-1841) was a Russian nobleman, who occupied his time with writing, poetry, and painting. He was described as having a "poisonous wit and cruel humour which would often earn him enemies." And in the end, his teasing nature got him killed in a duel after he had taunted former friend Nikolai Martynov about the way he dressed and acted.

A Hero of Our Time is partially autobiographical, "revolving around a single character, a disenchanted, bored and doomed young nobleman." The book earned Lermontov "recognition as one of the founding fathers of Russian prose." Parts of the story first appeared in a magazine in 1839, with the rest published in 1840.[242] The following excerpt from the book is not specifically about a Rusalka, although it could be interpreted that way from the character's perspective. It does give a literary flavor to how scandalous women were thought to be these sometimes-dangerous, wild spirits.

A Hero of Our Time (Lermontov, 1840, with 1916 translation)

The First Extract from Pechorin's Diary
Tamañ

Tamañ is the nastiest little hole of all the seaports of Russia. I was all but starved there, to say nothing of having a narrow escape of being drowned.

I arrived late at night by the post-car. The driver stopped the tired *trotka* [team of three horses abreast] at the gate of the only stone-built house that stood at the entrance to the town. The sentry, a Cossack from the Black Sea, hearing the jingle of the bell, cried out, sleepily, in his barbarous voice, "Who goes there?" An under-officer of Cossacks and a headborough [an officer like the old English tithing-man or headborough] came out. I explained that I was an officer bound for the active-service detachment on Government business, and I proceeded to demand official quarters. The headborough conducted us round the town. Whatever hut we drove up to we found to be occupied. The weather was cold; I had not slept for three nights; I was tired out, and I began to lose my temper.

"Take me somewhere or other, you scoundrel!" I cried; "to the devil himself, so long as there's a place to put up at!"

"There is one other lodging," answered the headborough, scratching his head. "Only you won't like it, sir. It is uncanny!"

Failing to grasp the exact signification of the last phrase, I ordered him to go on, and, after a lengthy peregrination through muddy byways, at the sides of which I could see nothing but old fences, we drove up to a small cabin, right on the shore of the sea.

The full moon was shining on the little reed-thatched roof and the white walls of my new dwelling. In the courtyard, which was surrounded by a wall of rubble-stone, there stood another miserable hovel, smaller and older than the first and all askew. The shore descended precipitously to the sea, almost from its very walls, and down below, with incessant murmur, plashed the dark-blue waves. The moon gazed softly upon the watery element, restless but obedient to it, and I was able by its light to distinguish two ships lying at some distance from the shore, their black rigging motionless and standing out, like cobwebs, against the pale line of the horizon.

"There are vessels in the harbour," I said to myself. "To-morrow I will set out for Gelenjik."

I had with me, in the capacity of soldier-servant, a Cossack of the frontier army. Ordering him to take down the portmanteau and dismiss the driver, I began to call the master of the house. No answer! I knocked—all was silent within! . . . What could it mean? At length a boy of about fourteen crept out from the hall.

"Where is the master?"

"There isn't one."

"What! No master?"

"None!"

"And the mistress?"

"She has gone off to the village."

"Who will open the door for me, then?" I said, giving it a kick.

The door opened of its own accord, and a breath of moisture-laden air was wafted from the hut. I struck a lucifer match and held it to the boy's face. It lit up two white eyes. He was totally blind, obviously so from birth.

He stood stock-still before me, and I began to examine his features.

I confess that I have a violent prejudice against all blind, one-eyed, deaf, dumb, legless, armless, hunchbacked, and such-like people. I have observed that there is always a certain strange connection between a man's exterior and his soul; as, if when the body loses a limb, the soul also loses some power of feeling.

And so I began to examine the blind boy's face. But what could be read upon a face from which the eyes are missing? . . . For a long time I gazed at him with involuntary compassion, when suddenly a scarcely perceptible smile flitted over his thin lips, producing, I know not why, a most unpleasant impression upon me. I began to feel a suspicion that the blind boy was not so blind as he appeared to be. In vain I endeavoured to convince myself that it was impossible to counterfeit cataracts; and besides, what reason could there be for doing such a thing? But I could not help my suspicions. I am easily swayed by prejudice. . .

"You are the master's son?" I asked at length.

"No."

"Who are you, then?"

"An orphan—a poor boy."

"Has the mistress any children?"

"No, her daughter ran away and crossed the sea with a Tartar."

"What sort of a Tartar?"

"The devil only knows! A Crimean Tartar, a boatman from Kerch."

I entered the hut. Its whole furniture consisted of two benches and a table, together with an enormous chest beside the stove. There was not a single ikon to be seen on the wall—a bad sign! The sea-wind burst in through the broken window-pane. I drew a wax candle-end from my portmanteau, lit it, and began to put my things out. My sabre and gun I placed in a corner, my pistols I laid on the table. I spread my felt cloak out on one bench, and the Cossack his on the other. In ten minutes the latter was snoring, but I could not go to sleep—the image of the boy with the white eyes kept hovering before me in the dark.

About an hour passed thus. The moon shone in at the window and its rays played along the earthen floor of the hut. Suddenly a shadow flitted across the bright strip of moonshine which intersected the floor. I raised myself up a little and glanced out of the window. Again somebody ran by it and disappeared—goodness knows where! It seemed impossible for anyone to descend the steep cliff overhanging the shore, but that was the only thing that could have happened. I rose, threw on my tunic, girded on a dagger, and with the utmost quietness went out of the hut. The blind boy was coming towards me. I hid by the fence, and he passed by me with a sure but cautious step. He was carrying a parcel under his arm. He turned towards the harbour and began to descend a steep and narrow path.

"On that day the dumb will cry out and the blind will see," I said to myself, following him just close enough to keep him in sight.

Meanwhile the moon was becoming overcast by clouds and a mist had risen upon the sea. The lantern alight in the stern of a ship close at hand was scarcely visible through the mist, and by the shore there glimmered the foam of the waves, which every moment threatened to submerge it. Descending with difficulty, I stole along the steep declivity, and all at once I saw the blind boy come to a standstill and then turn down to the right. He walked so close to the water's edge that it seemed as if the waves would straightway seize him and carry him off. But, judging by the confidence with which he stepped from rock to rock and avoided the water-channels, this was evidently not the first time that he had made that journey. Finally he stopped, as though listening for something, squatted down upon the ground, and laid the parcel beside him. Concealing myself behind a projecting rock on the shore, I kept watch on his movements. After a few minutes a white figure made its appearance from the opposite direction. It came up to the blind boy and sat down beside him. At times the wind wafted their conversation to me.

"Well?" said a woman's voice. "The storm is violent; Yanko will not be here."

"Yanko is not afraid of the storm!" the other replied.

"The mist is thickening," rejoined the woman's voice, sadness in its tone.

"In the mist it is all the easier to slip past the guardships," was the answer.

"And if he is drowned?"

"Well, what then? On Sunday you won't have a new ribbon to go to church in."

An interval of silence followed. One thing, however, struck me—in talking to me the blind boy spoke in the Little Russian dialect, but now he was expressing himself in pure Russian.

"You see, I am right!" the blind boy went on, clapping his hands. "Yanko is not afraid of sea, nor winds, nor mist, nor coastguards! Just listen! That is not the water plashing, you can't deceive me—it is his long oars."

The woman sprang up and began anxiously to gaze into the distance.

"You are raving!" she said. "I cannot see anything."

I confess that, much as I tried to make out in the distance something resembling a boat, my efforts were unsuccessful. About ten minutes passed thus, when a black speck appeared between the mountains of the waves! At one time it grew larger, at another smaller. Slowly rising upon the crests of the waves and swiftly descending from them, the boat drew near to the shore.

"He must be a brave sailor," I thought, "to have determined to cross the twenty versts of strait on a night like this, and he must have had a weighty reason for doing so."

Reflecting thus, I gazed with an involuntary beating of the heart at the poor boat. It dived like a duck, and then, with rapidly swinging oars—like wings—it sprang forth from the abyss amid the splashes of the foam. "Ah!" I thought, "it will be dashed against the shore with all its force and broken to pieces!" But it turned aside adroitly and leaped unharmed into a little creek. Out of it stepped a man of medium height, wearing a Tartar sheepskin cap. He waved his hand, and all three set to work to drag something out of the boat. The cargo was so large that, to this day, I cannot understand how it was that the boat did not sink.

Each of them shouldered a bundle, and they set off along the shore, and I soon lost sight of them. I had to return home; but I confess I was rendered uneasy by all these strange happenings, and I found it hard to await the morning.

My Cossack was very much astonished when, on waking up, he saw me fully dressed. I did not, however, tell him the reason. For some time I stood at the window, gazing admiringly at the blue sky all studded with wisps of cloud, and at the distant shore of the Crimea, stretching out in a lilac-coloured streak and ending in a cliff, on the summit of which the white tower of the lighthouse was gleaming. Then I betook myself to the fortress, Phanagoriya, in order to ascertain from the Commandant at what hour I should depart for Gelenjik.

But the Commandant, alas! could not give me any definite information. The vessels lying in the harbour were all either guard-ships or merchant-vessels which had not yet even begun to take in lading.

"Maybe in about three or four days' time a mail-boat will come in," said the Commandant, "and then we shall see."

I returned home sulky and wrathful. My Cossack met me at the door with a frightened countenance.

"Things are looking bad, sir!" he said.

"Yes, my friend; goodness only knows when we shall get away!"

Hereupon he became still more uneasy, and, bending towards me, he said in a whisper:

"It is uncanny here! I met an under-officer from the Black Sea to-day—he's an acquaintance of mine—he was in my detachment last year. When I told him where we were staying, he said, 'That place is uncanny, old fellow; they're wicked people there!' . . . And, indeed, what sort of a blind boy is that? He goes everywhere alone, to fetch water and to buy bread at the bazaar. It is evident they have become accustomed to that sort of thing here."

"Well, what then? Tell me, though, has the mistress of the place put in an appearance?"

"During your absence to-day, an old woman and her daughter arrived."

"What daughter? She has no daughter!"

"Goodness knows who it can be if it isn't her daughter; but the old woman is sitting over there in the hut now."

I entered the hovel. A blazing fire was burning in the stove, and they were cooking a dinner which struck me as being a rather luxurious one for poor people. To all my questions the old woman replied that she was deaf and could not hear me. There was nothing to be got out of her. I turned to the blind boy who was sitting in front of the stove, putting twigs into the fire.

"Now, then, you little blind devil," I said, taking him by the ear. "Tell me, where were you roaming with the bundle last night, eh?"

The blind boy suddenly burst out weeping, shrieking and wailing.

"Where did I go? I did not go anywhere . . . With the bundle? . . . What bundle?"

This time the old woman heard, and she began to mutter:

"Hark at them plotting, and against a poor boy too! What are you touching him for? What has he done to you?"

I had enough of it, and went out, firmly resolved to find the key to the riddle.

I wrapped myself up in my felt cloak and, sitting down on a rock by the fence, gazed into the distance. Before me stretched the sea, agitated by the storm of the previous night, and its monotonous roar, like the murmur of a town over which slumber is beginning to creep, recalled bygone years to my mind, and transported my thoughts northward to our cold Capital. Agitated by my recollections, I became oblivious of my surroundings.

About an hour passed thus, perhaps even longer. Suddenly something resembling a song struck upon my ear. It was a song, and the voice was a woman's, young and fresh—but, where was it coming from? . . . I listened; it was a harmonious melody—now long-drawn-out and plaintive, now swift and lively. I looked around me—there was nobody to be seen. I listened again—the sounds seemed to be falling from the sky. I raised my eyes. On the roof of my cabin was standing a young girl in a striped dress and with her hair hanging loose—a regular water-nymph. Shading her eyes from the sun's rays with the palm of her hand, she was gazing intently into the distance. At one time, she would laugh and talk to herself, at another, she would strike up her song anew.

I have retained that song in my memory, word for word:

At their own free will
They seem to wander
O'er the green sea yonder,
Those ships, as still
They are onward going,
With white sails flowing.
And among those ships
My eye can mark
My own dear barque:
By two oars guided
(All unprovided
With sails) it slips.
The storm-wind raves:
And the old ships—see!
With wings spread free,
Over the waves
They scatter and flee!
The sea I will hail
With obeisance deep:
"Thou base one, hark!
Thou must not fail
My little barque
From harm to keep!"
For lo! 'tis bearing
Most precious gear,
And brave and daring
The arms that steer
Within the dark
My little barque.

Involuntarily the thought occurred to me that I had heard the same voice the night before. I reflected for a moment, and when I looked up at the roof again there was no girl to be seen. Suddenly she darted past me, with another song on her lips, and, snapping her fingers, she ran up to the old woman. Thereupon a quarrel arose between them. The old woman grew angry, and the girl laughed loudly. And then I saw my Undine running and gambolling again. She came up to where I was, stopped, and gazed fixedly into my face as if surprised at my presence. Then she turned carelessly away and went quietly towards the harbour. But this was not all. The whole day she kept hovering around my lodging, singing and gambolling without a moment's interruption. Strange creature! There was not the slightest sign of insanity in her face; on the contrary, her eyes, which were continually resting upon me, were bright and piercing. Moreover, they seemed to be endowed with a certain magnetic power, and each time they looked at me they appeared to be expecting a question. But I had only to open my lips to speak, and away she would run, with a sly smile.

Certainly never before had I seen a woman like her. She was by no means beautiful; but, as in other matters, I have my own prepossessions on the subject of beauty. There was a good deal of breeding in her

. . . Breeding in women, as in horses, is a great thing: a discovery, the credit of which belongs to young France. It—that is to say, breeding, not young France—is chiefly to be detected in the gait, in the hands and feet; the nose, in particular, is of the greatest significance. In Russia a straight nose is rarer than a small foot.

My songstress appeared to be not more than eighteen years of age. The unusual suppleness of her figure, the characteristic and original way she had of inclining her head, her long, light-brown hair, the golden sheen of her slightly sunburnt neck and shoulders, and especially her straight nose—all these held me fascinated. Although in her sidelong glances I could read a certain wildness and disdain, although in her smile there was a certain vagueness, yet—such is the force of predilections—that straight nose of hers drove me crazy. I fancied that I had found Goethe's Mignon—that queer creature of his German imagination. And, indeed, there was a good deal of similarity between them; the same rapid transitions from the utmost restlessness to complete immobility, the same enigmatical speeches, the same gambols, the same strange songs.

Towards evening I stopped her at the door and entered into the following conversation with her.

"Tell me, my beauty," I asked, "what were you doing on the roof to-day?"

"I was looking to see from what direction the wind was blowing."

"What did you want to know for?"

"Whence the wind blows comes happiness."

"Well? Were you invoking happiness with your song?"

"Where there is singing there is also happiness."

"But what if your song were to bring you sorrow?"

"Well, what then? Where things won't be better, they will be worse; and from bad to good again is not far."

"And who taught you that song?"

"Nobody taught me; it comes into my head and I sing; whoever is to hear it, he will hear it, and whoever ought not to hear it, he will not understand it."

"What is your name, my songstress?"

"He who baptized me knows."

"And who baptized you?"

"How should I know?"

"What a secretive girl you are! But look here, I have learned something about you"—she neither changed countenance nor moved her lips, as though my discovery was of no concern to her—"I have learned that you went to the shore last night."

And, thereupon, I very gravely retailed to her all that I had seen, thinking that I should embarrass her. Not a bit of it! She burst out laughing heartily.

"You have seen much, but know little; and what you do know, see that you keep it under lock and key."

"But supposing, now, I was to take it into my head to inform the Commandant?" and here I assumed a very serious, not to say stern, demeanour.

She gave a sudden spring, began to sing, and hid herself like a bird frightened out of a thicket. My last words were altogether out of place. I had no suspicion then how momentous they were, but afterwards I had occasion to rue them.

As soon as the dusk of evening fell, I ordered the Cossack to heat the teapot, campaign fashion. I lighted a candle and sat down by the table, smoking my travelling-pipe. I was just about to finish my second tumbler of tea when suddenly the door creaked and I heard behind me the sound of footsteps and the light rustle of a dress. I started and turned round.

It was she—my Undine. Softly and without saying a word she sat down opposite to me and fixed her eyes upon me. Her glance seemed wondrously tender, I know not why; it reminded me of one of those glances which, in years gone by, so despotically played with my life. She seemed to be waiting for a question, but I kept silence, filled with an inexplicable sense of embarrassment. Mental agitation was evinced by the dull pallor which overspread her countenance; her hand, which I noticed was trembling slightly, moved aimlessly about the table. At one time her breast heaved, and at another she seemed to be holding her breath. This little comedy was beginning to pall upon me, and I was about to break the silence in a most prosaic manner, that is, by offering her a glass of tea; when suddenly, springing up, she threw her arms around my neck, and I felt her moist, fiery lips pressed upon mine. Darkness came before my eyes, my head began to swim. I embraced her with the whole strength of youthful passion. But, like a snake, she glided from between my arms, whispering in my ear as she did so:

"To-night, when everyone is asleep, go out to the shore."

Like an arrow she sprang from the room.

In the hall she upset the teapot and a candle which was standing on the floor.

"Little devil!" cried the Cossack, who had taken up his position on the straw and had contemplated warming himself with the remains of the tea.

It was only then that I recovered my senses.

In about two hours' time, when all had grown silent in the harbour, I awakened my Cossack.

"If I fire a pistol," I said, "run to the shore."

He stared open-eyed and answered mechanically:

"Very well, sir."

I stuffed a pistol in my belt and went out. She was waiting for me at the edge of the cliff. Her attire was more than light, and a small kerchief girded her supple waist.

"Follow me!" she said, taking me by the hand, and we began to descend.

I cannot understand how it was that I did not break my neck. Down below we turned to the right and proceeded to take the path along which I had followed the blind boy the evening before. The moon had not yet risen, and only two little stars, like two guardian lighthouses, were twinkling in the dark-blue vault of heaven. The heavy waves, with measured and even motion, rolled one after the other, scarcely lifting the solitary boat which was moored to the shore.

"Let us get into the boat," said my companion.

I hesitated. I am no lover of sentimental trips on the sea; but this was not the time to draw back. She leaped into the boat, and I after her; and I had not time to recover my wits before I observed that we were adrift.

"What is the meaning of this?" I said angrily.

"It means," she answered, seating me on the bench and throwing her arms around my waist, "it means that I love you!" . . .

Her cheek was pressed close to mine, and I felt her burning breath upon my face. Suddenly something fell noisily into the water. I clutched at my belt—my pistol was gone! Ah, now a terrible suspicion crept into my soul, and the blood rushed to my head! I looked round. We were about fifty fathoms from the shore, and I could not swim a stroke! I tried to thrust her away from me, but she clung like a cat to my clothes, and suddenly a violent wrench all but threw me into the sea. The boat rocked, but I righted myself, and a desperate struggle began.

Fury lent me strength, but I soon found that I was no match for my opponent in point of agility. . .

"What do you want?" I cried, firmly squeezing her little hands.

Her fingers crunched, but her serpent-like nature bore up against the torture, and she did not utter a cry.

"You saw us," she answered. "You will tell on us."

And, with a supernatural effort, she flung me on to the side of the boat; we both hung half overboard; her hair touched the water. The decisive moment had come. I planted my knee against the bottom of the boat, caught her by the tresses with one hand and by the throat with the other; she let go my clothes, and, in an instant, I had thrown her into the waves.

It was now rather dark; once or twice her head appeared for an instant amidst the sea foam, and I saw no more of her.

I found the half of an old oar at the bottom of the boat, and somehow or other, after lengthy efforts, I made fast to the harbour. Making my way along the shore towards my hut, I involuntarily gazed in the direction of the spot where, on the previous night, the blind boy had awaited the nocturnal mariner. The moon was already rolling through the sky, and it seemed to me that somebody in white was sitting on the shore. Spurred by curiosity, I crept up and crouched down in the grass on the top of the cliff. By thrusting my head out a little way I was able to get a good view of everything that was happening down below, and I was not very much astonished, but almost rejoiced, when I recognised my water-nymph. She was wringing the sea-foam from her long hair. Her wet garment outlined her supple figure and her high bosom.

Soon a boat appeared in the distance; it drew near rapidly; and, as on the night before, a man in a Tartar cap stepped out of it, but he now had his hair cropped round in the Cossack fashion, and a large knife was sticking out behind his leather belt.

"Yanko," the girl said, "all is lost!"

Then their conversation continued, but so softly that I could not catch a word of it.

"But where is the blind boy?" said Yanko at last, raising his voice.

"I have told him to come," was the reply.

After a few minutes the blind boy appeared, dragging on his back a sack, which they placed in the boat.

"Listen!" said Yanko to the blind boy. "Guard that place! You know where I mean? There are valuable goods there. Tell"—I could not catch the name—"that I am no longer his servant. Things have gone badly. He will see me no more. It is dangerous now. I will go seek work in another place, and he will never be able to find another dare-devil like me. Tell him also that if he had paid me a little better for my labours, I would not have forsaken him. For me there is a way anywhere, if only the wind blows and the sea roars."

After a short silence Yanko continued.

"She is coming with me. It is impossible for her to remain here. Tell the old woman that it is time for her to die; she has been here a long time, and the line must be drawn somewhere. As for us, she will never see us any more."

"And I?" said the blind boy in a plaintive voice.

"What use have I for you?" was the answer.

In the meantime my Undine had sprung into the boat. She beckoned to her companion with her hand. He placed something in the blind boy's hand and added:

"There, buy yourself some gingerbreads."

Water Depths. Дженеев Иван Алексеевич, 1907.
Дженеев Иван Алексеевич [Public domain or Public domain], via Wikimedia Commons.

"Is this all?" said the blind boy.

"Well, here is some more."

The money fell and jingled as it struck the rock.

The blind boy did not pick it up. Yanko took his seat in the boat; the wind was blowing from the shore; they hoisted the little sail and sped rapidly away. For a long time the white sail gleamed in the moonlight amid the dark waves. Still the blind boy remained seated upon the shore, and then I heard something which sounded like sobbing. The blind boy was, in fact, weeping, and for a long, long time his tears flowed. . . I grew heavy-hearted. For what reason should fate have thrown me into the peaceful circle of honourable smugglers? Like a stone cast into a smooth well, I had disturbed their quietude, and I barely escaped going to the bottom like a stone.

I returned home. In the hall the burnt-out candle was spluttering on a wooden platter, and my Cossack, contrary to orders, was fast asleep, with his gun held in both hands. I left him at rest, took the candle, and entered the hut. Alas! my cashbox, my sabre with the silver chasing, my Daghestan dagger—the gift of a friend—all had vanished! It was then that I guessed what articles the cursed blind boy had been dragging along. Roughly shaking the Cossack, I woke him up, rated him, and lost my temper. But what was the good of that? And would it not have been ridiculous to complain to the authorities that I had been robbed by a blind boy and all but drowned by an eighteen-year-old girl?

Thank heaven an opportunity of getting away presented itself in the morning, and I left Tamañ.

What became of the old woman and the poor blind boy I know not. And, besides, what are the joys and sorrows of mankind to me—me, a travelling officer, and one, moreover, with an order for post-horses on Government business?

Sacred Blood – Novel by Gippius

Zinaida Gippius (1869-1945) a Russian poet, playwright, essayist, novelist, editor, and religious thinker, has been described as exploring "mystical and covertly sexual themes"[243] in her writing. These topics certainly are evident in *Sacred Blood*, a play about a young Rusalka who wants a soul.

The following discussion will examine the similarities between Gippius' life and that of the Rusalka she wrote about. The full story is too long to be included here. Instead, I'll summarize most and provide excerpts of relevant sections to aid in the discussion.

Sacred Blood (Gippius, 1901)

A young Rusalka is bored watching her sisters sing and dance. Is that all there is for them before they become old and fade away into the mist after three or four hundred years?

She learns from an old Rusalka that humans have a soul, and she's intrigued, wanting to know more. What are the differences between Rusalki and humans? Blood for one thing, she discovers. The Rusalka learns that humans have blood flowing through their bodies, which makes them heavy (in comparison to the light Rusalki, who are made from water).

What's interesting here is that Rusalki don't originate from drowned girls who desire to harm people. Instead, they're born of water from the lake, to which they return as fog when they die. The song below is one the Rusalki sing about their lives.

> On the bank, in the rushes,
> a pale fog slips and melts away.
> We know: Summer yields to winter,
> winter—to spring, many times,
> and the secret hour will arrive,
> like all hours—blessed,
> when we'll melt into the pale fog,
> and the pale fog will melt away.
> And there will be new mermaids,
> and a moon will shine for them—
> and they too will melt into the fog.
>   Everything's a blessing: life! and us! and the world! and death![244]

Rusalki. Jacek Malczewski, 1888.
Jacek Malczewski [Public domain].

Rusalki being "born" of water has a significance in the rite of baptism. A historical reference calls Christ's followers "little fishes," which happens to be a nickname the Witch in this story calls the Rusalka. Another source talks figuratively about "fish as embodying the Christ-like trait of living without sin."[245] In the case of Rusalki, however, being "born" of water doesn't make them "saved" by water—at least not in the eyes of those who call them unclean and evil. This particular Rusalka, however, has goodness in her and seeks a soul to complete herself. All she lacks is the understanding of what it means.

Both baptism and blood, especially "holy" or "sacred" blood, are central to the story. A God shed his blood for humans and made their souls immortal. But this had an adverse effect on Rusalki. From that point onward, they no longer were immortal. They would eventually die, dissolve, and become one with the fog. A painless, peaceful death, but death nonetheless.

Before the arrival of Christianity, as mentioned earlier, people revered a powerful goddess, a nature deity with links to water.

> [T]ertullian and other early Christian leaders argue that the goddess, one of whose domains was water, the environment of the fish, has been replaced by Jesus the Christ; the goddess' life-giving waters, essential to all living things, have been replaced by the more esoteric and symbolic waters of baptism, possible only through conversion to the Christian faith.[246]

All this brings the Rusalka to a realization: "That means, He, this Man, or how did you say it, God—brought us death, but them life? Why do we have to die because of His blood?" To which the old Rusalka tells her, "Blood for blood. We don't have blood."[247] And if she wants to know more, she'll have to ask the Witch.

The Rusalka does want to know more. She has a longing for this soul people have, so she waits for the Witch. Ever looking for ways to cause mischief, the Witch tells the Rusalka to go where two men live (one old and one young), and while they're asleep, cosy up to one—preferably the younger one. (You'll later discover that they're monks.)

YOUNG MERMAID (*loudly*). And I'll have an immortal soul?

WITCH. Come, come how hasty you are! You won't have an immortal soul. And your blood won't be warm, like people's, but cold.

YOUNG MERMAID (*despondently*). Then why am I doing all this?

WITCH. Because for a human soul you need a human body. Without a body that looks human, people won't let you among them, and the Man who spilled his warm blood won't give you a soul.

YOUNG MERMAID. Well, all right, Auntie, but once I have a body—what else do I need?

WITCH. You need the people to baptize you.[248]

Baptism, the witch says, is "A sort of sign. The people will take you in, your blood will become warm, and the Man will give you an immortal soul."[249]

But, unfortunately, the Witch goes on, the men will be afraid of her because they think she's unclean. The Witch's advice is for the Rusalka to bide her time, saying nothing at first, so they get used to her and are no longer afraid. Then when one of the men starts to be kind to her, the Rusalka is to be kind to him. At that point, she can ask to be baptized. If he refuses, the Witch laughs and says, there's another way—but refuses to tell the Rusalka what it is.

The Rusalka does what the Witch tells her, and crawls into bed with the younger man while he's asleep. Nikodim, the young novice, beats her because he was tempted by her—this being "her" fault, because she's female, and not his fault for his lack of control. And he doesn't trust her, sensing that she's different from them. Father Pafnuty, the older monk, is more compassionate and is willing to believe that Rusalka is a human child who has been baptized because she performs the sign of the cross the Witch taught her. He agrees to let her stay and will teach her what she wants to know. Eventually, he agrees to baptize her.

But, it goes deeper than that. It's here that the role of the Church is evident. The two men represent two views: the letter of the law (the harsh, legalistic belief of Nikodim based on Old Testament laws) versus the spirit of the law (the compassionate, forgiving beliefs of mercy that Christ brought when he "fulfilled" the law with the blood he shed). And it's this "sacred blood" that the Rusalka wants to understand: why did the Man condemn them when he saved humans?

The beating the Rusalka is expected to endure is where Gippius' "covert sexual theme" comes into play. Although the Witch didn't explicitly tell the Rusalka to try to seduce the man, her words imply just that:

WITCH. … You just go into the little cell, make sure they don't see you, that they're asleep, and nestle up to one of them, close, warm yourself, have him breathe on you, touch him. He'll wake up and think he's seeing things; he'll start to say words over you, to drive you away, and perhaps he'll start to beat you—pay no attention, endure it, don't leave. He'll breathe on you and touch you—and you'll have a body like people do, with blood….[250]

And again later, the Witch adds:

> **WITCH**. ... Don't say anything to them at first, don't tell them anything, so they won't be afraid, and they'll get used to you. And keep living with them, warm yourself, and get a body. And then when one of them is… when one starts to be very kind to you, and you to him—then reveal yourself to him and ask to be baptized.
> **YOUNG MERMAID**. I'm kind to everyone.
> **WITCH**. Well, that doesn't count. It's when you start to be especially kind, to one in particular.[251]

Especially kind—sexually. Here the Rusalka represents what society thought of women. They were "soulless" beings whose "flesh" caused men to sin.

> This raises the ire of Pafnuty's ascetic novice Nikodim, who attempts to beat her when she first appears, naked, at the hermit's hut. The rusalka's gendered body haunts the stern ascetic, who labels her 'impure', 'unclean', and 'Satan's breed'.[252]

The "beating" the Witch mentioned also has a sexual meaning, referring to the possibility of violent intercourse, which the Witch says she must endure even if it's unpleasant so she can "acquire a warm-blooded human female body."[253]

In addition, the Rusalka represents people of other sexual persuasions, those not acceptable to the Church, such as Gippius herself.

But the Rusalka doesn't understand any of this. She's an innocent, ignorant child, "endowed with Christian virtues of sexual innocence and self-sacrificing love."[254] She says, "I'm kind to everyone," showing her innocence about what the Witch is implying might happen. It also demonstrates that Rusalki, as a species, know nothing about hate, jealousy, and lust that thrive among people. But neither do they know what love is, which is essential to the sacrifice the Man performed for people, and a key ingredient to the Rusalka getting her soul, as she later learns.

When she discovers that the old monk could lose his own soul if he baptizes her, the Rusalka decides to return to the lake because she now loves the monk, and would rather suffer herself than have harm come to him. The Witch comes by and offers her another solution, the one she withheld at the beginning. She hands the young spirit a knife and tells her it's the "means" so the old man doesn't lose his soul, but the Rusalka can still get a soul because she won't be able to talk the man out of performing the baptism. She will ultimately receive "spiritual enrichment through intolerable suffering."[255]

> **WITCH**. ... Listen. Walk up to your old man—don't let him start talking—and stab him immediately with this knife. What strong hands you have there. Stab him so that the knife goes in deeply, and as his blood splatters on you, everything in you will immediately change; you'll become as people are, warm, and a soul will enter your body. Well, do you understand? Why are you staring? How dumb you are!
> **YOUNG MERMAID** (*slowly*). That is… in order to… kill Grandpa?
> **WITCH**. Well, yes. So that his blood, spilled by your hand, touches you. His soul, you see, cannot be killed with a knife. This will make things even easier for his soul. It will be hard on yours, perhaps. People say that… He does not forgive the one who spills blood. He will even torment your soul as punishment. So people say.

YOUNG MERMAID. No…. It's probably not like that. Torment for what? Wasn't His blood spilled for the sake of people?... And if it were human blood—for His sake?

WITCH. Well, I don't know anything about it. That's what people say. I've told you—after that, it's not my business. Choose as you like. Be baptized, or else go to the lake without a soul. You know best.

YOUNG MERMAID (*looking aside*). Well all right…. But it's just that… Auntie! Have pity on me! (*Nearly screams.*) How can I kill him, when his pain—is more painful for me than my own? How can I enter into such torment myself? You see I love him, as if I were part of him, as if I were born of him, as if his blood were my blood! But no, that's not it! I don't have the right word for that pain! (*Throws the knife; it quietly and harmoniously rings.*) No, I'm better off going to the lake. (*After a moment of silence.*) Now I feel better.

WITCH (*laughing quietly*). I know you feel better, little fishie. It's much easier to go to the lake. I told you that, about the knife. I know how difficult this is; not a single person nor any other creature has been able to take it upon themselves. Creatures, who were in the lake just like you, could not, because they do not know love. People know love—but they cannot because of the torment. But without love, these means are of no use.

YOUNG MERMAID (*repeating*). Of no use?

WITCH. No. If you want eternal life—you must earn it through unbearable torment. And perhaps, as people say it will be eternal torment, if there is no forgiveness for blood.

YOUNG MERMAID. I don't care about that. I don't know. And if He wants my eternal soul in order to torment it—what does that matter? He wants it.[256]

Tormented, the Rusalka doesn't know what to do. But she finally determines that it must be God's will that she has this desire. Even the monk had said to her when he agreed to baptize her, "Let His holy will be done!"[257]

The Rusalka believes that the desire within her to have a soul was not her own feeling, but one that the God of people had instilled in her. And so, if he gave her this "pressing desire for an immortal soul [it] might mean that God actually wants to give it to her."[258]

YOUNG MERMAID. I don't have a soul! Do you understand? I don't! The man, Christ, God—came only for people; He didn't come for us. He forgot us! No, he didn't forget, because He brought us death with His death! We used to be immortal, but as soon as His blood fell on us—we began to die. As if it had scorched us!

…

The blood—scorched my soul, but it did not scorch the desire in me. I was born (*points to the clearing in the woods*) there, at the lake, I came from the water, from the mire. There are many of us there, living creatures, dying our deaths, bloodless. People despise us, call us unclean. You see, we melt away into the fog, and it's the end for all of us. The Lord despised them, people think, how can we not despise them? But just tell me, if God wanted to kill us, why did He leave us the desire for an immortal soul? And such a desire, such a will, that it's impossible to resist?[259]

And so, the Rusalka takes the knife and kills the old monk, whom she loved. When Nikodim condemns her, she replies:

> **YOUNG MERMAID**: Now I'm—like you. It was not my will that was done. Blood was spilled for me.
> **NIKODIM**. The cup of the Lord's patience overflows Holy blood…
> **YOUNG MERMAID**. Yes, holy blood. And the blood spilled by God for you—wasn't that holy?
> **NIKODIM**. There is no forgiveness for your soul. There is no limit to the Lord's wrath. Eternal torment awaits you.
> **YOUNG MERMAID**. Will He, whose will was done by me, give me eternal torment for my own torment? Because for His sake I spilled blood which was dearer to me than my own? He knows—dearer to me than my own! Where is the man who would fear torment after my torment? I am afraid of nothing. I went to the One Who called me, Who gave me the most difficult of paths, and He met me.[260]

Gippius herself can relate to the Rusalka's conflict. She was a lesbian (although some say she was bisexual or androgynous), called a "gender misfit,"[261] and therefore, "subhuman" in the eyes of the Church and society.[262] She lashed out in her written word, her provocative behavior, and her style of dress and became part of a "sexual dissidence and gender rebellion" that spread throughout Europe.[263] And yet, she was torn, wondering how she could reconcile her love for God with her love for another woman, which the Church considered a terrible sin. She, like the Rusalka, felt that God had made her that way. In her diary she wrote:

> Why do I rationalize, fear, complain? Everything will be as it should be. It is not my volition that there is such strange, such lively blood in me. For something, for somebody this blood is necessary. Let Him do with it whatever He wants.[264]

One way she strove for "God's love and acceptance" occurred around the time she was writing *Sacred Blood*. She and her husband (who was said to be homosexual) created their own church, a "new religious consciousness."[265]

> In this plan, the couple sought to publish a journal to propagate their new Christian ideas, to organize public discussions between Russian intellectuals and high-ranking Russian Orthodox clergy on religious issues, and—the project most cherished by Gippius—to create a new, private Church as an alternative to official Christian dogma.[266]

In her diary, Gippius talks about abandoning "her 'unclean' lifestyle for her new Christian aspirations" and refers to her religious project with the phrase about "going to the people."[267] The same words appear in *Sacred Blood* when the Witch is telling the Rusalka how to achieve her own "spiritual" desires.

> **WITCH**. … All right, little fishie, so you really want an immortal soul?
> **YOUNG MERMAID** (*lifting her eyes*). Yes.

WITCH. Does it bother you that… he spilled his blood for people, but not for you creatures?

YOUNG MERMAID (*thinking*). I don't know…. It should bother me.

WITCH. Well, then, listen, young lady: I'll teach you. You must approach [*go to*] people.[268]

And so it is that Gippius' Rusalka is a representation of her own life, love, and doubts.

"Ballad" – Poem by Gippius

Gippius felt estranged even among people who shared her sexuality. Even though she respected poet Poliksena Solovieva, Gippius made fun of the woman for holding female soirées for like-minded women. In 1903, she wrote and dedicated a poem to Solovieva, "which makes several allusions to lesbian sexuality," with the " 'gentle and timid' rusalka, underscoring her discomfort with same-sex attachments."[269]

Reading through the poem, it appears to be unrequited love between a man and a Rusalka. However, it has been described as radical concerning its "gender configuration."[270]

On first glance, Gippius seems true to the tradition. As the past tense verb endings indicate, the protagonist is masculine and the rusalka is feminine. However, as soon as we realize that the author herself was a woman, complications arise. It is true that Gippius always used masculine personae in her verse, but given a theme so dependent on gender stereotypes and a poem so intent on setting up expectations in order to break them, there is surely something more profound at work here.[271]

The fact that the poem is dedicated to Gippius' friend, who was also a lesbian, and that Gippius refused to conform to what people thought she should be as far as her sexuality,

it stands to reason that Solovieva would have been sensitive to the reversal of sex roles just beneath the surface of «Баллáда» [Ballad]. If nothing else, the dedication of this peculiar rusalka poem by a woman to a woman seems to extend the confused gender configuration implicit in the verses themselves beyond the text.[272]

"Ballad" (Gippius, 1903)

[For P. S. Solovieva]:
There are wood platforms in the garden, on the pond, in the reeds.
While taking a walk there one evening,
I saw a rusalka. She was sitting on the wood platform—
All tender, timid, evil.

I crept nearer. But a branch snapped—
The rusalka turned around cautiously,

She huddled up into a little ball, pulled herself tight, and—in a jump—
Melted into the white foam.

I go to the wood platforms to visit her every night.
The rusalka becomes bolder with me:
She is silent— but she sits, doesn't jump away,
Sits, showing white in the mist.

I have grown accustomed to remaining silent with her, the white one,
Through all the long, pale nights.
To look into the silence of waters growing ever colder
And into her bright, timid eyes.

And a joy was born between her and me,
Measureless, bright as bottomlessness;
It became entwined with sweetly-hot sadness,
And it became known as—being in love.

I am a beast for the rusalka, I have decay in my blood
And she seems to me a beast . . .
Our being in love is all the more ardent: we measure the strength of our love
By impossibility alone.

Oh, there is—alas!—too much flesh on me!
And on her, perhaps, too little . . .
And now, we burn in an incomprehensible fire
Of unprecedented love.

At times, above the water, the reeds barely rustle,
They babble about the joy of suffering ...
And in the midnight silence our meetings are
Ardently pure and mysteriously pure.

I will not give up my joy to anyone.
We are eternally desirable to each other,
And it is given to us to love eternally, because
Though loving, we are here unmerged![273]

A Modern Rusalka Story

The following is a prologue to an as-yet unpublished novel that the author (who wished to remain anonymous) was kind enough to allow me to use.

Untitled, Unpublished Modern Story

Prologue

Ash covered the ground, and a scorched veranda beam of the farmhouse sprouted like the gnarled branch of an ancient tree. Plastic tombstones and straw-stuffed goblins lay melted and charred—this year's Halloween display lay in ruins.

The wind died down and crickets stopped their incessant chirping. The night stilled as the moon shone bright.

Inside the den of the farmhouse, smothered in a smoky haze, the blood on a sooty handkerchief boiled. Crimson fluid altered from its dried state and bubbled from atop the cloth. The charred remains of a book spontaneously re-ignited for an instant and smoldered.

Puffs of smoke arose from the document as did a dark creature. The giant lizard reached down and gathered the blistering book with its scaly hands. It set the book onto what remained of a wooden mantelpiece. The red, glowing pages singed through the ledge and landed with a thud on the floor.

Venom dripped from the lizard's sharp fangs. Beady, red eyes surveyed the surroundings as the lizard stomped about the house. With flared nostrils and exhaled smoke, the creature watched a melted animatronic zombie lift its shoulders off the wooden floor.

A ghostly, little girl swayed on a backyard swing. "Come play with me," the mechanized girl said and then cackled.

The animatronic zombie with flesh half removed and an eyeball protruding from out of its socket crawled down the hall. Music played and the howl of a wolf cut through the silence to introduce the chords of the ominous melody.

The lizard spoke the rhythmic words of an ancient spell in its native Russian tongue. His scales disappeared, and he took human form. More words spilled from his pink lips, "*Cort porberi…*" and a thick fog rose at his feet and spilled across the floor, spreading an insidious evil, continuing beyond the damaged frame of the house. Voices emanated from the fog: soft, insistent, and deranged.

A river flowed through the eastern edge of the property. The fog rolled across the grounds and encased the river, infecting the water, as a young woman stood on the grassy bank. Tears fell from her eyes while she stared at the gentle waves. Bulrushes swayed lightly in the wind, motioning to her like the crook of a finger compelling her toward it, to enter its depths. As did a hypnotic voice that crept in around the woman like a blanket and called, 'Emily…Emily…'

"Who's there?" Her lip quivered.

The woman wore a white wedding gown. Her high heels lay haphazardly on the shore while she dipped her bare toe in the water. The crisp night air and the cold water raised goosebumps over her exposed skin. A silver locket pressed against her chest. She opened the clasp and stared at the picture inside. The man she loved—the one she was to marry—stared back at her. Her fingers trembled as she fumbled to close the clasp.

"How could he have cheated?" She sobbed and pleaded to the stars above for an answer. Silence. Her eyes lowered to the surface of the river when she realized no answer would come down from the heavens to soothe her, just a voice that kept calling her name.

'Emily.' The voice came from the river.

She rubbed the back of her neck. "I loved you so much. How could you do this to me? How could you make such a fool of me? On our wedding day." Her words choked out between her relentless crying. The pain was too much to bear.

'You're right, Emily. He should pay.' The soft voice echoed her thoughts.

She would have her revenge on the man who hurt her. He would never forgive himself for what he'd done. She would see to that. *He won't be able to live with himself knowing he's responsible.* Her lips curled up. *He'll feel so guilty.*

She stepped into the water, her body shaking from the cold, and stood knee deep with her feet sinking into the bottom. The mucky clay held her feet like wet cement. The train of her dress pulled her down like an anchor as she stepped once more—deeper, waist high. The clay encased her to her ankles while the train tugged her toward the murky floor of the river. Straining her thigh muscles, she slogged forward toward the middle until the surface reached just under her chin.

Rusalka. Ivan Bilibin, 1934.
Ivan Bilibin [Public domain].

One more step. She closed her eyes and clenched her fists, allowing the water to take her. Her nose filled first, then her mouth. She screamed but only a muffled sound came out. The water acted like a gag across her tongue.

He'll know how much he hurt me. Her tears mixed with the river as she succumbed to the depths.

The woman was not alone as she drowned. The suffocating fog had penetrated the river, filling her body like embalming fluid, and freeing her feet from the riverbed. Her corpse splayed out in the dead man's float before her head slowly rose above the water line. The whites of her eyes obliterated her pupils, as she swam down river—the lights of a close by town drawing her near.

Mystical Emona: Soul's Journey – Novel by Ronesa Aveela

As a final fiction example, you can read a re-enactment of the healing ritual that the *Rusalii* performed to cure people of the Rusalka disease. This is an excerpt from my romantic fantasy, *Mystical Emona: Soul's Journey*. A young girl has been cursed by an *uroki*, which you might call "the evil eye." The Rusalii are not present to heal her, but a *znahar* named Sultana is nearby. She's a woman people often called a witch, but is in reality someone who heals with herbs and incantations.

Mystical Emona: Soul's Journey (Aveela, 2014)

Taking hold of Sonia's face, Sultana opened the girl's eyes. She shook her head, grunted when she stood, and shuffled over to her medicine cabinet. A moment later, she returned with an assortment of odd items—bells, a white flag, a clove of garlic, a bouquet of herbs, white caps, a colorful stick decorated with strange symbols, and a ceramic pitcher full of vinegar.

Maria touched Stefan's shoulder. "Don't worry. Sultana has the power and knowledge to heal Sonia."

He swept his sweaty palm over the objects Sultana had laid out. "With *those*?" How were all of those things going to make Sonia well? He should have taken her to Varna, but he wouldn't make it there in time now. He had to let them perform their strange ritual and pray for the best.

"Yes. With those. Have faith." She patted his arm.

Their actions played out in front of Stefan like a bad dream. Maria gathered the herbs and attached them to the flag. Sultana placed the jug of vinegar on a three-legged stool. She ground the clove of garlic and added it to the vinegar. Peter handed each of them a cap and bells. Next, the three of them placed the caps on their heads and attached the bells to their ankles.

When Sonia began to convulse, Stefan paced the room, whispering, "Please help her."

In a low tone, Sultana said, "We ready."

She picked up the flag and chanted in a strange language. Peter and Maria followed her lead, dancing around Sonia, slow at first, but soon in a wild frenzy. The vinegar in the copper jug began to boil. Sultana dipped herbs into it and sprinkled the liquid on Sonia's head. Shaking even more, Sonia's body twisted on the floor. Foam poured out of her mouth.

Stefan's chest tightened. Sonia couldn't die.

Balkan growled at the door. Stefan walked over to the open window to see what was out there. His breath caught. A huge black wolf crouched near the cottage. Was it the same one?

A screech from the sky filled the night air. The white falcon hovered overhead. It descended toward the wolf, attacking with its beak and claws, forcing the animal to withdraw into the underbrush. The falcon circled the cottage a few times, then disappeared. Stefan shook his head. It had all been so sudden. Had it happened at all?

When he turned his attention back to the ritual, the dancing had ceased. Peter and Maria lifted the rug Sonia lay on. Sultana massaged Sonia's forehead with the vinegar mixture and lifted her chin to make her swallow some of the liquid.

Peter and Maria lowered Sonia to the ground, and Sultana began another chant. When she finished, she picked up the jug and smashed it with the colorful stick. The liquid flew all around, landing on them all. Peter and Sultana moved out of the way, leaving Maria to be covered with most of it. Within moments, Maria groaned and dropped to the floor and twisted in agony.

Stefan opened his mouth to scream.

"Daddy?" The weak voice drew his attention from Maria. Sonia struggled to get up, her face pale and her eyes wide open.

"Oh, sweetheart. I'm here." He hurried to her and squeezed her tight. "Everything's going to be fine now."[274]

Appendix:
The Little Mermaid
by Hans Christian Andersen

I've included Hans Christian Andersen's (1805-1875) *The Little Mermaid* here because it's influenced many other works about mermaids, including Slavic sources. You may be familiar with the Disney version, but that is but a shadow of the original story.

As an added bonus, you can read a modern, alternative fanfiction ending in which the little mermaid turns into a Rusalka. Written by Amy (DarkDancer07), the author describes the story as follows:

"Dark alternative ending to Hans Christian Andersen's *The Little Mermaid*. After choosing death instead of killing the Prince, the Little Mermaid is initiated into the rites of the Rusalki, a sisterhood of dark undead spirits of the sea. In her new existence as a Rusalka, she is given the chance to seek vengeance on those responsible for her death, but will she take it?"

The story is five chapters and begins here: https://www.fanfiction.net/s/10489855/1/The-Little-Rusalka.

The Little Mermaid (Andersen, 1836)

FAR out in the sea the water is as blue as the leaves of the loveliest cornflower and as clear as the purest glass, but it is very deep, deeper than ever anchor yet reached; many church-towers would have to be piled one on the top of the other to reach right up from the bottom to the surface of the water. Down there dwell the Sea-folk. Now you must by no means fancy that there is nothing there but a bare white sandbank; no, the most wondrous trees and plants grow there, the stalks and leaves of which are so supple that they move to and fro at the least motion of the water, just as if they were living beings. All the fish, small and great, dart about among the branches just as the birds do in the air up here. In the deepest spot of all lies the Sea-King's palace. The walls are of coral and the long, pointed windows of the clearest sort of amber, but the roof is of mussel-shells which open and shut according as the water flows; it looks lovely, for in every one of the shells lies a glistening pearl. Any one of these pearls would be the glory of a Queen's crown.

The Sea-King down there had been a widower for many years, but his old mother kept house for him; she was a wise woman, but proud of her noble birth, and that was why she always went about with twelve oysters on her tail, the other notabilities being only allowed to carry six. Nevertheless she was very popular, especially because she doted upon the little sea-princesses, her granddaughters. They were six pretty children, but the youngest was the loveliest of them all; her skin was as delicately tinted as a rose leaf, her eyes as blue as the deepest lake, but, like all the others, she had no feet, her body ended in a fish's tail. The livelong day they used to play in the palace down there in the great saloon where living flowers grew out of the walls. The large amber windows were opened and so the fishes swam into them just as the swallows fly in to us when we open our windows, but the fishes swam right up to the little princesses, ate out of their hands and let themselves be patted.

Outside the palace was a large garden full of blood-red and dark blue trees; the fruits there shone like gold, and the flowers like burning fire, and the stalks and leaves were always moving to and fro. The soil itself was of the finest sand, but as blue as sulphur-flames. A wondrous blue gleam lay over everything down there; one would be more inclined to fancy that one stood high up in the air and saw nothing but sky above and beneath than that one was at the bottom of the sea. During a calm, too, one could catch a glimpse of the sun; it looked like a purple flower from the cup of which all light streamed forth.

Every one of the little princesses had her own little garden-plot where she could dig and plant as she liked; one gave her flower-plot the form of a whale, another preferred hers to look like a little mermaid, but the youngest made hers quite round like the sun and would only have flowers which shone red like it. She was a strange child, silent and pensive, and when the other sisters adorned their gardens with the strangest things which they got from stranded vessels, all that she would have, besides the rosy-red flowers which resembled the sun up above, was a pretty marble statue of a lovely boy, hewn out of bright white stone, which had sunk to the bottom of the sea during a shipwreck. She planted by this statue a rosy-red weeping willow, it grew splendidly and hung over the statue with its fresh branches, right down towards the blue sandy bottom where the shadows took a violet hue and moved to and fro like the branches; it looked as if roots and tree-top were playing at kissing each other.

Her greatest joy was to hear about the world of mankind up above. She made her old grandmother tell her all she knew about ships and towns, men and beasts; and what especially struck her as wonderfully nice was that the flowers which grew upon the earth should give forth fragrance, which they did *not* do at the bottom of the sea; and that the woods there were green and the fish which were to be seen there among the branches could sing so loudly and beautifully that it was a joy to listen to them; it was the little birds that her grandmother called *fishes*, they would not otherwise have understood her, for they had never seen a bird.

"When you have reached your fifteenth year," said her grandmother, "you shall have leave to duck up out of the sea and sit in the moonshine on the rocks and see the big ships which sail by; woods and cities you shall also see."

In the following year one of the sisters would be fifteen years old, but how about the others? Each one was a year younger than the one before, and so the youngest had to wait five whole years before she could come up from the bottom of the sea and see how things are with us. But each one had promised to tell the others what she had seen and what she had thought the loveliest on the first day; for their grandmother did not tell them half enough, there was so much they wanted to know about.

None of them was so full of longing as the youngest, just the very one who had the longest time to wait and was so silent and pensive. Many a time she stood by the open window and looked up through the dark blue water where the fishes steered about with their fins and tails. She could see the moon and stars; of course, they shone quite faintly, but at the same time they looked twice as large through the water as they look to us, and when something like a dark cloud glided across them, she knew that it was either a whale swimming over them, or else a ship with many people on board; they certainly never dreamt that a pretty little mermaid stood down below and stretched her white arms up towards the keel.

And now the eldest princess was fifteen years old and might ascend to the surface of the water. When she came back she had hundreds of things to tell about, but the nicest of all, she said, was to lie in the

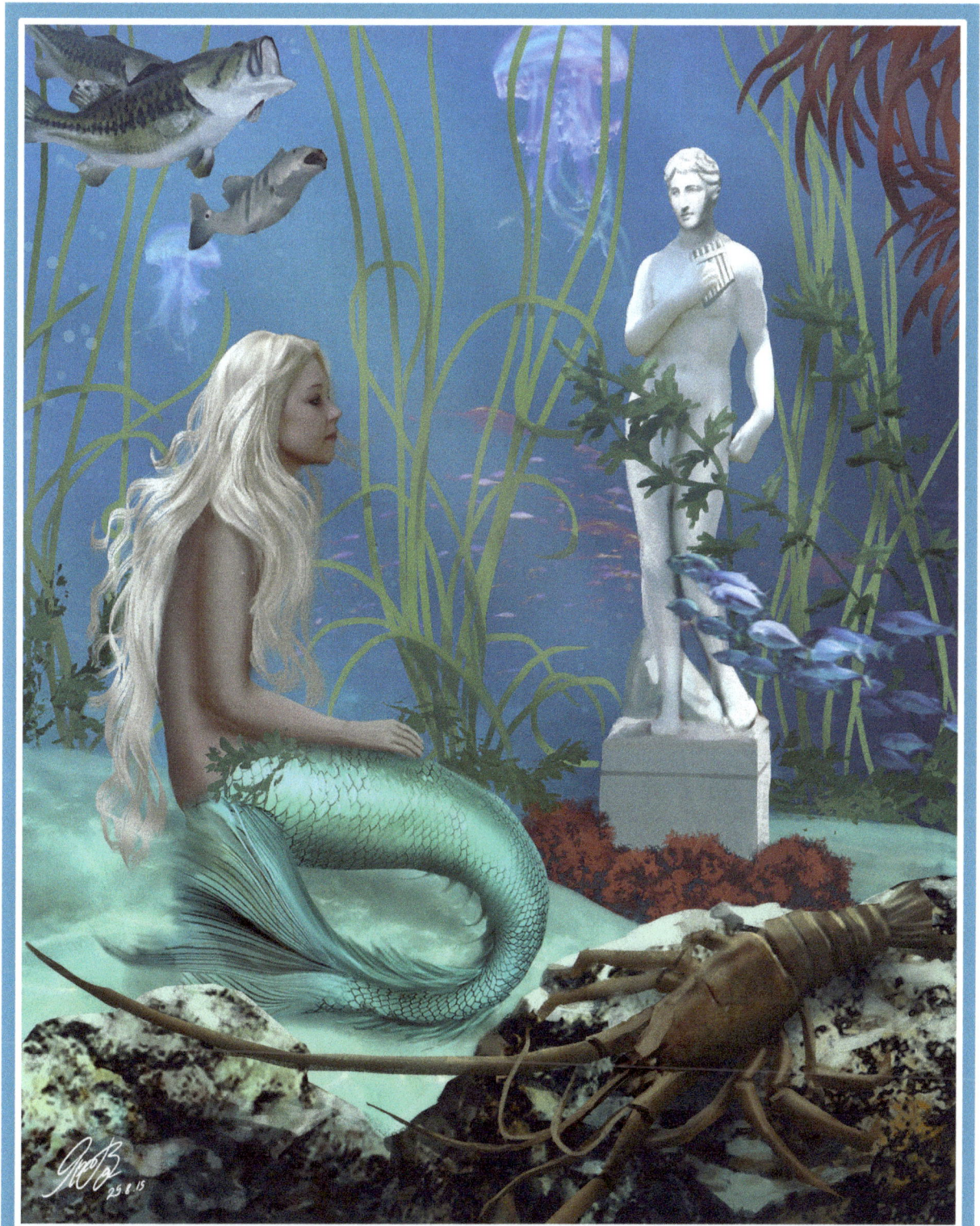

Little Mermaid and Statue.
Illustration by Dmitry Yakhovsky based off of original by Ivan Bilibin. © Bendideia Publishing.

moonshine on a sandbank in the calm sea, and see, close by the shore, the large town where the lights were twinkling, like hundreds of stars, and hear the music and the noise and bustle of carts and men, and look at the many church towers and spires, and hear the bells ringing; it was just because she could not go ashore that she longed so for all these things.

Oh! how the youngest sister listened, and ever afterwards, when she stood in the evening close by the open window, and looked up through the dark blue water, she thought of the great city with all its noise and hustle, and then she thought she heard the church bells ringing down where she was.

The next year the second sister got leave to mount up through the water and swim where she liked. She ducked up just as the sun was going down and she thought that the prettiest sight of all. The whole sky had looked like gold, she said, and the clouds—well, their beauty she absolutely could not describe. All red and violet they had sailed right over her; but far quicker than they, a flock of wild swans had flown right over the place where the sun stood, like a long white veil; she also swam towards the sun, but it sank; and the rosy gleam it left behind it was swallowed up by the sea and the clouds.

A year after that the third sister came up to the surface; she was the boldest of them all, so she swam up a broad river which ran into the sea. She saw pretty green hillocks with vines around them, castles and country houses peeped forth from among the woods; she heard all the birds singing and the sun shone so hotly that she frequently had to duck down under the water to cool her burning face. In a little creek she came upon a whole swarm of human children; they were running about quite naked and splashing about in the water. She wanted to play with them but they ran away in terror, and a little black beast came up. It was a dog, but she had never seen a dog before; it barked so savagely at her that she got frightened and sought the open sea again, but never could she forget the splendid woods, the green heights and the pretty children who could swim in the water although they had no fishes' tails.

The fourth sister was not so bold; she remained out in the middle of the wild sea and said that that was the nicest of all; you could see for miles and miles round about, and the sky above stood there just like a large glass bell. Ships she had seen too, but far away they looked like sea-mews; the merry dolphins had turned somersaults and the big whales had spirted water up out of their nostrils, so that it looked like hundreds of fountains playing all around.

And now it was the turn of the fifth sister. Her birthday happened to be in the winter time, and therefore she saw what the others had not seen the first time. The sea took quite a green colour and round about swam huge icebergs; each one looked like a pearl, she said, and yet was far larger than the church towers which men build. They showed themselves in the strangest shapes and gleamed like diamonds. She had sat upon one of the largest, and all vessels had cruised far out of their reach in terror while she sat there and let the blast flutter her long streaming hair; but towards evening the sky was overcast with clouds, it thundered and lightened while the black sea lifted the large ice-blocks high up and let them shine in the strong glare of the lightning. On all the ships they took in the sails; distress and horror were there, but she sat calmly on her swimming iceberg and saw the blue thunderbolts strike down in zigzags into the shining sea.

The first time any of the sisters rose to the surface of the water she was always enraptured at the new and beautiful things she saw, but when they now, as grown-up girls, had leave to go up whenever they chose, they became quite indifferent about it; they longed for home, and in about a month's time or so would say that it was nicest of all down below, for there one felt so thoroughly at home.

Very often in the evenings the five sisters would take each other's arms and mount up in a group to the surface of the water; they had nice voices, sweeter than any human voice, and when it was blowing a gale and they had good reason to believe that a ship might be lost, they would swim before that ship and sing so sweetly of how pleasant it was at the bottom of the sea, and bid the sailors not be afraid to come down. But the sailors could not understand their words. They fancied it was the storm, nor did they ever get to see any of the beautiful things down below, for when the ship sank the crew were drowned and only came as dead men to the Sea-King's palace.

Now when her sisters thus ascended, arm in arm, high up through the sea, the little sister would remain behind all alone and look up after them, and she felt as if she must cry; but the mermaid has no tears and so she suffers all the more.

"Oh, if only I were fifteen years old!" said she. "I know that I shall quite get to love the world up above there and the men who live and dwell there."

And at last she was fifteen years old.

"Well, now at last we have *you* off our hands," said her grandmother, the old Queen Dowager. "Come here and let me make you look nice like your sisters," and she placed a wreath of white lilies on her hair, but every petal in every flower was the half of a pearl, and the old lady made eight large oysters cling fast on to the Princess's tail to show her high rank.

"But it hurts me so!" said the little mermaid.

"Yes, one must suffer a little for the sake of appearances," said the old lady.

Oh, how much she would have liked to have torn off all this finery and laid aside her heavy wreath, the little red flowers from her garden suited her much better; but she dared not do it. "Farewell!" she said and mounted, light and bright as a bubble, up through the water.

The sun had just gone down as she lifted her head above the sea, but all the clouds were still shining like roses and gold, and in the midst of the pale pink sky sparkled the evening star, so clear and lovely. The air was mild and fresh and the sea as still as a mirror. A black ship with three masts lay upon it, only a single sail was up, for not a breath of wind was stirring and the sailors were sprawling all about on the masts and rigging. Music and singing were going on, and as the evening grew darker hundreds of variegated lamps were lit; it looked as if the flags of all nations were waving in the air. The little mermaid swam right up to the cabin window and every time the water raised her in the air she could look in through the mirror-bright panes where so many stylishly-dressed people were standing. The handsomest of them all was certainly the young Prince with the large black eyes (he could not have been more than sixteen years old); it was his birthday and that was why they were making all this display. The sailors were dancing upon the deck, and when the young Prince stepped out, more than a hundred rockets rose into the air; they shone as bright as day, so that the little mermaid was quite frightened and ducked down beneath the water, but she soon stuck up her head again and then it was as if all the stars of heaven were falling down to her. Never had she seen such fire-works. Large suns whizzed round and round, splendid fiery fish swung about in the blue air, and everything was reflected back from the clear, calm sea. On the ship itself it was so light that you could see every little rope and spar, to say nothing of the men. But oh! how lovely the young Prince was, and how he pressed people's hands and laughed and smiled while the music sounded through the lovely night.

It grew late, but the little mermaid could not tear her eyes away from the ship and the handsome Prince. The variegated lights were put out. No more rockets rose into the air, no more salvos were fired, but deep down in the sea there was a murmuring and a roaring. She meanwhile sat upon the water and rocked up and down with it so that she could look into the cabin. But the ship now took a swifter course, one sail spread out after the other, the roll of the billows grew stronger, it lightened far away. Oh! there will be a frightful storm, that is why the sailors are now reefing the sails. The huge ship rocked to and fro as it flew along the wild ocean; the water rose like big black mountains, which would roll right over the masts, but the ship ducked like a swan down among the lofty billows and let herself be lifted up again on the towering water. The little mermaid thought it rich sport, but not so the sailors; the ship strained and cracked, the thick planks bent at the violent shock of the sea, the mast snapped right in the middle like a reed, and the ship heeled over on her side while the water rushed into the cabin. And now the little mermaid saw that they were in danger, she herself had to beware of the spars and wreckage of the ship which drove along upon the water. For a moment it was so pitch dark that she could see nothing at all, but when it lightened it was bright enough for her to see everything on the ship. Everybody there was tumbling about anyhow. She looked out for the young Prince especially and she saw him, when the ship went to pieces, sink down into the deep sea. She immediately became quite delighted, for now he would come down to her, but then it occurred to her that men cannot live in the water and that it was only as a corpse that he could reach her father's palace. Die he must not, oh no; and so she swam among the spars and planks which were drifting about on the sea, quite forgetting that they might have crushed her, ducked down beneath the water and rose aloft again on the billows; and so, at last, she came up to the young Prince, who could scarcely swim a bit more in the raging sea. His arms and legs began to fail him, his beautiful eyes closed, he must have died if the little mermaid had not come up. She held his head above the water and let the billows drive him and her wherever they listed.

When morning dawned the storm had passed away, but not a fragment of the ship was to be seen. The sun rose so red and shining above the water, it seemed as if the Prince's cheeks regained the hue of life, but his eyes remained closed. The mermaid kissed his lofty handsome brow and stroked back his wet locks. He looked just like the marble statue down in her little garden; she kissed him again and wished that he might live.

And now she saw in front of her the mainland, the lofty blue mountains, on the summits of which the snow shone as if it were swans that lay there; down on the shore were lovely green woods and right in front lay a church or cloister, she did not exactly know what it was, but it was a building of some sort. Lemon and oranges trees grew in the garden there, and in front of the gate stood tall palm-trees. The sea formed a little creek here, it was quite calm but very deep, right up to the very cliff where the sea had washed up the fine white sand; thither she swam with the handsome Prince and laid him on the sand, taking particular care that his head should lie high in the warm sunshine.

And now the bells in the large white building fell a-ringing, and a number of young girls came walking through the garden. Then the little mermaid swam further out behind some lofty rocks which towered up out of the water, laid sea foam on her hair and breast that no one might see her face, and watched to see who would come to the poor Prince.

It was not very long before a young girl came by that way; she appeared quite frightened when she saw him, but only for a moment. Then she went and brought a lot of people, and the mermaid saw that the Prince came to life again, and smiled on all around him, but he did not send a smile to her, for of course he did not know that she had saved him. She felt so grieved that when he was carried away into the large building she ducked down under the water full of sorrow and sought her father's palace.

She had always been silent and pensive, but now she became still more so. Her sisters asked her what she had seen up there the first time, but she told them nothing. Many a morning and many an evening she ascended to the spot where she had seen the Prince. She saw how the fruits of the garden ripened and were plucked, she saw how the snow melted upon the lofty mountains, but the Prince she did not see, and therefore she returned home more and more sorrowful every time. Her only consolation was to sit in the little garden and wind her arms round the pretty marble statue which was so like the Prince. But she did not attend to her flowers at all; they grew as if in a wilderness right over the paths and wreathed their long stalks and leaves among the branches of the trees till it was quite gloomy there. At last she could endure it no longer, but told it to one of her sisters, and so all the others immediately got to know about it; but no one else knew it save they and a couple of other mermaids, who told it to nobody but their closest friends. One of these knew who the Prince was and all about him; she had also seen the merry-making on board the ship and knew whence he was and where his kingdom lay.

"Come, little sister!" said the other Princesses, and with their arms around each other's shoulders, they rose in a long row above the water in the place where they knew the Prince's palace lay. This palace was built of a light yellow glistening sort of stone with large marble staircases, one of which went straight down into the sea. Gorgeous gilded cupolas rose above the roof, and between the columns, which went round about the whole building, stood marble statues which looked like living beings. Through the clear glass in the lofty windows you looked into magnificent rooms hung with costly silk curtains and tapestries, and all the walls were adorned with large pictures, so that it was quite a pleasure to look at them. In the midst of the largest room plashed a large fountain, the water-jets rose high into the air towards the glass cupola, through which the sun shone upon the water and upon the beautiful plants which grew in the huge basin.

So now she knew where he dwelt, and many an evening and night she rose upon the water there. She swam much nearer to the land than any of the others had ventured to do; nay, she went right up the narrow canal, beneath the magnificent marble balcony which cast a long shadow across the water. Here she used to sit and look at the young Prince, who fancied he was quite alone in the bright moonshine.

Many an evening she saw him sail with music in his splendid boat where the banners waved; she peeped forth from the green rushes, and when the wind played with her long silvery white veil and people saw it, they fancied it was a swan lifting its wings.

Many a night when the fishermen were fishing by torch-light on the sea, she heard them speaking so well of the young Prince, and she was glad that she had saved his life when he was drifting half dead upon the billows, and she thought how fast his head had rested on her breast, and how ardently she then had kissed him; he knew nothing at all about it, he could not even dream about her.

And so she got to love mankind more and more, more and more she desired to be among them. Their world seemed to her far grander than her own; why, they could fly across the sea in ships, ascend the lofty mountains high above the clouds, and the lands they called their own extended with their woods and meadows farther than her eye could reach. There was so much she would have liked to know, but her sisters would not answer everything she asked, and therefore she asked her old grandmother, for she knew all about the upper world, which she very correctly called the lands above the sea.

"When men don't drown," asked the little mermaid, "can they live for ever? Don't they die as we do down in the sea here?"

"Yes," said the old grandmother, "they also must die; and indeed their life is even shorter than ours. We can last for three hundred years, but when at last we do cease to be, we become mere foam upon the water, we have not even a grave down here among our dear ones. We have no immortal soul; we never live again; we are like the green rushes, if once they be cut down, they cannot grow green again. Men, on the other hand, have souls which always live—live when the body has become earth; they rise up through the clear air, right up to the shining stars; just as we duck up out of the sea and see the lands of men, so they mount up to beautiful unknown places of which we shall never catch a glimpse."

"Why have not we got an immortal soul?" said the little mermaid sorrowfully. "I would give all the hundreds of years I have to live to be a human being but for a single day so that I might have my portion in the world above the sky!"

"You must not bother your head about that!" said the old grandmother, "we have a much better and happier lot than mankind up there."

"So I am to die and scud away like foam upon the sea, hear no more the music of the billows, see no more the pretty flowers and the red sun. Can I then do nothing at all to win an immortal soul?"

"No!" said the old grandmother, "only, if a man got to love thee so dearly that thou wert more to him than father or mother, if he clave to thee with all his heart and soul, and let the priest lay his right hand in thine and vow fidelity to thee here and in all eternity, then his soul would flow over into thy body and thou wouldst have thy portion of human bliss. He would have given thee a soul, and yet have kept his own. But that can never be! The very thing that is so pretty in the sea here, thy fish's tail, is looked upon as hideous upon earth; they don't know any better. Up there one must have a couple of clumsy columns called feet to be thought handsome!"

Then the little mermaid sighed and looked sorrowfully at her fish's tail.

"Let us be content with our lot," said the old grandmother, "we'll hop and skip about to our hearts' content in the three hundred years we have to live in. Upon my word we have a nice long time of it, and after it is all over one can rest all the more contentedly in one's grave. We'll have a court ball this very evening!"

And indeed it was a gorgeous sight such as one never sees on earth. The walls and ceiling of the vast dancing-hall were of glass, thick but clear. Many hundreds of colossal shells, rosy red and grass-green, stood in rows on each side full of a blue blazing fire which lit up the whole saloon and shone right through the walls so that the sea beyond them was quite illuminated. You could see all the countless fishes, both small and great, swimming towards the glass walls; the shells of some of them shone purple red, the shells of others seemed like gold and silver. In the midst of the saloon flowed a broad running stream, and on this danced the mermen and the mermaids to their own pretty songs. Such lovely voices are unknown on earth. The little mermaid sang sweetest of them all and they clapped her loudly, and for a moment her heart was glad, for she knew that she had the loveliest voice of all creatures on the earth or in the sea. But very soon she began once more to think of the world above her; she could not forget the handsome Prince and her sorrow at not possessing, like him, an immortal soul. So she stole quietly out of her father's palace, and while everything there was mirth and melody, she sat full of sorrow in her little garden. Then she heard the bugle-horn ringing down through the water and she thought, "Now I know *he* is sailing up there, *he* whom I love more than father or mother, he to whom the thoughts of my heart cleave and in whose hands I would willingly lay my life's happiness. Everything will I venture to win him and an immortal soul! While my sisters are dancing within my father's palace, I will go to the sea-witch; I have always been frightened of her, but she, perchance, may help and counsel me."

So the little mermaid went out of her own sea right towards the raging whirlpool behind which the witch dwelt. She had never gone that way before. No flowers, no sea-grasses grew there, only the bare grey sandy bottom stretched out towards the whirlpools where the water, like a rushing mill-wheel, whirled round and round, tearing everything it caught hold of away with it into the deep; she had to go right through the midst of these buffeting whirlpools to get to the sea-witch's domain, and here, for a long stretch, there was no other way than across hot bubbling mire which the witch called her turf moss. Right behind lay her house in the midst of a strange wood. All the trees and bushes were polypi, half animal, half vegetable, they

Little Mermaid and Sea-Witch.
Illustration by Dmitry Yakhovsky based off of original by Ivan Bilibin. © Bendideia Publishing.

looked like hundred-headed serpents growing out of the earth; all their branches were long slimy arms, with fingers like supple snakes, and joint by joint they were twisting and twirling from the roots to the outermost tips of their branches. Everything in the sea which they could catch hold of they wound themselves about and never let go of it again. The little Princess was quite terrified and remained standing outside there; her heart thumped for fear, she was very near turning back again, but then she thought of the Prince and of the human soul, and her courage came back to her. She bound her long fluttering hair close to her head so that the polypi might not grip hold of her thereby, then she crossed both hands over her breast, and away she flew through the water as only fishes can fly, right between the hideous polypi which stretched out their long supple arms and fingers after her. She saw that every one of them still had something which it had gripped, hundreds of little fingers held it like iron bands. Men who had perished in the sea and sunk down thither peeped forth from the arms of the polypi in the shape of white skeletons. Ships' rudders and coffers too they held fast; there were also the skeletons of land animals and even a little mermaid whom they had caught and tortured to death, and *that* was to her the most terrible sight of all.

And now she came to a large slimy open space in the wood where big fat water-snakes were wallowing and airing their ugly whitey-yellow bellies. In the midst of the empty space a house had been raised from the white bones of shipwrecked men; here sat the sea-witch and let a toad eat out of her mouth just as men let little canary-birds pick sugar. She called the hideous fat water-snakes her chicks and let them roll about over her large spongy bosom.

"I know very well what you want!" said the sea-witch; "you're a fool for your pains! Nevertheless you shall have your own way, for it will get you into trouble, my pretty Princess. You want to get rid of your fish's tail, eh? and have a couple of stumps to walk about on as men have, so that the young Prince may fall in love with you, and you may get him and an immortal soul into the bargain!" And with that, the witch laughed so loudly and hideously that the toad and the snakes fell down upon the ground and began wallowing there. "You have come at the very nick of time," said the witch; "if you had put it off till to-morrow, at sunrise, I should not have been able to help you for another year. I'll brew you a potion, but you must swim to land, sit down on the shore, and drink it off before sunrise, and then your tail will split and shrivel up into what men call nice legs; but it will hurt, it will be like a sharp sword piercing through you. All who see you will say that you are the loveliest child of man they ever saw. You will keep your lightsome gait, no dancing girl will be able to float along like you; but every stride you take will be to you like treading on some sharp knife till the blood flows. If you'd like to suffer all this, I'll help you."

"I will," said the little mermaid with a trembling voice; she thought of the Prince and of winning an immortal soul.

"But remember this," said the witch, "when once you have got a human shape you can never become a mermaid again! You can never again descend down through the water to your sisters and to your father's palace, and if you do not win the Prince's love so that, for your sake, he forgets father and mother and cleaves to you with all his soul, and lets the priest lay your hands together and make you man and wife, you will get no immortal soul at all! The very first morning after he has married another your heart will break and you will become foam upon the water!"

"Be it so!" said the little mermaid, but she was as pale as death.

"But you must pay me too," said the Witch, "and it will not be a small thing either that I demand. You have the loveliest voice of all things down below here at the bottom of the sea, you fancy you will enchant him with that, I know; not a bit of it, you must give that voice to me. I mean to have your best possession in return for my precious potion, for have I not to give you of my own blood in it, so that the potion may be as sharp as a two-edged sword?"

"But if you take my voice, what will be left for me?" asked the little mermaid.

"Your lovely shape," said the witch, "your lightsome gait and your speaking eye; you can fool a man's heart with them, I suppose? Well! have you lost heart, eh? Put out your little tongue and I'll cut it off in payment, and you shall have the precious potion!"

"Be it so, then!" said the little mermaid, and the witch put her kettle on to brew the magic potion. "Cleanliness is a good thing," said she, and she scoured out the cauldron with the snakes, which she tied into a knot; then she gashed herself in the breast and let her black blood drip down into the cauldron. The steam that rose from it took the strangest shapes, so that one could not but feel anguish and terror. Every moment the witch put something fresh into the cauldron, and when it was well on the boil it sounded like a crying crocodile. At last the drink was ready, it looked like the clearest water!

"There you are!" said the witch, and cut out the tongue of the little mermaid who was now quite dumb; she could neither sing nor talk.

"If the polypi grip at you when you go back through the wood," said the witch, "just you throw a single drop of this potion upon them, and their arms and fingers will burst into a thousand bits!" But the little mermaid had no need to do this, the polypi shrank back from her in terror when they saw the shining potion which sparkled in her hand like a dazzling star. So very soon she got through the wood, the morass and the raging whirlpool. She could see her father's palace; the lights in the long dancing-hall had been put out; all within there were doubtless sleeping; but she dared not venture thither to visit them now that she was dumb, and wanted to go away from them for ever. Yet her heart felt as if it must burst asunder for sorrow. She crept down into the garden, plucked a flower from each of her sister's flower-beds, threw a thousand kisses towards the palace, and ascended again through the dark blue sea. The sun had not yet risen when she beheld the Prince's palace, and mounted the splendid marble staircase. The moon was shining bright and beautiful. The little mermaid drank the sharp burning potion, and it was as though a two-edged sword pierced right through her body; she moaned with the agony and lay there as one dead.

When the sun shone over the sea she woke up and felt a sharp pang, but right in front of her stood the handsome young Prince. He fixed his coal-black eyes upon her, so that she cast her own eyes down and saw that her fish tail had gone, and that she had the prettiest little white legs, but she was quite naked, so she wrapped herself in her large long locks. The Prince asked who she was and how she came thither; and she looked at him with her dark blue eyes so mildly, and yet so sadly, for speak she could not. Then he took her by the hand and led her into his palace. Every step she took was, as the witch said it would be beforehand, as if she were treading on pointed awls or sharp knives, but she willingly bore it; holding the Prince's hand, she mounted the staircase as light as a bubble, and he and every one else were amazed at her graceful, lightsome gait. She was arrayed in the most costly garments, all silk and muslin, none in the whole palace was so lovely as she; but she was dumb, she could neither sing nor speak. Lovely slave-girls, clad in silk and gold, came forth and sang to the Prince and his royal parents; one of them sang more sweetly than all the rest, and the Prince clapped his hands and smiled at her. Then the little mermaid was troubled, she knew that she herself had sung far more sweetly, and she thought: "Oh, would that he might know that for the sake of being near him, I have given away my voice for ever and ever!"

And now the slave-girls danced the graceful, light-some dance to the loveliest music, and then the little mermaid raised on high her lovely white arms, raised herself on the tips of her toes, and danced and swept across the floor as none ever danced before; at every movement her loveliness became more and more visible and her eyes spoke more deeply to the heart than ever the songs of the slave-girl. They were all enchanted with her, especially the Prince, who called her his little foundling, and she danced more and more, though every time her feet touched the ground it was as if she trod upon a sharp knife. The Prince said she should always be with him, and she got leave to sit outside his door on a velvet cushion.

He had a male costume made for her that she might ride out with him. They rode through the fragrant woods where the green branches smote her on the shoulders and the little birds sang behind the fresh leaves. She clambered with the Prince right up the high mountains, and although her tender feet bled, so that the others could see it, she only laughed at it and followed him till they saw the clouds sailing below them like flocks of birds departing to a foreign land.

At night, in the Prince's palace, while others slept, she went out upon the broad marble staircase, and it cooled her burning feet to stand in the cold sea-water, and then she thought of them in the depths below.

One night her sisters came up arm in arm, they sang so sorrowfully as they swam in the water, and she nodded to them, and they recognised her, and told her how miserable she had made them all. After that, they visited her every night, and one night she saw, a long way out, her old grandmother who had not been above the sea for many years, and the Sea-King with his crown upon his head; they stretched out their hands towards her, but dared not come so close to land as her sisters.

She became dearer to the Prince every day. He loved her as one might love a dear, good child; but to make her his queen never entered his mind, and his wife she must be, or she would never have an immortal soul, but would become foam upon the sea upon his bridal morn.

"Do you love me most of all?" the eyes of the little mermaid seemed to say when he took her in his arms and kissed her fair brow.

"Yes, you are dearest of all to me," said the Prince, "for you have the best heart of them all, you are most devoted to me, and you are just like a young girl I once saw but certainly shall never see again. I was on a ship which was wrecked, the billows drifted me ashore near a holy temple, where many young girls were the ministrants. The youngest, who found me on the sea-shore and saved my life, I only saw twice; she is the only girl I can love in this world, but you are like her, you almost expel her image from my soul; she belongs to that holy temple, and therefore my good fortune has sent me you instead, we will never part!"

"Alas! he knows not that 'twas I who saved his life!" thought the little mermaid. "I bore him right over the sea to the wood where the temple stands, I sat behind the foam and looked to see if any one would come; I saw the pretty girl whom he loves better than me!" And the mermaid drew a deep sigh, weep she could not. "He says the girl belongs to that holy temple, she will never come forth into the world, they will never meet again. I am with him, I see him every day, I will cherish him, love him, sacrifice my life for him!"

But now the Prince was to be married and take the lovely daughter of the neighbouring king to wife, and that was why he now set about equipping a splendid ship. The Prince is travelling to see the land of the neighbouring king, that is what they said; but it was to see the neighbouring king's daughter that he went forth with such a grand retinue. But the little mermaid shook her head and laughed; she knew the Prince's thoughts much better than all the others. "I must travel," he had said to her, "I must see the fair Princess, my parents require it of me; but they shall not compel me to bring her home as my bride. I cannot love her, she is not like the lovely girl in the temple whom you are like. Should I ever choose me a bride, it would rather be you, my dumb foundling with the speaking eyes!" And he kissed her red mouth, played with her long hair, and laid his head close to her heart till her heart dreamt of human bliss and an immortal soul.

"Surely you are not frightened at the sea, my dumb child!" said he, as they stood on the gorgeous ship which was to carry him to the land of the neighbouring king; and he told her about storm and calm, about the strange fishes of the deep, and what the divers had seen down there, and she smiled at his telling, for she knew better than any one else all about the bottom of the sea.

In the moonlight nights when all were asleep save the man at the helm, she sat at the side of the ship and looked down through the clear water and seemed to see her father's palace, and at the very top of it stood the old grandmother with the silver crown upon her head, and stared up at the ship's keel through the contrary currents. Then her sisters came up to the surface of the water, they gazed sadly at her and wrung their white hands. She beckoned to them, smiled, and would have told them that everything was going on well and happily, but the cabin-boy drew near at that moment and her sisters ducked down again, so that she half fancied that the white things she had seen were the foam upon the sea.

The next morning the ship sailed into the haven of the neighbouring king's splendid capital. All the church bells were ringing, they blew blasts with the bassoons from the tops of the high towers, while the soldiers stood drawn up with waving banners and flashing bayonets. Every day had its own special feast. Balls and assemblies followed each other in rapid succession, but the Princess was not yet there, she had been brought up in a holy temple far away, they said, where she had learnt all royal virtues. At last she arrived.

Full of eagerness, the little mermaid stood there to see her loveliness; and recognise it she must, a more beauteous shape she had never seen. Her skin was so transparently fine, and from behind the long dark eyelashes smiled a pair of dark blue, faithful eyes.

" 'Tis thou!" said the Prince, "thou who hast saved me when I lay like a corpse on the sea-shore!" and he embraced his blushing bride. "Oh! I am so happy, I don't know what to do!" said he to the little mermaid. "The very best I dared to hope has come to pass. You too will rejoice at my good fortune, for you love me more than them all!" And the little mermaid kissed his hand, and she felt that her heart was like to break. Yes, his bridal-morn would be the death of her, and change her into sea-foam.

All the bells were ringing, and the heralds rode about the streets to proclaim the espousals.

Fragrant oil in precious silver lamps burned upon every altar. The priests swung their censors, and the bride and bridegroom gave each other their hands and received the bishop's benediction. The little mermaid stood there in cloth of gold and held the bride's train, but her ears did not hear the festal music, her eyes did not see the sacred ceremony, she thought of her night of death, she thought of all she had lost in this world.

The same evening the bride and bridegroom went on board the ship, the cannons were fired, all the flags waved, and in the midst of the ship a royal tent was raised of cloth of gold and purple and precious furs; there the bridal pair were to sleep in the still, cool night.

The sails swelled out in the breeze, and the ship glided, lightly rocking, away over the bright ocean. When it grew dark, coloured lamps were lit, and the mariners danced merry dances on the deck. The little mermaid could not help thinking of the first time she had ducked up above the sea, and seen the self-same gaiety and splendour, and she whirled round and round in the dance, skimming along as the swallow skims when it is pursued, and they all applauded her enthusiastically, never before had she danced so splendidly. There was a piercing as of sharp knives in her feet, but she felt it not; the anguish of her heart was far more piercing. She knew it was the last evening she was to see *him* for whom she had forsaken house and home, surrendered her lovely voice, and suffered endless tortures day by day, without his having any idea of it all. It was the last night she was to breathe the same air as he, and look upon the deep sea and the star-lit sky;

an eternal night without a thought, without a dream, awaited her who had no soul and could not win one. And all was joy and jollity on board the ship till long past midnight, and she laughed and danced with the thought of death in her heart. The Prince kissed his lovely bride, and she toyed with his black hair, and arm in arm they went to rest in the gorgeous tent.

It grew dark and still on board; only the steersman was there, standing at the helm. The little mermaid laid her white arms on the railing and looked towards the cast for the rosy dawn, the first sunbeam, she knew it well, must kill her. Then she saw her sisters rise up from the sea, they were as pale as she was; their long fair hair fluttered no longer in the breeze, it was all cut off.

"We have given it to the witch that she might bring help so that you may not die to-night! She has given us a knife, here it is, look how sharp it is! Before the sun rises you must thrust it into the Prince's heart, and then, when his warm blood sprinkles your feet, they will grow together into a fish's tail, and you will become a mermaid again, and may sink down through the water to us, and live out your three hundred years before you become dead, salt sea-foam. But hasten! Either you or he must die before sun-rise. Our old grandmother has sorrowed so that her hair has fallen off, just as ours has fallen off beneath the witch's shears. Kill the Prince and come back to us! Hasten! Don't you see the red strip in the sky yonder? A few minutes more and the sun will rise and you must die." And they heaved a wondrously deep sigh and sank beneath the billows.

The little mermaid drew aside the purple curtains from the tent door, and she saw the beauteous bride sleeping with her head on the Prince's breast, and she bent down, kissed him on his fair brow, looked at the sky where the red dawn shone brighter and brighter, looked at the sharp knife, and again fixed her eyes on the Prince, who, in his dreams, named his wife by her name, she alone was in his thoughts. And the knife quivered in the mermaid's hand—but then she cast it out far into the billows, they shone red where it fell, it looked as if drops of blood were there bubbling up out of the water. Once again she looked with half-breaking eyes at the Prince, plunged from the ship into the sea, and felt her whole body dissolving into foam.

And now the sun rose out of the sea, his rays fell with so gentle a warmth upon the death-cold sea foam, and the little mermaid did not feel death; she saw the bright sun, and right above her hundreds of beauteous, transparent shapes were hovering. Through them she could see the white sails of the ship and the red clouds of the sky, their voice was all melody, but so ethereal that no human ear could hear it, just as no human eye could see them; they had no wings, but their very lightness wafted them up and down in the air. The little mermaid saw that she had a body like them, it rose higher and higher out of the foam. "To whom have I come?" said she, and her voice sounded like the voices of the other beings, so ethereal that no earthly music can render it.

"To the daughters of the air," answered the others; "the mermaid has no immortal soul and can never have one unless she wins a man's love, her eternal existence depends upon a Power beyond her. The daughters of the air, likewise, have no immortal soul, but they can make themselves one by good deeds. We fly to the hot countries, where the sultry, pestilential air slays the children of men; there we waft coolness. We spread the fragrance of flowers through the air and send refreshment and healing. When for three hundred years we have striven to do all the good we can, we get an immortal soul and have a share in the eternal destinies of mankind. Thou, poor little mermaid, thou also hast striven after good with thy whole heart; like us, thou hast suffered and endured, and raised thyself into the sphere of the spirits of the air; now, therefore, thou canst also win for thyself an immortal soul after three hundred years of good deeds."

And the little mermaid raised her bright arms towards God's sun, and for the first time she felt tears in her eyes. There was life and bustle on board the ship again, she saw the Prince with his fair bride looking for her, and they gazed sadly down upon the bubbling foam, as if they knew she had plunged into the billows. Invisible as she was, she kissed the bride's brow, smiled upon the Prince, and ascended with the other children of the air up to the rosy red clouds which were sailing along in the sky. "For three hundred years we shall float and float till we float right into God's kingdom."

"Yea, and we may also get there still sooner," whispered one of them. "Invisibly we sweep into the houses of men, where there are children, and every day we find there a good child who gladdens his parents' hearts, and deserves their love, God shortens our time of trial. The child does not know when we fly through the room, but when we can smile with joy over it, a whole year is taken from off the three hundred; but whenever we see a bad, naughty child, we must, perforce, weep tears of sorrow, and every tear adds a day to our time of trial!" [275]

Special Offer

Would you like to learn more about folklore and mythology? Sign up for our periodic newsletter and also get updates about book releases and promotions. As a thank you, follow this link to receive a FREE supplement to our "Spirits and Creatures" book series. From time to time, we'll change this free gift. The first installment is about a malicious water spirit: Vodyanoy or Vodnik. Discover where he comes from, how to protect yourself from him, how to make him "somewhat" happy, and more. Written in a conversational way, rather than dull academia, it will engage you, the reader. Illustrations and stories help provide you with an overall picture of this spirit.

Link to download: https://dl.bookfunnel.com/1rq3ku0fa9

About the Author

Ronesa Aveela is "the creative power of two." Two authors that is. The main force behind the work, the creative genius, was born in Bulgaria and moved to the US in the 1990s. She grew up with stories of wild Samodivi, Kikimora, the dragons Zmey and Lamia, Baba Yaga, and much more. She's a freelance artist and writer. She likes writing mystery romance inspired by legends and tales. In her free time, she paints. Her artistic interests include the female figure, Greek and Thracian mythology, folklore tales, and the natural world interpreted through her eyes. She is married and has two children.

Her writing partner was born and raised in the New England area. She has a background in writing and editing, as well as having a love of all things from different cultures. She's learned so much about Bulgarian culture, folklore, and rituals, and writes to share that knowledge with others.

Connect with Us!

Social Media: Website/Blog | Newsletter | Facebook | Twitter | Instagram | Pinterest | Goodreads | Bookbub | LinkedIn | YouTube |

Promo products: Redbubble

Ronesa's Books

Fiction
Mystical Emona: Soul's Journey
The Unborn Hero of Dragon Village
Zmeykovo (Bulgarian version of *The Unborn Hero of Dragon Village*)
La profezia del Villaggio del Drago (Italian version of *The Unborn Hero of Dragon Village*)

Nonfiction
Light Love Rituals: Bulgarian Myths, Legends, and Folklore
A Study of Household Spirits of Eastern Europe
A Study of Rusalki – Slavic Mermaids of Eastern Europe

Children's short stories, activity & coloring books
Baba Treasure Chest series
The Christmas Thief
The Miracle Stork
Born From the Ashes
Mermaid's Gift
Baba Treasure Chest: A Collection of Modern Bulgarian Tales (contains all four short stories)

Coloring Books
Mermaids Around the World
More Mermaids Around the World
Little Zoi

Cookbook
Mediterranean & Bulgarian Cuisine: 12 Easy Traditional Favorites

Reviews

PLEASE HELP AUTHORS BY LEAVING A REVIEW!

We hope you've enjoyed this book, and that its illustrations and words have inspired you. As an author with a small publisher, we would appreciate your gift of a review. Good or bad, we'd love to hear your honest thoughts.

Artist Profiles

Nelinda is the artistic side of Ronesa. Not only does she have thousands of ideas for stories about her Bulgarian heritage, but she is a talented artist. You can see more of her work at www.nelinda.com.

Andy Paciorek is a graphic artist and writer, drawn mainly to the worlds of myth, folklore, symbolism, decadence, curiosa, anomaly, dark romanticism and otherworldly experience. His published books include *Black Earth: A Field Guide to the Slavic Otherworld, Strange Lands: A Field Guide to the Celtic Otherworld* and *The Human Chimaera: Slideshow Prodigies & Other Exceptional People*. He is also the creator of the Folk Horror Revival multimedia project.

Books available at: www.blurb.co.uk/user/andypaciorek
Email: andypaciorek@yahoo.co.uk

Dmitry Yakhovsky has received education at the Academy of Art in Minsk, Belarus. He mostly works for authors and publishers all over the world to illustrate books in both digital and traditional ways but is also regularly commissioned for smaller projects. Dmitry writes and illustrates his own books. Examples of this are the graphic novel series "The Shadow of the Cross" and two coloring books for adults which were all published by the British publisher MadeGlobal and two historical graphic novels set in medieval Netherlands published by the Dutch publisher Pear Productions. He is a winner of a big comic contest in the Netherlands. Dmitry is besides this specialized in portrait and landscape paintings which are usually done in oil paint or watercolor and regularly exhibited.

Facebook: https://www.facebook.com/entaroart/
DeviantArt: https://www.deviantart.com/entar0178

Books by Andy Paciorek

Andy Paciorek is a graphic artist and writer, drawn mainly to the worlds of myth, folklore, symbolism, decadence, curiosa, anomaly, dark romanticism and otherworldly experience.

His published books include Black Earth: A Field Guide to the Slavic Otherworld, Strange Lands: A Field Guide to the Celtic Otherworld and The Human Chimaera: Sideshow Prodigies & Other Exceptional People.

He is also the creator of the Folk Horror Revival multimedia project

www.blurb.co.uk/user/andypaciorek

email: andypaciorek@yahoo.co.uk

Bibliography

Abrahamson, Valerie (2002). "The Orante and the Goddess in the Roman Catacombs." *Journal of Higher Criticism* 9, no 1 (Spring):1-15. http://depts.drew.edu/jhc/AbrahamsenOrante.pdf.

Alice, "Slavic Mythology I: Water Spirits, Demons, and Creatures," June 12, 2011. http://nokkandmyling.blogspot.com/2011/06/slavic-mythology-i-water-spirits-and.html.

Andersen, Hans Christian. *The Little Mermaid and Other Stories*, translated by Nisbet Bain. London: Lawrence and Bullen, 1893.

Anne, Martha, and Dorothy Myers Imel. *Goddesses in World Mythology*. Santa Barbara, California: ABC-CLIO, 1993.

Anonymous. "Naturalist and Sportsman Gossip." *The Speaker* 13 (1896):452-454. [London]: [Mather & Crowther], [1890-].

Antonin-dvorak.cz. "Rusalka." http://www.antonin-dvorak.cz/en/rusalka.

Aveela, Ronesa. *Light Love Rituals: Bulgarian Myths, Legends, and Folklore*. U.S.: Bendideia Publishing, 2015.

Aveela, Ronesa. *The Wanderer*. U.S.: Bendideia Publishing, forthcoming.

Barber, Elizabeth Wayland. T*he Dancing Goddesses: Folklore, Archaeology, and the Origins of European Dance*. New York: W. W. Norton & Company, 2013.

Bassett, Fletcher S. *Sea Phantoms: or, Legends and Superstitions of the Sea and of Sailors in All Lands and at All Times*. Chicago: Morrill, Higgins & Co., 1892.

Beard, Valeriu DG. "Hora românilor – ceea ce nu știai…" ("Romanian's time - what you didn't know…"). June 4, 2018. https://www.vocativ-plus.com/hora-romanilor-ceea-ce-nu-stiai/.

Bestiary.us. "Русалки" ("Rusalki"). https://www.bestiary.us/rusalki.

Bezovska, Albena. "Green walnut tree growing." Translated by Milena Daynova. April 19, 2019. https://www.bnr.bg/en/post/100546558/green-walnut-growing.

Bezovska, Albena. "St. Spas or Ascension Day." Translated by Milena Daynova. May 29, 2014. https://www.bnr.bg/en/post/100413842/st-spas-or-ascension-day.

Boneva, Rada N. "Folklore Elements And Influences In Metal Music." Sofia, Bulgaria: National High School for Ancient Languages and Cultures "Constantine Cyril the Philosopher," April 2015. https://www.academia.edu/35129897/Folklore_Elements_And_Influences_In_Metal_Music_-_a_study_by_Rada_Boneva_Bulgaria_2015_.

Castro, Carlos Mario. "The Mermaid: Lake of the Dead - Ending Explained." February 10, 2019. https://sabanerox.com/2019/02/10/the-mermaid-lake-of-the-dead-ending-explained/.

Chelariu, Ana Radu. "The Most Prevalent Feminine Mythical Characters in Romanian Folklore." https://limbaromana.org/en/the-most-prevalent-feminine-mythical-characters-in-romanian-folklore/.

Cooke, Brett. "Constraining the Other in Kvapil and Dvorak's Rusalka." In *The Fantastic Other: An Interface of Perespectives*, edited by Brett Cooke, George E. Slusser, and Jaume Marti-Olivella, 121-42. Amsterdam: Editions Rodopi, 1998. https://www.academia.edu/843913/Constraining_the_Other_in_Kvapil_and_Dvor_%C3%A1ks_Rusalka.

Cox, Benjamin D., and Susan Ackerman. "Rachel's Tomb." *Journal of Biblical Literature* 128, no. 1 (2009):135-48. doi:10.2307/25610171.

Dargomyzhsky, Alexander Sergeyevich. "Русалка" ("Rusalka"). http://home.tiscali.cz:8080/ist987/libreta/rusalka.html.

Dimova, Elitsa. "Обредът 'Русалии' лекува целия свят чрез мълчаната вода" (" 'Rusalii' ritual heals the whole world through silent water"). January 7, 2019. http://www.elitsa-dimova-rozeta.com/post/obred-t-rusalii-lekuva-celiya-svyat-chrez-m-lchanata-voda.

Dixon-Kennedy, Mike. *Encyclopedia of Russian & Slavic Myth and Legend*. Oxford: ABC CLIO, 1998.

Dobrovolsky, V.N. "Русалки: Глава из книги Добровольского 'Нечистая сила в народных верованиях' ("Rusalki: Chapter from Dobrovolsky's book Unclean power in popular beliefs"). https://www.bestiary.us/rusalki-v-knige-dobrovolskogo-nechistaja-sila-v-narodnyh-verovanijah.

Dynda, Jiří. "Rusalki: Anthropology of time, death, and sexuality in Slavic folklore." *Studia Mythologica Slavica* 20, no. 1 (2017):83-109. https://www.academia.edu/34620531/Rusalki_Anthropology_of_time_death_and_sexuality_in_Slavic_folklore.

Emerson, Caryl. "To What End Rusalka? Pushkin's Folk Tragedy and Dargomyzhskii's Opera." *Slavonic and East European Review* 97 no. 1 (2019):169-200.

Firică, Camelia. "The Romanian Căluş: Symbol of National Identity." *Journal of Ethnology and Folkloristics* 4, no. 2 (2010):3-18. https://www.jef.ee/index.php/journal/article/viewFile/52/pdf_50.

Georgieva, Ivanichka. *Bulgarian Mythology*. Sofia: Svyat Publishers, 1985.

Gippius, Zinaida. *Sacred Blood in Eight Twentieth-Century Russian Plays*. Langen, Timothy and Justin Weir, eds. Evanston, Illinois: Northwestern University Press, 2000.

Green, Garry, compiled by. "Slavic Pagan World." http://www.rodnovery.ru/attachments/article/526/slavic-pagan-world.pdf.

Gogol, Nikolaï Vasil'evich. "A May Night," 175-186. In *The Mantle, and Other Stories*, by Nicholas Gogol, translated by Claud Field. New York: Frederick A. Stokes, [1916?].

Goscilo, Helena. "Watery Maidens: Rusalki as Sirens and Slippery Signs," 50-70. https://www.academia.edu/5879011/Rusalki_Sirens_Watery_Maidens..._Helena_Goscilo.

Gura, Aleksandr V. "Coitus in the Symbolic Language of Slavic Culture." *Folklore* 30, 135-154. https://www.folklore.ee/folklore/vol30/gura.pdf.

Hehn, Victor. *The Wanderings of Plants and Animals from their First Home*. London: S. Sonnenschein and Co., 1885.

Hetherington, Philippa. "Mythos and Eros in Fin de Siecle Russia: Zinaida Gippius' Sexual Revolution." A thesis submitted in partial fulfilment of the requirements of the degree of ba (hons) in history. University of Sydney. October 2006. http://hdl.handle.net/2123/1548.

Hindus, Maurice Gerschon. *Broken Earth*. New York: International Publishers, 1926.

Hubbs, Joanna. *Mother Russia: The Feminine Myth in Russian Culture*. Bloomington and Indianapolis: Indiana University Press, 1988.

Igabi7. "«Русалка» Александр Петров, 1996 The Mermaid, Aleksandr Petrov." June 2, 2014. https://www.youtube.com/watch?v=Js6biCftfks.

Interreg. "eTourist." http://www.maritza.info/1.1_Annex_Database_sites_eng.pdf.

Ivanits, Linda J. *Russian Folk Belief*. Armonk, New York: M. E. Sharpe, Inc., 1989.

iVideos. "Русалка. Озеро мертвых — Трейлер (2018)" ("Rusalka. Lake of the Dead"). April 11, 2018. https://www.youtube.com/watch?v=bTJ9RdH6BWk.

Johnson, Kenneth. *Slavic Sorcery: Shamanic Journey of Initiation*. St. Paul, Minnesota: Llewellyn Publications, 1998.

Journeying to the Goddess. "The Rousalii." June 23, 2012. https://journeyingtothegoddess.wordpress.com/tag/rusalki/.

Kenealy, Edward Vaughan. *A New Pantomime*. London: Reeves and Turner, 1865.

Konstantinova, Daniela. "Ascension Day and Pentecost." June 13, 2013. https://www.bnr.bg/en/post/100201761/ascension-day-and-pentecost.

Konstantinova, Daniela, trans. "Rousalii and kaloushari: shamans and witch-doctors." June 18, 2019. https://www.bnr.bg/en/post/100202514/rousalii-and-kaloushari-shamans-and-witch-doctors.

Kropej, Monika. *Supernatural Beings from Slovenian Myth and Folktales*. Ljubljana: Založba ZRC/ZRC Publishing, 2012. https://www.academia.edu/7119416/Supernatural_Beings_from_Slovenian_Myth_and_Folktales.

Kubijovyč, Volodymyr, ed. *Ukraine, a Concise Encyclopedia Prepared by Shevchenko Scientific Society*, v. 1. Toronto: University of Toronto Press, 1963.

Larson, K. Maya. "Why Does the Rusalka Have to Die? The Call of the Other in Zinaida Gippius's *Sacred Blood*." *Amaltea. Revista de mitocrítica* 6 (2014):161-186. http://revistas.ucm.es/index.php/AMAL/article/viewFile/46520/43708.

Lermontov, Mikhail Yurevich. "The First Extract from Pechorin's Diary." In *A Hero of Our Time*, translated by J. H. Wisdom & Marr, 117-141. New York: A. A. Knopf, 1916.

Máchal, Jan. "Slavic." In *The Mythology of All the Races*, vol. 3, edited by Herbert Louis Gray with consulting editor George Foot Moore, 217-330. Boston: Marshall Jones Company, 1918.

MacDermott, Mercia. *Bulgarian Folk Customs*. London: Jessica Kingsley Publishers, 1998.

Maclaren, Archibald. "The Rusalka." In *The Fairy Family: A Series of Ballads & Metrical Tales Illustrating the Fairy Mythology of Europe*, 247-252. London: Longman, Brown, Green, Longmans, & Roberts, 1857.

Mickelson, Jane L. "The Rusalki." October 23, 2018. https://parabola.org/2018/10/23/the-rusalki-by-jane-l-mickelson/.

MIGHTYJLY. "Frederica Von Stade – Rusalka (Moon Song)." November 25, 2012. https://www.youtube.com/watch?v=UwVYFpY3VL4.

Miller, Dean. "Supernatural Beings and 'Song and Dance': Celtic and Slavic Exemplars." *Studia Celto-Slavica* 6, 101-112. http://uir.ulster.ac.uk/25529/1/00-214_StudiaCeltoSlavica6_c.pdf.

Milne, Louise. "Mermaids and Dreams in Visual Culture." *Cosmos* 22 (2006):65-104. https://www.academia.edu/236114/Milne_Louise_S_2008_Mermaids_and_Dreams_In_Visual_Culture_Cosmos_22_65-104.

Molina-Moreno, Francisco. "La Vida Amorosa de las *Rusalki* (The Love Life of the *Rusalki*)." *Liburna* (May 10, 2017):101-142. https://www.academia.edu/34097979/La_vida_amorosa_de_las_rusalki_The_Love_Life_of_the_Rusalki_en_Liburna_10_mayo_de_2017_pp._101-42.

Monaghan, Patricia. *Encyclopedia of Goddesses and Heroines*, vol. 2. ABC-CLIO: Santa Barbara, CA, 2010.

Murav, Harriet. "Engendering the Russian Body Politic." *Genders* 22: Postcommunism and the Body Politic, edited by Berry Ellen E., 32-56. New York; London: NYU Press, 1995. http://www.jstor.org/stable/j.ctt9qfv6g.5.

Mythcrafts Team. "Dancing for the Queen of the Fairies: Doamna Zînelor and the Călușari." May 23, 2019. https://mythcrafts.com/2019/05/23/dancing-for-the-queen-of-the-fairies-doamna-zinelor-and-the-calusari/.

Nilot. "Rusalka – The Slavic 'Mermaid.' " June 8, 2017. http://slavicchronicles.com/mythology/rusalka-the-slavic-mermaid/.

Ofmosquitos, Nikolai. "Русалка 1910 Mermaid Puskin's Rusalka by Vasili Goncharov." March 28, 2018. https://www.youtube.com/watch?v=ViMEzISLej4.

Operas Arias Composers. "Rusalka Libretto." https://www.opera-arias.com/dvorak/rusalka/libretto/english/. (In Czech: https://www.opera-arias.com/dvorak/rusalka/libretto/).

Osipovich, Tatiana. "God's Other Children: Gender Marginality and Intertextuality in Zinaida Gippius's Play 'Sacred Blood' (Святая кровь, 1901)." Lewis & Clark College, Portland, Oregon. https://www.academia.edu/7459102/God_s_Other_Children_Gender_Marginality_and_Intertextuality_in_Zinaida_Gippius_s_Play_Sacred_Blood_Святая_кровь_1901_.

Periclieva, Violeta. "Спасовден и Русалска неделя" ("Spasadden and Rusalka Sunday"). May 29, 2019. https://balgarskaetnografia.com/praznici-i-obichai/kalendarni-praznici-i-obichai/2019-05-29-06-21-10.html.

Petkova, Rossitsa. "The Sunday of Mermaids (Rusalska Nedelya)." June 1, 2012. https://www.bnr.bg/en/post/100155961/the-sunday-of-mermaids-rusalska-nedelya.

Pushkin, Alexander. "The Water Nymph." In *Alexander Pushkin: Selected Works in Two Volumes. Volume One: Poetry*, 161-183. Moscow: Progress Publishers, 1922.

Radenković, Ljubinko. "Slav Beliefs on Changelings." *Balcanica*, Institute for Balkan Studies, Belgrade (2003):32-33. https://www.academia.edu/36285069/Slav_beliefs_on_changelings.

Radulescu, Pierre. "Aleksandr Petrov: Rusalka (1997)." April 8, 2011. http://updateslive.blogspot.com/2011/04/aleksandr-petrov-rusalka-1997.html.

Radulović, Nemanja. "The Feminine Imaginarium in Traditional Legends about Fate (The Predestined Death – ATU 934)." *Studia Mythologica Slavica* 18 (2015):63-79. https://www.academia.edu/14533084/The_Feminine_Imaginarium_in_Traditional_Legends_about_Fate_The_Predestined_Death_ATU_934_.

Ralston, William. *The Songs of the Russian People, as Illustrative of Slavonic Mythology and Russian Social Life*, 2nd. ed. London: Ellis & Green, 1872.

Rappopo, Philippa. "If It Dries Out, It's No Good: Women, Hair and Rusalki Beliefs." *SEEFA Journal* 4, no. 1 (1999):55-64. https://journals.ku.edu/folklorica/article/download/3689/3532/.

Rubchak, Marian J. "Evolution of a Feminist Consciousness in Ukraine and Russia." *The European Journal of Women's Studies* 8, no. 2, 149-160.

Rubchak, Marian J. "Ukraine's Ancient Matriarch as a Topos in Constructing a Feminine Identity." *Feminist Review*, no. 92 (2009):129-50. http://www.jstor.org/stable/40664036.

Salmon, Arthur L. "Folklore Jottings." *The Gentleman's Magazine* 296 (Jan.-June 1904):178-184. [London: Bradbury, Evans,1868-1907].

Sarah in Romania. "Rusalii (Pentecost) - legends, fairies and dances." June 19, 2016. http://sarahinromania.canalblog.com/archives/2016/06/19/33984649.html.

Sedgley, M. "The Rusalque." *The Athenaeum* 2 (1847):814-815. London: British Periodicals Ltd.

Shubnaya, Ekaterina. "Prominent Russians: Aleksandr Pushkin." http://russiapedia.rt.com/prominent-russians/literature/aleksandr-pushkin/.

Sinnett, A. P. *Incidents in the Life of Madame Blavatsky*. London: Theosophical Publishing Society, 1913.

Stewart, Hugh. *Provincial Russia, Painted by F. De Haenen, Described by Hugh Stewart*. London: A. and C. Black, 1913.

Stewie, Lukecza. "Antonín Dvořák: Rusalka." August 15, 2015. https://www.youtube.com/watch?v=kobTXKUBe3w.

Thraxus Ares. "CĂLUȘUL ROMÂNESC, TRADIȚIE ȘI ÎN ANGLIA." Oct 10, 2015. https://www.youtube.com/watch?v=xcHufgrCSKU.

Tryfanenkava, Maryna A. "The Current Status of Belarusian Calendar-Ritual Tradition." *SEEFA Journal* VI, no. 2 (2001):39-48. Belarusian State University, Minsk. https://journals.ku.edu/folklorica/article/view/3709/3552

Valodzina, Tatyana. " 'Unchristened Flesh': The Woman's Breast and Breastfeeding in Traditional Slavic Culture, with Especial Reference to Belorussian." *Forum for Anthropology and Culture* 3, 168-192. https://www.academia.edu/31134027/Unchristened_Flesh_The_Womans_Breast_and_Breastfeeding_in_Traditional_Slavic_Culture_with_Especial_Reference_to_Belorussian.

Vivod, Maria. "The Fairy Seers of Eastern Serbia: Seeing Fairies—Speaking through Trance." *Oral Tradition* 32, no. 1 (2018):53-70. http://admin.oraltradition.org/wp-content/uploads/files/articles/32i/04_32.1.pdf.

Vivod, Maria. "Radmila—the Fairy-clairvoyant. Rethinking Ethnopsychiatry—a Case Study from Serbia." *Journal of Medical Anthropology* 37 (2014):8-17. https://www.academia.edu/20502427/Radmila_the_Fairy-clairvoyant._Rethinking_Ethnopsychiatry_a_Case_Study_from_Serbia.

Vizigot, Metko. "Stribog – Rusalka." June 18, 2010. https://www.youtube.com/watch?v=uMNegVAWp5M.

Vuia, R. "The Roumanian Hobby-Horse, the Călușari." *Journal of the English Folk Dance and Song Society* 2 (1935):97-108. http://www.jstor.org/stable/4521071.

Wachtel, Michael. *The Cambridge Introduction to Russian Poetry*. New York: Cambridge University Press, 2004.

Wagenvoort, H. "The Journey of the Souls of the Dead to the Isles of the Blessed." *Mnemosyne*, Fourth Series, 24, no. 2 (1971):113-61. http://www.jstor.org/stable/4429971.

Warner, Elizabeth. *Russian Myths*. Austin, Texas: University of Texas Press, 2002.

Whishaw, Frederick. *The Romance of the Woods*. London: Longmans Green & Co., 1895.

Wikipedia. "Alexander Dargomyzhsky." https://en.wikipedia.org/wiki/Alexander_Dargomyzhsky.

Wikipedia. "Alexander Pushkin." https://en.wikipedia.org/wiki/Alexander_Pushkin.

Wikipedia. "Antonín Dvořák." https://en.wikipedia.org/wiki/Antonín_Dvořák.

Wikipedia. "Korybantes." https://en.wikipedia.org/wiki/Korybantes.

Wikipedia. "Mikhail Lermontov." https://en.wikipedia.org/wiki/Mikhail_Lermontov.

Wikipedia. "The Rape of the Sabine Women." https://en.wikipedia.org/wiki/The_Rape_of_the_Sabine_Women.

Wikipedia. "Rosalia (festival)." https://en.wikipedia.org/wiki/Rosalia_(festival).

Wikipedia. "Rusalka." https://en.wikipedia.org/wiki/Rusalka.

Wikipedia. "Rusalka (Dargomyzhsky)." https://en.wikipedia.org/wiki/Rusalka_(Dargomyzhsky).

Wikipedia. "Rusalka (opera)." https://en.wikipedia.org/wiki/Rusalka_(opera).

Wikipedia, Bulgarian. "Възнесение Господне." https://bg.wikipedia.org/wiki/Възнесение_Господне.

Wikipedia, Bulgarian. "Русалка." https://bg.wikipedia.org/wiki/Русалка.

Wikipedia, Russian. "Русалка." https://ru.wikipedia.org/wiki/Русалка.

Wikipedia. "Salii." https://en.wikipedia.org/wiki/Salii.

Wikipedia. "Slavic water spirits." https://en.wikipedia.org/wiki/Slavic_water_spirits.

Wikipedia. "Zinaida Gippius." https://en.wikipedia.org/wiki/Zinaida_Gippius.

Worobec, Christine D. "Death Ritual among Russian and Ukrainian Peasants: Linkages between the Living and the Dead." In *Cultures in Flux: Lower-class Values, Practices, and Rsesistance in Late Imperial Russia*, edited by Stephen P. Frank and Mark D. Steinberg, 11-33. Princeton, N.J.: Princeton University Press, 1994.

End Notes

[1] Kenealy, *A New Pantomime*, 434.

[2] Ivanits, *Russian Folk Belief*, 77-78.

[3] Dynda, "Rusalki: Anthropology," 85.

[4] Wikipedia, "Rusalka."

[5] Larson, "Why Does the Rusalka Have to Die?" 16.

[6] Abrahamson, "The Orante," 5.

[7] Rubchak, "Evolution of a Feminist Consciousness," 152.

[8] Anne, *Goddesses in World Mythology*, Intro xx.

[9] Rubchak, "Evolution of a Feminist Consciousness," 149.

[10] Anne, *Goddesses in World Mythology*, 57.

[11] Dynda, "Rusalki: Anthropology," 87.

[12] Dobrovolsky, "Rusalki."

[13] Cooke, "Dvorak's Rusalka."

[14] Dynda, "Rusalki: Anthropology," 91.

[15] Ivanits, *Russian Folk Belief*, 188.

[16] Molina-Moreno, "La Vida Amorosa de las *Rusalki*," 120.

[17] Molina-Moreno, "La Vida Amorosa de las *Rusalki*," 117.

[18] Ralston, *Songs of the Russian People*, 146.

[19] Sedgley, "The Rusalque," 815.

[20] Anonymous, "Naturalist and Sportsman Gossip," 543.

[21] Whishaw, *Romance of the Woods*, 204.

[22] Radenković, "Slav Beliefs on Changelings," 150.

[23] Dynda, "Rusalki: Anthropology," 102-103.

[24] Ivanits, *Russian Folk Belief*, 76.

[25] Whishaw, *Romance of the Woods*, 204.

[26] Dynda, "Rusalki: Anthropology," 84, footnote 3.

[27] Milne, "Mermaids and Dreams," 69.

[28] Barber, *Dancing Goddesses*, 21.

[29] Milne, "Mermaids and Dreams," 69.

[30] Ivanits, *Russian Folk Belief*, 185-186.

[31] Goscilo, "Watery Maidens," 63.

[32] Goscilo, "Watery Maidens," 58.

[33] Dixon-Kennedy, *Russian & Slavic Myth and Legend*, 258.

[34] Valodzina, "Unchristened Flesh," 185.

[35] Valodzina, "Unchristened Flesh," 185.

[36] Gogol, "A May Night," 178-179.

[37] Anne, *Goddesses in World Mythology*, 64.

[38] Gołębiowski, Łukasz (1831). *Gry i zabawy różnych stanów w kraju całym...* [*Games and Plays of Various Estates...*]. 279–280, as referenced on Wikipedia, "Rusalka."

[39] Ralston, *Songs of the Russian People*, 139-140.

[40] Dynda, "Rusalki: Anthropology," 86.

[41] Warner, *Russian Myths*, 44.

[42] Johnson, *Slavic Sorcery*, 155.

[43] Ralston, *Songs of the Russian People*, 146.

Getting to Know Rusalki

[44] Milne, "Mermaids and Dreams," 69.

[45] Ancient civilizations considered nature sacred, and they deeply venerated the World Tree as a force of strength and protection. The three parts of the tree symbolize the nature of the universe. Branches represent the heavens where divine spirits reside. The trunk signifies Earth, which is the home of men and preternatural creatures like nymphs and fairies. And roots represent the underworld and the dead who dwell there. Like nature itself, all these creatures live in harmony with one another. Also demonstrating the world's unity were Thracian deities, who performed their designated functions, working together as a triad, none having dominion over the others. From my book *Light Love Rituals: Bulgarian Myths, Legends, and Folklore*, 9.

[46] Johnson, *Slavic Sorcery*, 155.

[47] Ralston, *Songs of the Russian People*, 146.

[48] Sedgley, "The Rusalque," 815.

[49] Ralston, *Songs of the Russian People*, 356-357.

[50] Máchal, "Slavic," 255.

[51] Kropej, *Supernatural Beings*, 155.

[52] Ralston, *Songs of the Russian People*, 146.

[53] Goscilo, "Watery Maidens," 64.

[54] Rappopo, "If It Dries Out," 59.

[55] Dynda, "Rusalki: Anthropology," 94.

[56] Barber, *Dancing Goddesses*, 3.

[57] Dynda, "Rusalki: Anthropology," 96.

[58] Barber, *Dancing Goddesses*, 52.

[59] Barber, *Dancing Goddesses*, 18.

[60] Murav, "Engendering the Russian Body Politic," 37.

[61] Barber, *Dancing Goddesses*, 21. From Dobrovol'skiy, 1908, 13.

[62] Dynda, "Rusalki: Anthropology," 93.

[63] Dynda, "Rusalki: Anthropology," 94. Referencing Propp, Vladimir Jakovlevič 1963: *Russkie agrarnye prazdniki (Opyt istoriko-ėtnografičeskogo issledovanija)*, Leningrad: Izdatel'stvo Leningradskogo Universiteta, 133.

[64] Dynda, "Rusalki: Anthropology," 94.

[65] Dynda, "Rusalki: Anthropology," 91.

[66] Dynda, "Rusalki: Anthropology," 93-94.

[67] Dynda, "Rusalki: Anthropology," 94. Referencing Propp, Vladimir Jakovlevič, 1963: *Russkie agrarnye prazdniki (Opyt istoriko-ėtnografičeskogo issledovanija)*, Leningrad: Izdatel'stvo Leningradskogo Universiteta, 133.

[68] Molina-Moreno, "La Vida Amorosa de las *Rusalki*," 135.

[69] Murav, "Engendering the Russian Body Politic," 41. The quoted note comes from a discussion of Vasilii Belov's *Raising Children According to Doctor Spock*, 317 (Воспитание по доктору Споку, 1974, short stories).

[70] Rappopo, "If It Dries Out," 61. Referencing Kononenko, Natalie, "Women as Performers of Oral Literature: A Reexamination of Epic and Lament," *Women Writers in Russian Literature* 00. Toby W. Clyman and Diana Greene (Westport, Connecticut and London, England: Greenwood Press, 1994) 23.

[71] Gura, "Coitus in the Symbolic Language," 135.

[72] Molina-Moreno, "La Vida Amorosa de las *Rusalki*," 126.

[73] Barber, *Dancing Goddesses*, 53-54.

[74] You can read about more pre-wedding bathhouse rituals in my first book of this series, *A Study of Household Spirits of Eastern Europe*, in the Bannik chapter on page 122.

[75] Rappopo, "If It Dries Out," 62.

[76] Dynda, "Rusalki: Anthropology," 93, footnote 20.

[77] Gura, "Coitus in the Symbolic Language," 136.

[78] Big & Rich, "Save A Horse [Ride A Cowboy]," https://www.youtube.com/watch?v=HflDc7PUT2g.

[79] Dynda, "Rusalki: Anthropology," 93.

[80] Rubchak, "Ukraine's Ancient Matriarch," 135, footnote 4.

[81] Rubchak, "Evolution of a Feminist Consciousness," 155.

[82] You can read about more childbirth bathhouse rituals in my first book of this series, *A Study of Household Spirits of Eastern Europe*, in the Bannik chapter on pages 119-120.

[83] Cox, "Rachel's Tomb," 143.

[84] Dynda, "Rusalki: Anthropology," 98.

[85] Dynda, "Rusalki: Anthropology," 88.

[86] Molina-Moreno, "La Vida Amorosa de las *Rusalki*," 133.

[87] You can read about other funeral rituals in my first book of this series, *A Study of Household Spirits of Eastern Europe*, in the Bannik chapter, 122. Plus, additional Bulgarian funeral rites are discussed in *Light Love Rituals: Bulgarian Myths, Legends, and Folklore* in the Arkhageloven chapter, 115-119.

[88] Molina-Moreno, "La Vida Amorosa de las *Rusalki*," 133.

[89] Molina-Moreno, "La Vida Amorosa de las *Rusalki*," 104.

[90] Rappopo, "If It Dries Out," 61.

[91] Molina-Moreno, "La Vida Amorosa de las *Rusalki*," 110-111. The story, published in 1995, is thought to have been told before 1929, due to the mention of the "Samara" government.

[92] Dixon-Kennedy, *Russian & Slavic Myth and Legend*, 125.

[93] Barber, *Dancing Goddesses*, 26.

[94] Molina-Moreno, "La Vida Amorosa de las *Rusalki*," 126.

[95] Molina-Moreno, "La Vida Amorosa de las *Rusalki*," 125.

[96] Kropej, *Supernatural Beings*, 155.

[97] Molina-Moreno, "La Vida Amorosa de las *Rusalki*," 129-130.

[98] Milne, "Mermaids and Dreams," 79.

[99] Kropej, *Supernatural Beings*, 156.

[100] Dynda, "Rusalki: Anthropology," 91.

[101] Barber, *Dancing Goddesses*, 23, quoting from Gogol, *May Night*, chapter 13.

[102] Ralston, *Songs of the Russian People*, 140, footnote 6.

[103] Dynda, "Rusalki: Anthropology," 90.

[104] Dynda, "Rusalki: Anthropology," 91.

[105] Russian Wikipedia, "Русалка."

[106] Dobrovolsky, "Rusalki."

[107] Dobrovolsky, "Rusalki."

[108] Ralston, *Songs of the Russian People*, 144.

[109] Barber, *Dancing Goddesses*, 24.

[110] Dobrovolsky, "Rusalki."

[111] Journeying to the Goddess, "The Rousalii." Taken from Tesco, *365 Goddess: A Daily Guide to the Magic and Inspiration of the Goddess*.

[112] Hindus, *Broken Earth*, 163-165.

[113] Comments from Nilot, "Rusalka – The Slavic 'Mermaid.' "

[114] You can read more about one of Madame Blavatsky's encounters with spirits in my first book in this series: *A Study of Household Spirits of Eastern Europe*, in the Domovoi chapter, 43-45.

[115] Sinnett, *Life of Madame Blavatsky*, 14, 15.

[116] Sinnett, *Life of Madame Blavatsky*, 16-17.

Rusalka Week

[117] Vivod, "Radmila—the Fairy-clairvoyant," 13.

[118] Molina-Moreno, "La Vida Amorosa de las *Rusalki*," 127.

[119] Petkova, "The Sunday of Mermaids."

[120] Bezovska, "St. Spas or Ascension Day."

[121] Bezovska, "St. Spas or Ascension Day."

[122] Bezovska, "St. Spas or Ascension Day."

[123] Ginchev, *In a Few Words*, 216.

[124] Barber, *Dancing Goddesses*, 69.

[125] Mickelson, "The Rusalki."

[126] Ralston, *Songs of the Russian People*, 216-217.

[127] Green, *Slavic Pagan World*, 54.

[128] Barber, *Dancing Goddesses*, 57.

[129] Rubchak, "Ukraine's Ancient Matriarch," 133.

[130] Rappopo, "If It Dries Out," 60.

[131] Barber, *Dancing Goddesses*, 37. From Propp, Vladimir, 1963, 60-61.

[132] Barber, *Dancing Goddesses*, 57. From Propp, Vladimir, 1987, 143.

[133] Ivanits, *Russian Folk Belief*, 81.

[134] Green, *Slavic Pagan World*, 54.

[135] Green, *Slavic Pagan World*, 83-84.

[136] Ivanits, *Russian Folk Belief*, 80.

[137] Ralston, *Songs of the Russian People*, 145.

[138] Hubbs, *Mother Russia*, 73.

[139] Green, *Slavic Pagan World*, 53, as quoted from Reeder, Roberta, *Russian Folk Lyrics*, 101.

[140] Barber, *Dancing Goddesses*, footnote on 58.

[141] Maclaren, "The Rusalka," 249-252.

[142] Konstantinova, "Ascension Day and Pentecost."

[143] Barber, *Dancing Goddesses*, 106.

[144] Warner, *Russian Myths*, 44.

[145] Dynda, "Rusalki: Anthropology," 98.

Magical Healers

[146] Barber, *Dancing Goddesses*, 70.

[147] Georgieva, *Bulgarian Mythology*, 80.

[148] Dynda, "Rusalki: Anthropology," 96.

[149] MacDermott, *Bulgarian Folk Customs*, 172.

[150] Barber, *Dancing Goddesses*, 36.

[151] Kubijovyč, *Ukraine, a Concise Encyclopedia*, 329.

[152] Máchal, "Slavic," 311.

[153] Georgieva, *Bulgarian Mythology*, 80.

[154] Kubijovyč, *Ukraine, a Concise Encyclopedia*, 329.

[155] Wikipedia, "Rosalia (festival)."

[156] Georgieva, *Bulgarian Mythology*, 80.

[157] Barber, *Dancing Goddesses*, 30.

[158] MacDermott, *Bulgarian Folk Customs*, 229.

[159] Konstantinova, "Rousalii and kaloushari."

[160] Firică, "The Romanian Căluș," 13.

[161] Dimova, "Обредът 'Русалии.' "

[162] Barber, *Dancing Goddesses*, 48.

[163] Barber, *Dancing Goddesses*, 72.

[164] Konstantinova, "Rousalii and kaloushari."

[165] Barber, *Dancing Goddesses*, 71.

[166] MacDermott, *Bulgarian Folk Customs*, 172.

[167] Konstantinova, "Rousalii and kaloushari."

[168] MacDermott, *Bulgarian Folk Customs*, 173.

[169] Konstantinova, "Rousalii and kaloushari."

[170] Barber, Dancing Goddesses, 77.

[171] Barber, *Dancing Goddesses*, 76.

[172] Barber, *Dancing Goddesses*, 70-71.

[173] MacDermott, *Bulgarian Folk Customs*, 173.

[174] Firică, "The Romanian Căluş," 3.

[175] Firică, "The Romanian Căluş," 4.

[176] Vuia, "The Roumanian Hobby-Horse," 97.

[177] Wikipedia, "Salii."

[178] Wikipedia, "The Rape of the Sabine Women."

[179] Firică, "The Romanian Căluş," 6.

[180] Firică, "The Romanian Căluş," 6.

[181] Wikipedia, "Korybantes."

[182] Firică, "The Romanian Căluş," 6.

[183] Firică, "The Romanian Căluş," 4.

[184] You can learn more about the *kukeri* in my book *Light Love Rituals: Bulgarian Myths, Legends, and Folklore.*

[185] Firică, "The Romanian Căluş," 13.

[186] Firică, "The Romanian Căluş," 5.

[187] Firică, "The Romanian Căluş," 14.

[188] Vuia, "The Roumanian Hobby-Horse," 99.

[189] Chelariu, "The Most Prevalent Feminine Mythical Characters."

[190] Vuia, "The Roumanian Hobby-Horse," 106.

[191] Wikipedia, "Statues (game)," https://en.wikipedia.org/wiki/Statues_(game).

[192] Firică, "The Romanian Căluş," 7.

[193] Vuia, "The Roumanian Hobby-Horse," 99.

[194] Firică, "The Romanian Căluş," 14.

[195] Vuia, "The Roumanian Hobby-Horse," 97.

[196] Firică, "The Romanian Căluş," 12.

[197] Vivod, "The Fairy Seers of Eastern Serbia," 53.

[198] Vivod, "Radmila—the Fairy-clairvoyant," 9.

[199] Vivod, "The Fairy Seers of Eastern Serbia," 59.

[200] This is a term used by Vivod to describe these women. She says, "I choose to use this term in an attempt to cover and to depict a vast range of more or less similar phenomena across the Balkans with an English term, with the goal of creating an "umbrella term" in the English language (nowadays a *lingua franca*) for working purposes." (Vivod, "The Fairy Seers of Eastern Serbia," 53.)

[201] Vivod, "The Fairy Seers of Eastern Serbia," 56.

[202] Vivod, "The Fairy Seers of Eastern Serbia," 57.

[203] Vivod, "Radmila—the Fairy-clairvoyant," 8.

[204] Vivod, "Radmila—the Fairy-clairvoyant," 10.

[205] Vivod, "The Fairy Seers of Eastern Serbia," 61 and following.

[206] Vivod, "The Fairy Seers of Eastern Serbia," 61.

[207] Vivod, "The Fairy Seers of Eastern Serbia," 61.

[208] Vivod, "The Fairy Seers of Eastern Serbia," 62.

[209] Vivod, "The Fairy Seers of Eastern Serbia," 61-62.

[210] Vivod, "The Fairy Seers of Eastern Serbia," 62.

[211] Johnson, *Slavic Sorcery*, 196.

[212] Vivod, "Radmila—the Fairy-clairvoyant," 9 and following.

[213] Vivod, "Radmila—the Fairy-clairvoyant," 9.
[214] Vivod, "Radmila—the Fairy-clairvoyant," 12.

Rusalki in Literature
[215] Cooke, "Dvorak's Rusalka," footnote 20.
[216] Emerson, "To What End Rusalka?" 181.
[217] Cooke, "Dvorak's Rusalka."
[218] Larson, "Why Does the Rusalka Have to Die?" 7-8.
[219] Whishaw, *Romance of the Woods*, 253-272.
[220] Shubnaya, "Prominent Russians: Aleksandr Pushkin."
[221] Goscilo, "Watery Maidens," 69.
[222] Radulescu, "Aleksandr Petrov: Rusalka."
[223] Larson, "Why Does the Rusalka Have to Die?" 166.
[224] Radulescu, "Aleksandr Petrov: Rusalka."
[225] Radulescu, "Aleksandr Petrov: Rusalka."
[226] Radulescu, "Aleksandr Petrov: Rusalka."
[227] Pushkin, "The Water Nymph," 161-183.
[228] Emerson, "To What End Rusalka?" 173, footnote 11.
[229] Emerson, "To What End Rusalka?" 175, footnote 15.
[230] Radulescu, "Aleksandr Petrov: Rusalka."
[231] *Terem* refers to the separate living quarters occupied by elite women in Russia.
[232] Emerson, "To What End Rusalka?" 183.
[233] Emerson, "To What End Rusalka?" 185.
[234] Emerson, "To What End Rusalka?" 188.
[235] Emerson, "To What End Rusalka?" 189.
[236] Emerson, "To What End Rusalka?" 189-190.
[237] Antonin-dvorak.cz, "Rusalka."
[238] Cooke, "Dvorak's Rusalka."
[239] Stewie, "Antonín Dvořák: Rusalka."
[240] MIGHTYJLY, "Frederica Von Stade – Rusalka (Moon Song)."
[241] Used with permission from Operas Arias Composers, "Rusalka Libretto" (with modifications): https://www.opera-arias.com/dvorak/rusalka/libretto/english/.
[242] Quotes from Wikipedia, "Mikhail Lermontov."
[243] Wikipedia, "Zinaida Gippius."
[244] Gippius, *Sacred Blood*, 6.
[245] Larson, "Why Does the Rusalka Have to Die?" 173.
[246] Larson, "Why Does the Rusalka Have to Die?" 183.
[247] Gippius, *Sacred Blood*, 8.
[248] Gippius, *Sacred Blood*, 12.
[249] Gippius, *Sacred Blood*, 12.
[250] Gippius, *Sacred Blood*, 12.
[251] Gippius, *Sacred Blood*, 13.
[252] Hetherington, "Zinaida Gippius' Sexual Revolution," 56.
[253] Osipovich, "God's Other Children," 19.
[254] Larson, "Why Does the Rusalka Have to Die?" 168.
[255] Goscilo, "Watery Maidens," 69.
[256] Gippius, *Sacred Blood*, 33-34.
[257] Gippius, *Sacred Blood*, 35.
[258] Osipovich, "God's Other Children," 21.

[259] Gippius, *Sacred Blood*, 27.

[260] Gippius, *Sacred Blood*, 37-38.

[261] Larson, "Why Does the Rusalka Have to Die?" 162.

[262] Osipovich, "God's Other Children," 2.

[263] Hetherington, "Zinaida Gippius' Sexual Revolution," 4.

[264] Osipovich, "God's Other Children," 22.

[265] Osipovich, "God's Other Children," 3.

[266] Osipovich, "God's Other Children," 3.

[267] Osipovich, "God's Other Children," 16.

[268] Gippius, *Sacred Blood*, 11-12.

[269] Osipovich, "God's Other Children," 17.

[270] Wachtel, *The Cambridge Introduction to Russian Poetry*, 92.

[271] Wachtel, *The Cambridge Introduction to Russian Poetry*, 92-93.

[272] Wachtel, *The Cambridge Introduction to Russian Poetry*, 93.

[273] Wachtel, *The Cambridge Introduction to Russian Poetry*, 90-91.

[274] Aveela, *Mystical Emona*, 252-253.

Appendix

[275] *The Little Mermaid*, 1-36.

www.ingramcontent.com/pod-product-compliance
Lightning Source LLC
Chambersburg PA
CBHW051311020426
42333CB00027B/3296